The Ontology of Becoming
and
The Ethics of Particularity

....

M. C. DILLON

EDITED BY
LAWRENCE HASS

OHIO UNIVERSITY PRESS / ATHENS

Ohio University Press, Athens, Ohio 45701
ohioswallow.com
© 2012 by Ohio University Press
All rights reserved

To obtain permission to quote, reprint, or otherwise reproduce or distribute
material from Ohio University Press publications, please contact our rights and
permissions department at (740) 593-1154 or (740) 593-4536 (fax).

Printed in the United States of America
Ohio University Press books are printed on acid-free paper ∞

20 19 18 17 16 15 14 13 12   5 4 3 2 1

Library of Congress Cataloging-in-Publication Data

Dillon, M. C. (Martin C.), 1938–2005.
 [Art, truth, and illusion]
 The ontology of becoming ; and, The ethics of particularity / M.C. Dillon ;
edited by Lawrence Hass.
   p. cm. — (Series in Continental thought)
 Includes bibliographical references (p. 221) and index.
 ISBN 978-0-8214-1999-1 (hc : alk. paper) — ISBN 978-0-8214-4415-3
(electronic)
   1. Nietzsche, Friedrich Wilhelm, 1844–1900. 2. Ontology. 3. Becoming
(Philosophy) 4. Merleau-Ponty, Maurice, 1908–1961. 5. Ethics. 6.
Intersubjectivity. I. Hass, Lawrence. II. Dillon, M. C. (Martin C.), 1938–
2005. Ethics of particularity. III. Title.
 B3318.O5D55 2012
 193—dc23   2011043452

Dedicated to all of Mike Dillon's students near and far,
and
to the memory of Keith Nintzel

CONTENTS

ACKNOWLEDGMENTS

In my work on these posthumous manuscripts, I have sought to honor Mike Dillon and his memory by presenting them as it seems he intended. That is a daunting task and I am especially indebted to several people for their insights, efforts, and support of my work on this project.

Above all, my deepest thanks go to Joanne Dillon, who entrusted me with the project in late 2005—an extraordinary honor. Not only did Joanne give me full rein to edit and present Dillon's writings as I saw fit, she also provided constant friendship along the way. Joanne was as much a companion in my process of bringing these manuscripts to print as she had been a companion to them when Mike was writing them. It is certain to say that you would not be holding this book in your hands without Joanne's loving commitment to Mike's work. Even so, responsibility for all the editorial decisions is solely mine. For anything else, you have to blame Dillon!

In these efforts, I have also received remarkable support from friends and colleagues. It is my pleasure to thank Duane Davis, Galen Johnson, Len Lawlor, Jim Morley, Susan O'Shaughnessy, Dorothea Olkowski, Jonathan D. Singer, and Ted Toadvine for their advice and encouragement. Special thanks, too, are in order for many people at Ohio University Press, including Ted Toadvine (editor of the Series in Continental Thought), Kevin Haworth (executive editor), the editorial board, and the production team. I also want to acknowledge the constant love and support of my family: Marjorie, Cameron, and Jessica.

A small number of these chapters have seen print previously as essays, and so I am very appreciative to the following editors and publications for permission to publish a later version of those essays here. My sincere thanks go to:

- Antonio Calcagno, editor of *Symposium*, for "Art, Truth, and Illusion: Nietzsche's Metaphysical Skepticism," vol. 8, no. 2 (2004): 299–312.

- Renaud Barbaras, Mauro Carbone, and Leonard Lawlor, editors of *Chiasmi International*, for "Conscience and Authenticity," vol. 5 (2003): 15–28; and for "Life-Death," vol. 9 (2008): 449–58.
- Diane Perpich and Daniel Smith, editors of the *Journal of French Philosophy*, for "Reversibility and Ethics: The Question of Violence," vol. 10, no. 2 (1998): 82–101.
- State University of New York Press for "Merleau-Ponty and the Ontology of Ecology, or Apocalypse Later," in Suzanne L. Cataldi and William S. Hamrick, eds., *Merleau-Ponty and Environmental Philosophy: Dwelling on the Landscapes of Thought* (Albany, NY: 2007), 259–71.

The reader will have observed that this book is dedicated to all of Mike's students. This seemed fitting to Joanne and me, given the extraordinary extent to which Dillon developed his ideas in classes, courses, and dialogue with students. I know for a fact that Dillon thought of himself as a teacher first and then a scholar, and he dedicated himself, above all, to excellence in the classroom. For those of you who had Dillon as a teacher and a mentor, I hope that you enjoy experiencing his "voice" and his thoughts one more time, and on topics that you probably already engaged with him. Knowing Mike as I did, I can tell you that you brought out the best of Dillon as, hopefully, he brought out the best in you.

Finally, this book is also dedicated to the memory of Keith Nintzel. Keith was a young engineering student who took one of Mike's philosophy classes and became completely smitten with the subject—a rather familiar story at Binghamton. In fall 2004, Keith took Dillon's Nietzsche course and was helping Dillon with the translations for the Nietzsche manuscript. However, in an unspeakable tragedy, Keith was killed in an automobile accident while returning to Binghamton after Thanksgiving that fall. With Joanne's permission and the permission of Keith's parents, I share an excerpt from a letter Mike wrote to them in February 2005, less than three weeks before his own death:

> I have been trying to write to you for some time now, but haven't been able to get my thoughts into words. I doubt that I will do any better now. I really have not been able to come to terms with Keith's death, to confront it directly. Keith was helping me research Nietzsche's unpublished writings for a book I am writing. . . . His understanding of both Nietzsche and the German language was

phenomenal. Although the tragedy of his untimely death cut short our collaboration, his contribution to this project is substantial, and he will be acknowledged in the final manuscript. . . .

His absence from the Nietzsche seminar in the last weeks of the semester was palpable. Questions would come up that only he could answer, but he was not there to answer them, and his empty seat evoked silent mourning on the part of us all.

The promise of this good and gentle, brilliant and diligent young scholar will go unfulfilled. The world to come will be a lesser place than it would have been had that absurd accident not intervened.

His memory will linger as long as I do, as long as the others who knew and cared for him are alive. Our lives are richer for having known him, and poorer for having lost his graceful presence. . . .

I am not yet ready to say goodbye to Keith. I doubt that I ever will.

These are profoundly moving words. They are words that honor Keith's memory and remind us of our deep loss at Mike's passing. May my own words and efforts in this book find themselves to be half so eloquent.

Lawrence Hass
Sherman, Texas
April 2011

ABBREVIATIONS

. . . .

Abbreviations of Texts by Nietzsche

BGE: *Beyond Good and Evil*

BT: *The Birth of Tragedy*

EH: *Ecce Homo*

GM: *On the Genealogy of Morals*

GS: *The Gay Science*

HH: *Human All Too Human*

TL: "On Truth and Lies in a Nonmoral Sense"

PN: *The Portable Nietzsche*

PT: *Philosophy and Truth*

TI: *The Twilight of the Idols*

W1: *Werke, Band 1*

W2: *Werke, Band 2*

Z: *Thus Spoke Zarathustra*

Abbreviations of Texts by Merleau-Ponty

AD: *Adventures of the Dialectic*

HT: *Humanism and Terror*

PP: *Phenomenology of Perception*

S: *Signs*

S-F: *Signes*

TD: *Texts and Dialogues*

VI: *The Visible and the Invisible*

VI-F: *Le Visible et l'invisible*

In his foreword to Merleau-Ponty's *The Visible and the Invisible*, editor Claude Lefort writes:

> However expected it may sometimes be, the death of a . . . friend opens an abyss before us. How much more so when it comes absolutely unannounced . . . when, moreover, he who dies is so alive that habitually we had come . . . to count him among the truest witnesses of our undertakings. Such was the sudden death of Maurice Merleau-Ponty. (*VI*, xi)

Such, too, I must add, was the death of philosopher Martin C. Dillon. In March 2005, while skiing in the Swiss Alps with his wife, Joanne, Dillon felt overcome with nausea and was taken to the emergency room at a nearby hospital. Shortly after being taken to the examination room, he peacefully expired. The light that had burned so brightly and with such energy—Mike Dillon was a vital soul indeed—had suddenly gone out.

Just as Lefort describes the strange, stunned silence that attended the death of his friend, so, too, were we confronted with Dillon's sudden loss. While Mike's wife, daughters, and family were grieving in the most personal ways, his friends, colleagues, and students also were facing an abyss. Dillon was gone; he had been with us a few moments ago, and now he was gone. There could be no more conversations, no more classes with this master teacher, no more intimate moments over glasses of fine wine and gourmet steaks. There could be no more opportunities to say the unsaid things (words of appreciation or of rapprochement); no more questions or criticisms to be raised; no more remarkable learning through Dillon's famous give-and-take. As Lefort says, at this terrible point of loss we are returned to the thinker's work: "The work has come to an end, and, simply because everything in it is said, we are suddenly confronted with it" (*VI*, xi).

The good news is that Dillon has left us more "work" than many people knew. Indeed, he left two mostly finished book manuscripts among his papers: *Art, Truth, and Illusion: Nietzsche's Ontology* and *The Ethics of Particularity*, both of which had been written in the last seven years of his life. While the titles, subject matter, and tables of contents suggest that these manuscripts are discrete, I believe (and will argue below) that—whether Dillon fully realized it or not—they offer two distinct yet inseparable sides of a complex, unified project to reconcile an ontology of becoming (*à la* Nietzsche) with a detailed Merleau-Pontian ethics and social theory. This highly ambitious project—realized in the pages of this book—is an achievement that, I believe, helps us better understand the entirety of Mike Dillon's philosophical orientation, previously published books, and even style. Indeed, it makes possible a new understanding of Dillon's philosophy as a whole. How often does *that* happen? How often does a posthumous text provide a kind of "capstone" to a thinker's entire lifework? Not all that often.

Thus it is with great enthusiasm that I present Dillon's final manuscripts to you. When I began my editing work on the manuscripts (more details on that below), I had no idea if there was one book here or two distinct books, let alone if they would be sufficiently developed to publish. But it didn't take long to realize that these manuscripts *had to* be published together—that a reader of only one manuscript or the other simply would not understand the whole of Dillon's late thinking. And it didn't take long either to recognize that in these writings Dillon was working at the peak of his powers as a thinker and a writer, that his light was burning very bright indeed. In the pages that follow, I will talk a bit about Dillon's life and work as they led to these final manuscripts. Then I will offer a general discussion of the philosophical contents of the manuscripts themselves and their complex interrelationship. I will close my introduction by describing the state of the manuscripts as I found them and the nature of my editorial interventions in bringing these works to publication.

I. LIFE AND WORK

Born in 1938, Martin Dillon received his bachelor of arts, with a major in philosophy, from the University of Virginia in 1960. Within one month of graduation, he was serving as a commissioned officer in the United States Navy, eventually serving as a staff member of the Sixth Fleet command. He

was discharged from the Navy in July 1963, and began nineteen years of service in the naval reserve—which included two different stints as commanding
officer: for the 3-47 Surface Division (1973–1975) and for the Military Sea-
lift Command Office (1979–1981). In short, along with all his achievements
as a scholar and a teacher, Mike Dillon was a military man—a fact reflected, I
think, in his rather no-nonsense approach to things; his succinct, clear prose;
and his assertive style of thinking and being.

While the military was an important part of Dillon's life for twenty years,
still more formative was his devotion to philosophy. After his discharge from
the Navy in 1963, Dillon received his master of arts in philosophy in 1964
from the University of California at Berkeley, and then continued his studies
at Yale—receiving his master of philosophy in 1968 and his doctorate in
1970 with a dissertation on Merleau-Ponty. At that point, Dillon had already
been teaching for two years as an instructor at the State University of New
York—Binghamton, now known as Binghamton University. With doctorate
in hand, Dillon became an assistant professor of philosophy at Binghamton
in 1970, and went on to become an associate professor in 1974 and professor in 1988; indeed, he spent his entire career at that institution.

I am told that right from the start, Mike Dillon was a "star" in the classroom. In the course of my research for this project, I have spoken with countless of his students. What emerges from their myriad tales and memories is
a picture of Dillon as a most revered teacher—well reflected by the fact that
in 1993 he was given the rare honor of being named Distinguished Teaching
Professor at Binghamton. Apparently in most of Dillon's courses and classes
it was "standing room only," no matter the topic. And what transpired in
class was an energetic and interactive performance of inspired thinking. By
all accounts, he brought *waves* of students to philosophy, many of whom
went on to academic careers. Dillon was never my teacher in a classroom setting, but as I talked to his students, and studied syllabi and course notes from
the entire length of his career, it became evident to me that all of Dillon's
courses were informed by his profound conviction that philosophy really
matters and *should matter*, that philosophy has the promise to change—if
not the world, then at least the hearts, minds, and sensibilities of the people
who live in it. This is powerful stuff indeed.

When Mike Dillon wasn't teaching, he was engaged in two or three other
primary activities. In 1974 he bought five acres of land in the northern Pennsylvania woods and invited Joanne Bubela to help him build a house there.
The house, the space, and the idea came to be called "Ambremerine," from

a book of fantasy by E. R. Eddison titled *Mistress of Mistresses*. Mike and Joanne really did "build it all": Every few summers, they would buy the lumber, strap on the tool belts, and carry out a major project, such as building a second floor, an extension for a bedroom, or a wraparound deck. Over the years, project by project, Ambremerine became something remarkable: a substantial, beautiful, handmade house surrounded by glorious nature and blooming, buzzing natural life. I have gone on about Ambremerine because it was such an important part of Mike Dillon's sensibilities; this natural setting and home were the deep context of Dillon's thinking and writings. Students and colleagues were always welcome at Ambremerine, and I am sure that many readers of this book will have vivid memories of their days and nights there. Perhaps, too, they will have memories of chopping wood for the winter, helping to lay a foundation, or waking up to the tip-tapping sound of Dillon writing on his Mac.

This last activity was fairly constant: Dillon was always writing on some project or another. No doubt, his life was already full. He made a remarkable, loving relationship with Joanne; he had lots to do with Ambremerine; he was dedicated to teaching and the business of university life; he helped to raise three daughters (Kathleen, Liz, and Sarah). Even so, Dillon was passionately committed to writing and presenting his philosophical ideas and concepts. In the course of his career, he published more than fifty essays and made more than one hundred presentations at conferences and colleges and universities. Between 1970 and 1988, his presentations and publications moved through two large regions: the phenomenology of love and sex and the philosophy of Merleau-Ponty. He presented a paper at the second meeting of the Merleau-Ponty Circle in 1977 (now known as the International Merleau-Ponty Circle), and he became a constant participant in its meetings. So much so, in fact, that in the early 1980s he was made the organization's general secretary—a position he held until his death. Throughout this time, Dillon was working to transform his dissertation into a fully developed presentation of Merleau-Ponty's philosophy. And so, after nearly twenty years of study, writing, and rewriting, in 1988 Dillon published *Merleau-Ponty's Ontology* (Indiana University Press).

Merleau-Ponty's Ontology is generally acknowledged to be one of the most important English-language books on Merleau-Ponty and a genuine classic in the field. In fact, the book went into a second edition with Northwestern University Press in 1997—something that is quite unusual for an academic monograph. This introduction is not the place to fully sing its praises,

but part of the book's excellence is that it offers a clear, detailed, and systematic presentation of Merleau-Ponty's ontology as a whole. It also shows how
his philosophy is able to resolve both traditional philosophical problems and
problems inherent in the projects of previous Continental thinkers (such as
Husserl, Sartre, and Heidegger). Further, at the time of publication, Dillon's
book had that rare quality of more or less setting the terms, problems, and
debates for nearly a generation of scholarship about Merleau-Ponty. I can
attest to this fact personally. Dillon's book was published when I was in the
second year of work on my own dissertation on Merleau-Ponty. It didn't take
long for me to realize that the scope and organizational power of the book
required that I start over in writing my dissertation. If I didn't, I would be
just "reinventing the wheel" or missing the whole new discourse on Merleau-
Ponty. Moreover, Dillon made my project much easier because he offered
such clear representations and arguments about central themes in Merleau-
Ponty's thought. It is not too much to say that *Merleau-Ponty's Ontology*
was the air that existential phenomenologists breathed for many years, and
it remains mandatory reading for any contemporary student or scholar of
Merleau-Ponty.

But Dillon was not letting any moss grow; by the time *Merleau-Ponty's
Ontology* was published (in 1988), his next book was already well under
way: *Semiological Reductionism: A Critique of the Deconstructionist Movement in Postmodern Thought* (SUNY Press, 1995). In fact, when I first heard
and met Dillon at the Twelfth Annual Meeting of the Merleau-Ponty Circle
(in 1987), he was already mounting his impassioned phenomenological criticisms of Derrida and of deconstructionist philosophy in general. Dillon was
entirely focused on this critique for five or six years, during which time he
was, step-by-step, writing the chapters for *Semiological Reductionism*. This
focus also led Dillon to edit a collection of essays on the Merleau-Ponty–
Derrida relation: *Écart and Différance: Merleau-Ponty and Derrida on Seeing
and Writing* (Humanities, 1997).

Of all Dillon's books, I think it is fair to say that *Semiological Reductionism* is the most vexed and vexing. This synoptic introduction is not the
place to carry out a detailed analysis of this complex book, and it is not
my intention to pass judgment on it, but its chilly reception and disregard
constituted a significant episode in Dillon's professional career and require
some commentary. Part of the difficulty, I think, is the book's fairly aggres-
sive tone: While *Merleau-Ponty's Ontology* was essentially affirmational and
constructive, *Semiological Reductionism* is flat-out confrontational; it rejects

the value and plausibility of Derrida's thought. True, Dillon asserts in his introduction that his "critique is intended to be balanced and fair: a critical interpretation, not a polemic,"[1] but the book doesn't really read that way. However, I think a deeper difficulty for the book is that it is built upon a highly controversial and contested interpretation of Derrida's thought. In brief, Dillon's arguments are predicated on a foundational assertion that Derrida's deconstructive philosophy is committed to what Dillon calls "the semiological reduction," that is, a reduction of the world and the body to a "linguistic text" or to what Dillon calls "linguistic immanence."[2] On this interpretation, Derrida's philosophy is a new form of transcendental idealism in which language constitutes the world rather than, as with Kant, the categories of the transcendental subject—a view that, Dillon argues, results in abject relativism and skepticism.

Dillon was not the first scholar, nor the last, to impute this kind of view to Derrida. The problem with this interpretation—a problem already pressed upon Dillon by several scholars before the book was published—is that this interpretation doesn't seem correct. It is true that Derrida wrote, "There is nothing outside of the text,"[3] but rigorous scholars were not persuaded that Derrida's sentence and his overall project insisted upon or implied a reduction of the world to language—particularly given Derrida's own repeated insistence *against* this reading. Having said that, it is true that when Dillon was writing this book in the late 1980s and early 1990s, what we might call days of "high postmodernism" in American universities, a significant number of presumptively Derridean literary theorists and a few Continental philosophers were talking about Derrida and deconstruction in exactly the way that Dillon was criticizing. Thus, with all the power of hindsight and the benefits of an additional fifteen years of more work *by* Derrida and of more careful scholarship *about* Derrida, it is my sense that *Semiological Reductionism* is marked by a strange problem. That is, while its interpretation and many of its arguments are telling against some "Derrideans" of the day, they miss Derrida's view and his deconstructive project.[4]

It is clear that Dillon was disturbed by the reception to his critical work on Derrida and to *Semiological Reductionism*. After the great appreciation and international success of *Merleau-Ponty's Ontology*, he found himself embattled. Even good friends (myself included) were challenging his interpretation of Derrida. A glimmer of his experience can be seen in the acknowledgments section of the book: "This book has changed the tenor of my relations with the colleagues and friends whose thoughts and sentiments bear on my own.

My struggles with this alien but enticing style of thinking have opened a distance between their minds and mine, a space of solitude within the community."[5] I believe that the language and the tone of this passage are important for understanding certain aspects of Dillon's later professional career: "distance from colleagues," "solitude within the community." To the best of my knowledge, Dillon never withdrew his interpretation of Derrida—in fact, some passages in his later writings repeat it—and his experience of being at odds with his larger intellectual community settled in as an aspect of his style. (I will have more to say about this in the next section.)

Nonetheless, after finishing *Semiological Reductionism*, Dillon immediately launched into writing *Beyond Romance* (SUNY Press, 2001). After the frustrations of the previous book, Dillon intended this book about love to reach an audience both inside and beyond the academy.[6] There is no question that Dillon saw this book as a culmination of one long line of his thinking; he had been regularly teaching courses on love and sex at Binghamton since 1976. And for him the topic was of singular and passionate importance. As he puts it: "I believe that love, more than anything else, determines the quality of our lives. Fame, fortune, power, and the like do not guarantee happiness (whatever that might be), nor does the failure to attain all or any of these condemn us to a life unfulfilled. But failure in love *does* guarantee misery. . . . That is the credo upon which this book is built. No good love, no good life."[7]

"No good love, no good life": What follows after this fecund beginning is Dillon's attempt to articulate a rigorous theory of love and sex (what he calls "sexlove") that overturns the binary categories and structures of existing theories of love from Plato through Romanticism to some contemporary models. More specifically, drawing upon Merleau-Ponty's late ontology, Dillon argues that the myriad phenomena of love and sex must be understood as grounded in our carnal lives that are reversibly intertwined with others'. However, going well beyond Merleau-Ponty, Dillon articulates the specific dynamics of these relationships that explains their absolute centrality in human life while respecting the obvious plurality of their forms.

The project I have just described is no small feat. Indeed, *Beyond Romance* is an ambitious and important book. It may even be Dillon's best book—his most personal and passionate one; the one where he makes his most original contribution to philosophy, where he advances the phenomenology of embodied life beyond obvious gaps and limits in Merleau-Ponty's thought. If this is not yet widely perceived, I suspect part of the reason is that, after all the struggles with Dillon about Derrida, a number of scholars did not read *Beyond Romance*. Or they might have assumed they understood his theory of love from hearing short versions of some chapters at conferences, or both of those things. For my part, when I did finally read and study the book (much too late, shortly before his death), I quickly discovered that I had gotten virtually no understanding of Dillon's theory from hearing partial chapters at conferences. Indeed, for all its immediacy and passion, *Beyond Romance* is a complex book and things move fast; close reading and careful study are necessary to understand it. Nonetheless, I have taught the book to undergraduate students on multiple occasions, and they have found Dillon's theory of love to be affecting and inspirational. For that matter, I do, too. In my view (for what it is worth), there are some significant difficulties along the way, but they are ameliorated by Dillon's success in offering an original and fully articulated incarnate theory of loving relationships. I think the theory is a "player" in contemporary discussions of the subject and deserves extensive consideration, far more than it has so far received.

Dillon finished writing *Beyond Romance* in 1998. It was the culmination of a lifelong course of teaching and research, and it would have made a fitting capstone to his career. But he was far from done; he immediately began working in tandem on the two manuscripts collected here: a book on Nietzsche (inspired by years of teaching Nietzsche and a renewed interest in him) and a long-promised book that would elucidate a full-fledged ethical theory rooted in the phenomenology of our embodied relations with others. In several respects, Dillon's work on these two manuscripts was nothing less than astonishing. Between 1998 and March 2005, with scarcely a break, he wrote chapters for one book or the other, back and forth; clearly he intended to finish these books. In fact, in Dillon's proposal for sabbatical during the spring semester of 2005 (which he was awarded), he promised to finish both manuscripts by the end of the summer, something he almost surely would have done had he not passed away in March.

In this section, I have traced one path through Dillon's professional career, through his writing and his thinking, which brings us to his work on these two final manuscripts. In the next section, I will discuss in a general way the character and content of the two manuscripts, and then argue for something about them that is not necessarily apparent: that they offer two complex, distinct sides of a relatively unified philosophical worldview.

2. THE MANUSCRIPTS

As indicated above, Dillon was equally committed to both of these book projects. However, one of them must be presented first in this book, and for minor thematic reasons I have chosen to start with the Nietzsche manuscript, *Art, Truth, and Illusion: Nietzsche's Ontology*. As can be learned from my table of contents, the Nietzsche manuscript, as it exists, consists of six completed chapters and an appendix that contains Dillon's fairly detailed template for the seventh chapter. While Dillon wrote each chapter as an individual essay, he noted on each of the final drafts "ATI: chapter one," "ATI: chapter two," and so on. In other words, there is no question whatsoever about his intended order for these existing chapters. What is not clear from any of his notes, papers, or conversations is whether there would have been one, two, or three additional chapters beyond chapter 7; indeed, Dillon left no outlines for the book of any sort.

Joanne recalls Mike saying in early 2005 that he had *two* more chapters to finish, although in keeping with his practice on *Semiological Reductionism* and *Beyond Romance*, one of those two might have been an overarching preface or introduction. I suspect that there would have been a chapter on *Ecce Homo* because, in fall semester 2004, when Dillon was teaching his Nietzsche course, he went to considerable trouble to type new lecture notes on that book—the clear beginnings of a template for that chapter. More, we can tell from his Nietzsche course notes that Dillon had a special fondness for *Ecce Homo*; he used the book to pull the themes of the course together. However, Dillon also spent many classes toward the end of his last Nietzsche course on *Twilight of the Idols* and *The Will to Power*. So it is possible that he envisioned a chapter on each of these books as well. Possible, but unlikely I think, because Dillon's new *Ecce Homo* notes incorporated some of the material from his previous sketchy notes about *The Will to Power*. In the end, then, my best guess is that Dillon was intending to include a chapter 8 on *Twilight*, a concluding chapter 9 on *Ecce Homo*, and probably then to write a short overarching preface. But again, he left no documentary evidence to confirm this.

The Nietzsche manuscript is thus incomplete. Nonetheless, I believe that by the end of chapter 6 Dillon had largely made his primary case: that by 1878, Nietzsche had abandoned a latent quasi-Schopenhauerian ontology of Being and had articulated a radical, new ontology of becoming. Indeed, Dillon argues that Nietzsche underwent a dramatic self-transformation as a thinker—a transformation that allowed him to fully articulate and embrace a one-world ontology of contingent, partial, and painful truths. For Dillon, careful attention to Nietzsche's self-transformation and his new ontology allows for a rigorous and fairly systematic interpretation of the big themes in Nietzsche's later texts. These themes include, for example, Nietzsche's perspectivism and his new theory of truth, his critique of religion, his articulation of Zarathustra as an exemplar of nobility, and his famous views of *Übermensch*, eternal return, and the like. As Dillon's study of Nietzsche moves forward, step-by-step, from *The Birth of Tragedy* to the late works, he gives detailed and typically fresh interpretations of those big themes by studying them through the organizing lens of Nietzsche's radicalized ontology. What occurs then in the existing manuscript is a sophisticated double movement. On one hand, Dillon grounds Nietzsche's big themes in an interpretation of his mature ontology of becoming. At the same time, Dillon more fully elucidates the ontology as he is articulating Nietzsche's themes. While it is clear that Dillon's final one or two chapters would have discussed further themes, nonetheless I believe that by the end of his chapter 6 the reader will feel the organizing force of Dillon's ontological approach and appreciate his rigorous interpretations of Nietzsche's most famous concepts. Even though the reader will wish the rest of the book were there, the manuscript is extensive, expansive, and satisfying.

The second manuscript collected in this book is titled *The Ethics of Particularity*—a title that Dillon announced in his very last curriculum vitae. (That document also authoritatively establishes the intended order of the essays.) While, as stated above, the exact length of the final Nietzsche book is unclear, I am cautiously confident that with *The Ethics of Particularity* we have the entire book that Dillon intended and that we have it in near-publication condition. For example, the last existing chapter, chapter 8, has as its title the title of the book itself—a significant choice that signals the end of the book. And that chapter reads as a conclusion; that is, it pulls the overarching argument of the book together, but then works to address the important subject of freedom. About this manuscript, Joanne reports that Dillon said there was one more chapter to write, but I believe he probably intended that to be a fairly substantial organizing introduction. Indeed, this manuscript, much more than the one on Nietzsche, reads like a collection of separate papers on ethical topics and would have required such an introduction. However that may be, *The Ethics of Particularity* is virtually complete and its core project is weighty and provocative: It sets out to develop a ranging normative theory that both starts from and integrates the ethical content-structures that imbue our deeply particular, embodied relationships with others. In other words, in this manuscript Dillon articulates an ethical, political, and social-practice theory that builds upon Merleau-Ponty's account of chiasmatic intersubjectivity. In a phrase, he offers a full-blown Merleau-Pontian ethics.

There is nothing superficial or quick in Dillon's handling of this project. At its core, it is a fulsome extension of the account of carnal intersubjectivity he argued for in *Beyond Romance*. Thus, Dillon begins the manuscript of *The Ethics of Particularity* where *Beyond Romance* left off, by arguing that the recognition, vulnerability, pain, empathy, desire, and respect that imbue our prethematic carnal relations with others also constitute the "ground phenomena" of ethics. Further, he argues that these facts of embodied relations are deeply particular and essential to life as we know it; they both underlie and motivate our universal discourses about what is good, right, wrong, and the like. As a result of this complex conjunction—deep particularity at the core of universalizing discourse—Dillon shows that the Kantian and post-Kantian tendency to treat the particular as pathos and the universal as ethics is itself a flawed binary. He argues then that what is required is a normative theory that acknowledges the "ethics of particularity"—one that articulates the values that flow from embodied beings in social relations and the discursive practices that are required for such beings to adjudicate the good. As the chapters of the manuscript unfold, Dillon elucidates these values and discursive practices by showing their application to a range of ethical themes, such as shame, conscience, violence, politics, ecology, human finitude, authenticity, and freedom.

It is neither possible nor desirable in this introduction to *summarize* Dillon's two manuscripts. Indeed, no summary could suffice, and now with their publication none is needed. My intention here has only been to say enough about the two manuscripts at a general level to establish that both of these manuscripts are doing substantial philosophical work and are richly deserving of our attention. In fact, I hope to have shown that if the reader is at all interested in Nietzsche, naturalism, Merleau-Ponty, normative theory, and the phenomenology of embodied life (to name a few things), these two manuscripts are mandatory reading. However, in the remainder of this section I want to argue for a feature of the manuscripts that may not be obvious to a first-time or casual reader. That is, that there are hidden, but essential relations between these manuscripts—relations that reveal them as two aspects of one coherent philosophical outlook rather than two independent projects. I think this argument is important to make, not only because these relations are hidden and subtle, but also because it is by no means evident how a Nietzschean ontology and epistemology could fit together with a Merleau-Pontian ethics and social theory. Prima facie, those things would seem incommensurable. This worry about incoherence is also exacerbated, I think, by Dillon's voice in the Nietzsche manuscript. Indeed, as you will discover, Dillon doesn't write that manuscript with the quasi-objective style of measuring strengths and weaknesses. Rather, he embraces Nietzsche's outlook and elaborates his views with enthusiastic vigor. It is not that Dillon is agreeing with everything Nietzsche says, but rather that Dillon's disposition is to passionately defend what he sees as the best of Nietzsche and to more or less ignore problem areas. Once again, it seems hard to grasp how Dillon's embrace of Nietzsche's firebrand approach could be consistent with an ethics of embodied intersubjectivity and mediating discourse.

However, to launch my argument about hidden interconnections, I want to focus on a singular place in the Nietzsche manuscript where Dillon's enthusiasm breaks down—where the voice shifts from Dillon-Nietzsche to Dillon *on* Nietzsche. This unusual shift happens in chapter 6 of the Nietzsche manuscript, that is to say, very late in it, the place where Dillon turns his focused attention to the question of "morality in a god-forsaken world." He begins the section by saying he wants "to put his cards on the table," and to "divulge his own position," "right from the start." Dillon then says: "I think that Nietzsche's revaluation of all values is many things: a breath of fresh air; an attempt to think through a radical position honestly and to follow the thought wherever it leads even if it leads to unpalatable conclusions; a much-needed critique of contemporary ethics and morality; and maybe even partly right (which is to say probably partly wrong)" (p. 00).

There is a lot of enthusiasm here, and yet the final clause ("probably partly wrong") foreshadows a moment of explicit disagreement that is uncharacteristic of the Nietzsche manuscript so far. Dillon then proceeds to situate Nietzsche's ethical viewpoint as one side of a long-standing binary for depicting our relations with others. On one side of the binary is what Dillon calls "an ecological model" in which "the welfare of each is bound up with the welfare of the whole, not only other humans, but every element of the ecosystem. . . . If some identifiable element threatens the whole, we have to band together to remove the threat, be it a virus, a hurricane, or a sociopath" (p. 00). The other side of the binary is an oppositional model for those relations in which, Dillon says, "the interest of the self is intrinsically in opposition to the interest of the collective. With regard to power . . . each of us wants [more], hence is reluctant to relegate any of it to other persons" (p. 00). Dillon concludes this passage by arguing that Nietzsche clearly adopts the oppositional model and rejects the ecological model because he insists that the tension between self and others-collective-herd is irremediable.

At this junction—with the binary identified and Nietzsche on one side of it—at this important junction, Dillon says:

> In my view, the truth lies between these two models. There are ways in which self and others will always be in tension, just because variations in perspective are inevitable. Universal accord will never be reached, and there is some question in my mind as to whether such accord should be assumed to be the supreme goal or regulative ideal that drives political and moral theorizing. On the other side, some degree of harmony, based on acknowledgment of our interdependency, is necessary for the survival of each of us just because many of our interests are common. (p. 00)

This is a portentous passage with the promise of riches because an "in-between" theory of ethics and social theory is *exactly* what Dillon is concurrently developing in *The Ethics of Particularity*. Furthermore, such a theory would effectively counter some of the most troubling elements of Nietzsche's thought, for instance, his late notion of a strict "order of rank" among people and his autocratic, antidemocratic political philosophy. However, Dillon has nothing more to say about his own normative theory in chapter 6 of the Nietzsche manuscript and nowhere in that text mentions the ethics manuscript. Further, in chapter 3 of the ethics manuscript, Dillon makes substantial criticisms against Nietzsche's oppositional account of authenticity, but he does not carry out the natural extension of that critique to Nietzsche's larger social and political theory. My point here is not to criticize Dillon for these omissions—for all we know, he would have added those things as he finished the books—but rather to establish one specific, yet unarticulated way the ethics manuscript completes a major argument that is merely started in the Nietzsche manuscript. In a phrase, we are beginning to see that the relation of the two manuscripts is greater than the sum of its parts.

There are some other important ways in which the ethics manuscript, along with *Beyond Romance*, qualifies the Nietzschean perspective that Dillon otherwise seems to embrace. For one thing, both of those texts emphasize

something that Nietzsche could scarcely imagine: the centrality of love relationships in the good life. As I suggested earlier, this idea is so important
to Dillon that it serves as the foundational premise or credo of *Beyond Romance*: "No good love, no good life." Coupled with Dillon's foundational
commitment to "good love" is his distinctive account in both the ethics manuscript and *Beyond Romance* of *to kalon* as the recognition of nobility in
my beloved other—a nobility I want to affirm and emulate, and which I hope
she comes to recognize in me. Indeed, beyond the Nietzschean virtues that
Dillon applauds in the Nietzsche manuscript, for example, lucidity, honesty,
joyful affirmation of suffering and finitude, and living without supernatural illusions, it is clear to me that Dillon would have added the vulnerable,
self-suspending, intersubjective movement of *to kalon*. I believe that Dillon
would say that this movement of *to kalon* demands a kind of strength beyond
power or will to power; it involves a kind of letting-go-ness into the contingent, uncertain places where love and desire grow, where I stand revealed,
responsible to, and inspired by others.

There are some other important ways that *The Ethics of Particularity* tacitly qualifies the Nietzsche manuscript. For example, in chapter 7 of the ethics manuscript, titled "Life-Death," Dillon attempts to answer the age-old
question of what makes life worth living in the absence of fantasies about an
afterlife. While he acknowledges Nietzsche's suspicion that trying to vindicate life from within life is a form of circular reasoning, Dillon nonetheless
proceeds to develop an answer that, while partial and perspectival (in Nietzschean fashion), is sufficiently robust for a living being to embrace. Part of the
answer to what makes life worth living, Dillon says, is pleasure: "Anyone as
fond of Scotch whiskey as I am knows that the vindication of drinking it does
not lie in the consequences it frequently produces the following morning. *Au
contraire*, it is a "now" kind of thing: consequences be damned. . . . Speaking
as the Irishman I am, I can say that pleasure is surely part of the meaning life
has for me" (p. 00).

But immediately Dillon insists that isn't the whole story, because our reversible relationships with others—with their pain, suffering, and regard—
take us well beyond the pleasure of now. In a beautiful passage, he says:

> There is reversibility in the intercorporeity of the dying during the
> advent of death we call life. And it pervades the entirety of life. This
> pervasiveness is the basis of the peculiar qualitative aspect of life we
> place under such headings as intersubjectivity, morality, and love. To

the extent we care about others—that is, that we care about the ways in which they care about us, care being a preeminently reversible relation—we care about things that will take place in the world from which we have departed. The quality of life for those alive now is necessarily bound up with anticipations about the hereafter because it matters to us now what will happen to others later when we are dead and gone. (p. 00)

While Dillon has much more to add to his vindication of life and living well, already in this quote we see intersubjective elements that flatly contradict Nietzsche's late "Dionysian pessimism," that is, Nietzsche's wildly affirmative, yet profoundly lonely image of life and death.[8]

Thus far I have elaborated three significant ways that Dillon's texts on ethics and love provide an essential, yet unstated horizon for understanding the nature and the limits of the Nietzsche manuscript. But the "horizontal" relationship goes the other way, too. That is, Dillon's robust engagement with Nietzsche in the last years of his life helps us understand important aspects of the ethics text. One example of this unstated yet constitutive influence can be seen by considering chapter 6 of *The Ethics of Particularity*, the essentially critical chapter about ecology and environmentalism. At first glance this critique is puzzling and disturbing. I distinctly remember the uproar an oral version of this paper caused at the Merleau-Ponty conference in St. Louis in 2002. (It probably didn't help that the conference theme of environmentalism inspired attendance by many working ecologists.) However, close reading of this chapter, with the Nietzsche manuscript as a horizon, brings more understanding of his critique. Throughout the chapter, Dillon is concerned to criticize the concept of nature as a home or protective hold and also the concept of environmental balance or equilibrium. The crux of his challenge is that all these concepts involve subtle forms of anthropocentric or onto-theological projection: "There are, indeed, awesome powers at work in the universe, but they did not contrive Being for human dwelling. . . . Anthropomorphic design, intention, and intelligence belong in the sphere of *anthropos*, which is but one part intertwined with others in the flesh of the world. So, it would be wise and prudent to think and speak differently about the uncanny place mutating around us" (p. 00). A bit later he adds: "I believe . . . that much . . . ecological discourse covertly presupposes some sort of appeal to a natural teleology that is onto-theological at its core. For example, the notion of a cosmic balance upset by self-seeking human projects . . . is largely crypto-onto-theology. Balance is stasis, rest, and per-fection, none of which is apparent in the turmoil of continental drift . . . and the chaos of weather" (p. 00).

What Dillon does not tell us here, does not even reference in a footnote, is that this type of argument about nature is Nietzsche's. As Nietzsche puts it in the rather well-known section 109 in *The Gay Science*:

> Let us beware of thinking that the world is a living being. . . . Let us beware of positing generally and everywhere anything as elegant as the cyclical movements of our neighboring stars. . . . The total char-acter of the world . . . is in all eternity chaos—in the sense not of a lack of necessity but of a lack of order, arrangement, form, beauty, wisdom, and whatever other names there are for our aesthetic an-thropomorphisms. (*GS*, 167–68)

The similarity between Dillon's and Nietzsche's passages is remarkable; whether or not Dillon explicitly knew it, there is no doubt in my mind that Nietzsche is informing his critique of ecology in chapter 6 of the ethics manu-script. This means that Dillon's at first puzzling, disturbing critique becomes more understandable because it has a substantial intellectual antecedent and must be engaged on those terms.

Of course that doesn't mean Dillon's Nietzschean view of nature in chapter 6 of the ethics manuscript is correct. To be honest, I am not at all persuaded by this type of argument. If Nietzsche or Dillon wants to reject attributing arrangement, form, or balance to nature because it is anthropomorphic pro-jection, so, too, goes Nietzsche's language of chaos. Indeed, if attributions of form are projection, so, too, are attributions of *no* form. From my point of view, this means then that Nietzsche's and Dillon's anthropomorphic pro-jection argument ends up refusing meaningful reference to nature. And that position is a throwback to Nietzsche's early skepticism about reality—the very position, Dillon argues, that Nietzsche correctly supersedes. Ironically enough, Dillon himself shows in chapter 3 of the Nietzsche manuscript that Nietzsche's breakthrough is to see that "appearances" and language do not *screen* reality. Rather, "appearances" and language are our perspectival ac-cess to reality itself. Thus, for the mature Nietzsche—the Nietzsche who finally embraces becoming—the fact that such things flow from a human perspective is no objection to them; instead, we need to evaluate those per-spectives in terms of their expansiveness, life affirmation, and correctness. To

say it again, consistently applied, Nietzsche's mature thought, his perspectivism, doesn't reject views qua "projection," because that very concept—with
its accompanying notions of "screen" and "true reality beyond"—remains
mired in the post-Kantian ontology of Being. Instead, as Dillon himself
shows, Nietzsche's new task is to evaluate which of our reality concepts and
attributions is most expansive, rich, affirmative, and correct about reality.

So I think Dillon's particular way of arguing against ecology in chapter
6 of the ethics manuscript is deeply flawed. And, while I cannot develop
it here, I also think in this chapter that Dillon fails to recognize how his
Merleau-Pontian carnal ethics entails that we have responsibilities toward at
least some animal species. This is no small oversight on Dillon's part, and it
leads him to a kind of sanguinity about despecification that I would vigor-
ously challenge. But I do not make these arguments in a triumphal way. On
the contrary, I do so with sadness about the fact that Dillon and I cannot discuss them together over dinner and a glass of wine. And who knows how he
would have responded? My primary point in this section is not to show that
Dillon was mistaken, but rather to establish that we need to understand his
final writings as coiling over and back on one another in subtle folds of mutual elaboration and limitation. Again, this means that the final manuscripts
are not paradoxically diverse or disconnected, but rather different aspects of
a mature, coherent philosophical worldview that would be incorrect to call
either Nietzschean or Merleau-Pontian. Instead, I think we must understand
it as distinctly "Dillon."

This subtle synergy between the manuscripts is the primary reason I have
compiled them into this single book rather than separately publishing them.
I had no idea I would compile them when I started my editing work, but it
is now unimaginable to me to have done otherwise; too much would be lost
to the reader of only one or the other. How much of this "coiling over and
back" did Dillon himself see or intend? It is impossible to say, for he left no
working notes and there is not a single reference from one manuscript to the
other. Perhaps Dillon's final, completed manuscripts would have made these
interconnections clear, but with his sudden, untimely death, the work has
been left to us.

I do have one final thought for this section, an insight that came to me
after close study of these two manuscripts. Any previous reader of Dillon
will have encountered his occasional polemic on all things postmodern, and
on some things called "feminist." As you probably have discerned by now,
I did not follow Dillon in this, and, truth be told, he and I had some feisty

disagreements about it. Nonetheless, I think people who don't read Dillon because they have heard of this aspect of his thought are missing something important. That is, in my view, while some of Dillon's interpretations and arguments are flawed, his criticisms and polemics often speak truths and expose error; they sometimes miss the philosopher (such as Derrida in *Semiological Reductionism*), but hit square-on certain trends or fashions in academic or intellectual culture that were the result. Perhaps this last clause already indicates where I am heading, for the originator of this polemical style is none other than Nietzsche himself. Indeed, we celebrate Nietzsche as an "unfashionable thinker," a masterful critic who blurred the line between rhetoric and argument in his effort to expose deep-lying lenses or constitutive paradigms of cultural accretions. For Nietzsche, the deepest, least acknowledged of these lenses went by the names of "religion" and "morality"—safe enough from our perspective of one hundred years after the fact. But for Dillon, working in the distinctive intellectual culture of the late twentieth century, the deep lenses he perceived went by the names of "postmodernism" and "radical feminism."

Please do not misunderstand me: in making this connection, I am *not* saying that therefore either Nietzsche or Dillon is correct in their arguments, nor am I endorsing this kind of approach. (I suspect you can tell that is not my style of philosophy.) What I *am* arguing is that there is something philosophical going on in this aspect of Dillon's writings. Given Nietzsche's precedent, Dillon's occasional polemics should not be flatly rejected as "irrational" or "reactionary." Nor, conversely, should they be politely ignored in the name of memory or friendship. Instead, the truth is more complex: this aspect of Dillon's thought is a more or less intentional manifestation of Nietzsche's maverick approach and must be evaluated in these terms. Thus we see one more fold in the subtle synergy that Dillon's late thought performs between Merleau-Ponty, Nietzsche, and himself—a synergy that helps us better understand each of his books and his style as parts of a more or less coherent whole.

To underscore this point, and at the risk of immodesty, I want to share a few words that Mike wrote in a reader's report of an early version of my book *Merleau-Ponty's Philosophy*. He says: "I think Hass is wise to engage feminist criticisms of Merleau-Ponty, which he does adroitly and without compromising either himself or Merleau-Ponty. . . . The same sort of observation could be made about postmodern critics. I want to challenge and provoke them, Hass invites them aboard. He is probably wiser, but I have more fun."

Mike Dillon says: "I have more fun." It is possible that he did, but that is not my point. Rather, it is that Nietzsche would scarcely have said different.

3. EDITORIAL PROCESS

In the previous section I mentioned how the titles of the manuscripts and the chapter orders were established by Mike's Dillon's final curriculum vitae. In other words, no editorial intervention was required there. But along the editorial way I made several decisions that have shaped this book, and it seems important to say some things about the process through which the manuscripts were transferred from Dillon's desk to this book.

First of all, while Dillon was extremely tight-lipped about their contents, many friends and colleagues knew that he was working intensely on "a Nietzsche book" and "an ethics book." In the wake of Dillon's death, friends and colleagues wondered about the state of the manuscripts, excited by Joanne's revelation that he had finished chapter 6 of the Nietzsche manuscript days before his death, by her inclusion of some passages from it in a handout at one of his memorial services, and by her stated belief that the two manuscripts were mostly complete and sitting there on his computer. In late 2005, I offered my services as editor to Joanne, and she enthusiastically agreed. In February 2006, my wife, Marjorie, and I visited Ambremerine so I could spend time in Mike's study, reviewing his papers, files, and computer files. Needless to say, our hearts were heavy that weekend as the anniversary of Mike's death approached and many memories were shared. The bright side, however, was that with only a couple of days of excavation, I found computer copies of all the essays (that is, chapters) and paper files that contained all the hard drafts of each of them. And each of those paper files had the latest version clearly marked, with all the previous ones labeled "superseded"—thank heavens for Dillon's military habits! I also had other paper files of materials that seemed relevant to the two manuscripts: course notes, curriculum vitae, proposals, and the like. We returned home with two large boxes of material.

Between February 2006 and the end of August 2006, I completed a close reading of the essays, making detailed notes about their contents and their publication and presentation history. Additionally, I carried out a detailed editing of the electronic versions of the essays—now making them chapters in keeping with Mike's intentions. At this stage, I was mostly making format and font changes for consistency, even though some substantial editorial decisions needed to be made. For example, with one chapter (*Ethics*, chapter 3), the only existing electronic version was a shortened version that had been published in *Chiasmi International*. This short version conflicted with the long version of the essay that was found in the paper file, and so the deleted text had to be reinserted. In the three or four cases in which the electronic version had been shortened, I reinserted the content as it appeared in the paper version. I did this with confidence because it was evident from Dillon's notations that he understood the latest paper version to be his last word on the content of each essay. In this regard, it is also important to report that Dillon made frequent notes in the margins of the paper versions—word or sentence changes, deletions—that were obviously intended to be incorporated. Since Dillon's intentions were evident, I made those incorporations without noting them in the text.

In the summer of 2007, I made a third close reading of the manuscripts so I could write a detailed book proposal—one that included both general synopses of the two manuscripts and detailed discussions of each of the chapters. On the basis of the favorable response this proposal received from colleagues, I spent the summer of 2008 carrying out a final, systematic editing of the manuscript, which included regularizing the system of textual abbreviations and footnotes, hunting down references, fixing punctuation and citations, creating the bibliography, and writing this introduction and all the prefatory material.[9] Many of these changes were made merely to format and so were made without comment. However, every interjection I made into or about the content of the manuscripts is marked with an endnote that begins "Editor's note." If an endnote does not begin with that phrase, Dillon wrote the note. This will be important for the reader to remember, because some of Dillon's endnotes read like an editor's interjection although the notes were written by him.

As I write these words, my work on this project is nearly complete. At every step, I have attempted to edit with a very light touch. Indeed, Dillon was such an orderly, careful writer that nothing more was required. Thus the reader can have confidence that, unless I indicate otherwise, the chapters that follow are pure Dillon, from first to last and start to stop. Not that you will need my assurances: Dillon's distinctive tone and style will shine through every sentence and paragraph. The most controversial decision I made as editor—the decision I thought about longest—was whether or not to include the template for chapter 7 of the Nietzsche manuscript. As you will see, in the end I decided to include it as an appendix to that manuscript. Although it is self-evidently unfinished, sometimes even with incomplete sentences, I decided that the course of Dillon's intended argument was sufficiently clear and interesting for the template to be included. I trust that colleagues will tread lightly when drawing upon or citing material from it. But also, I thought readers might like to see what one of Dillon's chapters looked like at one stage *before* he sat down to turn it into copy that was ready for presentation or publication. Indeed, I can report from comparing other templates to their finished versions that while the finished version is fleshed out and polished in fine detail (with additional arguments here or there), for the most part, the core of the argument had been already laid down in the template.

In the end, I remain honored to have been entrusted with this task. At times, I have been deeply saddened by the work. Can anyone who knew Mike read the chapter "Life-Death" (*Ethics*, chapter 7) without feeling his sudden loss and one's own mortality? At other times, I felt a pressing need to *talk* to him: "Did you really intend to say *that*?" or "How would you respond to *this*?" And at every step, I have felt the privilege of my position as editor to be reading and studying Mike Dillon's final words and thoughts, his final developing positions on becoming and ethics—what should probably be called his "ethics of becoming." I am delighted that these manuscripts are now available to everyone who knew him and also to those who never had the chance. For as I mentioned at the outset of this introduction, Mike Dillon's light shone very brightly indeed—in his life, in his classrooms, and in his philosophy. And while he left us much too soon, we still have his work. We will always have his work. As Claude Lefort reminds us, when a thinker leaves us, we must go back to the work.

Lawrence Hass

Art, Truth, and Illusion: Nietzsche's Ontology
by
M. C. Dillon

. . . .

CHAPTER ONE

ART, TRUTH, AND ILLUSION: NIETZSCHE'S METAPHYSICAL SKEPTICISM

> I feel myself impelled to the metaphysical assumption that the truly existent primal unity, eternally suffering and contradictory, also needs the rapturous vision, the pleasurable illusion, for its continuous redemption.
>
> —Friedrich Nietzsche, *The Birth of Tragedy*

I. ART AND ILLUSION, REALITY AND TRUTH

Art creates illusions that vindicate reality. This is Nietzsche's claim in *The Birth of Tragedy*. What is the argument Nietzsche offers in support of this claim?

Reality is inaccessible to human cognition because it is finite and perspectival. A finite perspective, taken to be Real,[1] can only be an illusion. The illusions that displace reality become, for us, Reality. The only reality we can experience is reality-for-us. Reality, what we construe to be real independently of us, is an illusion because it is only real-for-us. If Truth is conceived as measured by adequacy to Reality, then the truth-for-us is that there is no Truth for us. Truth is an illusion produced through the perspectival nature of human cognition. This production is the source of art. Art devises illusions that displace reality.

Is this argument sound? That is, are the premises true and is the reasoning valid? What do the terms "truth" and "validity" signify in this context?

This problem-nexus collects many of the issues Nietzsche addresses: the attack on religion and metaphysics; the revaluation of values dependent upon Western religion and metaphysics; the critique of resentment and affirmation of honesty; the thesis of radical perspectivalism; the reconstitution of the project of science; the foundation of art in will to power, and so on.

The focus here is on the issue of truth in art. Nietzsche displaces science as the exemplar of truth: science is born of art, human creation; art sets an ideal of truth from which science draws. The supporting argument might be expressed as follows.

Science models truth on adequacy to divine creation: a statement is true if it reflects what is the case independent of us, or what is the case from the divine (non-)perspective. The measure of truth is God's creation. But God is a human creation, a product of art. Therefore, the model of scientific truth must derive from finite human creation or art.

What is the model of truth operative here? Is it true from all perspectives that we create (all models of) truth? Or is it equally valid—from other perspectives—to say that the measure of truth lies beyond us?

A. Nietzsche's Early Writings

> It is only as an *aesthetic phenomenon* that existence and the world are eternally *justified*. (BT, 52)

The most famous statement in *The Birth of Tragedy* calls upon art to justify or vindicate reality. What is it to justify reality? In what senses does reality require vindication? If reality, as we conceive it, is the product of human art, then does art implicitly involve the burden of self-vindication? If art is required to justify its own creation, Reality, then how, concretely, would art go about doing this? Does every artistic endeavor require a metaphysical vindication? As, for example, the art of medieval painting, sculpture, music, architecture, based itself upon Christian theology and vindicated itself by appeal to that context. How could we measure the success or failure of any given attempt at self-vindication on the part of art?

If art, finally, appeals to itself to justify itself, is this not a vicious form of circularity, a radical form of begging the question of its own truth? How would one go about adjudicating between competing artistic claims to truth? If Diego Rivera's art is true, can Fragonard's art also be true? If Bach's *Magnificat* is true, can Richard Strauss's *Also Sprach Zarathustra* also be true? What conception of truth is at work here?

Nietzsche argues again and again that it is impossible to judge or evaluate a perspective from within that perspective. The question of the value of existence cannot be decided from within existence.[2] His argument is based on denial of the validity of circular reasoning. Life cannot take a perspective upon itself; therefore, its attempts to vindicate itself are laughable because they beg the question, the question of the legitimacy of life's own perspective.

Why would this argument not weigh equally against the attempt on the part of art to justify itself?

What, then, of truth in art? What kind of truth is this?

In *The Birth of Tragedy*, Nietzsche argues that Greek tragedy justifies existence and the world by offering metaphysical comfort. The view of the world it presents makes life bearable by making it meaningful. The appeal here is to aesthetic values: seeing things as beautiful vindicates them.

The Birth of Tragedy was first published in 1872. A second edition, little changed, came out in 1878. In 1886, Nietzsche published a third edition containing his "Attempt at a Self-Criticism." In that "Attempt," he emphatically rejected the notion of metaphysical comfortizing, characterizing it as romantic and Christian.[3]

What does this portend for the dictum that "it is only as an aesthetic phenomenon that existence and the world are eternally justified"? What ramifications does this turnabout have for the concept of truth in art or for the role of art in determining truth?

Here I develop the thesis that Nietzsche initially adopts, but subsequently rejects: the notion of Truth as it is defined within the context of an ontology of Being. In this context, "True" means eternal and unchanging, and necessarily appeals to a divine or infinite knower. The truths that he subsequently asserts are those commensurate with an ontology of becoming, where things come into existence and pass away, where truth about things evolves as things and our understanding of them change. A consistency problem arises when one asks the critical or recursive question: Is it abidingly true that truth changes with time?

In the "Attempt," Nietzsche says: "All of life is based on semblance [*Schein*], art, deception [*Täuschung*], points of view, and the necessity of perspectives and error" (*BT*, 23; W1, 15). This allows me to sharpen the question: What content can be given to the notion of truth within the context of Nietzsche's perspectivalism? Are all points of view equally semblance and deception? Or are some appearances [*Erscheinung*] truer or better than others?

Is it possible to adjudicate among the truth claims of competing perspectives? I think it is. More evidence supports the perspective that says the earth is spherical than supports the claim that it is flat. But both remain perspectives.

Problems remain, nonetheless. Is this an appeal to utility, to a pragmatic theory of truth? Does it depend on the "all-too-human" aspects of human pleasures and pains and pursuits? Would it then be true to say that god exists, if belief in god can be shown to be useful? What about ugly truths that seem, at least, to have no utility? For example, the Dionysian truth that we shall all die after a period of suffering. Or the truth contained in the wisdom of Silenus that the greatest good for humans is never to have been born.[4]

2. THE NOBLE LIE: NIETZSCHE'S EARLY SKEPTICISM
AND TOTALITARIANISM

Nietzsche has become famous as an advocate of the "useful fiction." There are arguments that tend in this direction throughout Nietzsche's work—as well as arguments to the contrary. In fact, even in his early work, Nietzsche expresses contempt for taking pleasure and happiness as viable human ends.[5] We shall return to this, but even now it seems clear that Nietzsche does not espouse the doctrine of truth as utility as it is typically propounded: he calls for the affirmation of life in its harshest aspects, even when it threatens our comfort and security. "Useful fiction" means—in my interpretation of Nietzsche—finite truth: it is not True; it is necessary for life, but "necessary for life" means empirically grounded, like causal reasoning. And, like causal reasoning, finite truth permits us to adjudicate among competitive views. The point here is that the usefulness criterion tacitly appeals to a notion of truth. In the short run, luck may produce a useful result from a false belief— as Kepler's hypothesis that the ratios among geometrical solids matched the spatial relations between planets led to his discovery of their elliptical orbits—but, in the long run, one depends on luck as a last resort. To entrust one's fortune to luck is to abandon *phronesis*, and in that sense is antiphilosophical. As we witness in *Ecce Homo*, Nietzsche assiduously incorporates phronesis in his own living—he pays serious attention to his diet.

There is another notion of "useful fiction" that needs to be mentioned. In "The Philosopher: Reflections on the Struggle Between Art and Knowledge," an unpublished manuscript drafted in 1872, Nietzsche argues that cultural unity transcends utility: happiness does not produce great achievement, but cultural unity does.[6] Cultural unity is achieved by mastery on the part of creator-commanders, mastery that entails subjugation of those who are small. The noble lie or "beautiful illusion"[7] is one of the means by which this process of unification by mastery takes place.

It is generally acknowledged that Nietzsche is an elitist. This elitism can be mitigated by taking it to be an affirmation of the lonely and vulnerable individual who exposes himself to the "flies of the marketplace" out of altruistic motives. The solitary truth-seeker is also a bodhisattva, one who returns to the cave to shed light, knowing ahead of time that he is taking his life into his own hands. The *Untergehen* of Zarathustra can be read this way.

The political (as opposed to individual) elitism in early Nietzsche, however, is more troublesome. Nietzsche's great contempt for democracy and socialism as political institutions is well known. His arguments are consonant with Plato's argument in *Republic VIII* that if power is vested in the demos, then the lowest common denominator will prevail: pleasure and sloth will govern the social entity; it will lose its vitality, lapse into heteronomy, and fall prey to tyranny. Nietzsche's specific concern was that democracy endangers the cultural unity required for the production of great art. The task of the artist-philosopher is to generate—and enforce—the unifying vision.

In his early works Nietzsche affirms a form of political elitism pointed in the direction of totalitarianism.[8] The program for bringing about cultural unity that he advocates requires creator-commanders, artists and philosophers, to circumscribe the quest for unlimited knowledge—dissipated into heteronomy by science—within the parameters of a governing metaphor or vision, just as world religions have generated cultural unity through promulgation and enforcement of their visions of Reality. "The philosopher of the future? He must become the supreme tribunal of an artistic culture, *the police force, as it were, against all transgressions.*"[9]

The philosopher-artist is the myth builder who creates an illusion among the masses that allows him to manifest his conception of greatness and nobility. Like Plato's philosopher-king—but with one important difference. Although Plato advocates making use of the noble lie on the part of his rulers, he is in general opposed to myth because it is mere illusion, divorced from truth. In this early work, Nietzsche takes the contrary view: the only value criterion he admits is aesthetic; neither moral nor epistemological foundations survive in the context of Nietzsche's skepticism:

> All that philosophy can do [in this time of cultural vacuum] is to emphasize the relativity and anthropomorphic character of all knowledge, as well as the all pervasive ruling power of illusion. . . .
>
> Whether or not a religion is able to establish itself here within this vacuum depends upon its strength. We are committed to *culture*:

the "German" as a *redeeming* force! In any case, that religion which would be able so to establish itself would have to possess an immense *power of love*—against which knowledge would shatter as it does against the language of art.

But might not art itself perhaps be capable of creating a religion, of giving birth to myth? This was the case among the Greeks." ("The Philosopher," in *PT*, 13)

The prime example of the use of the beautiful lie for political ends in Nietzsche is the myths or lies used by the "priestly caste" to control their flocks, to bend the wills of the lesser to the ends of the greater. This strategy is affirmed in the writings—both published and unpublished—of the 1870s, that is, during the phase in which he wrote *The Birth of Tragedy*.

Later, however, in "On the Genealogy of Morals," Nietzsche opposes this strategy. He condemns the priestly caste who mobilize the *ressentiment* of the masses and turn it to their own purposes. He repudiates religion, exactly the kind of myth used to foster a set of values that allowed the priests to overthrow the warrior class.

What led Nietzsche to this about-face? My claim is that one can do more than merely speculate about his motives and reasons; it is possible, I think, to be confident about the flaws in the early position, and the nature of the standpoint Nietzsche adopted later on. One can trace the drift of the thought that guided Nietzsche, find it articulating itself in his writings. That is what I am attempting to do here.

The rift with Wagner is significant. When he wrote *The Birth of Tragedy*, Wagner was, for Nietzsche, the heroic artist who created the myth that would unify German culture. By 1886, Nietzsche regarded Wagner as a posturing Svengali who sought popularity by pandering to the rising tide of German nationalism. In my view, this is emblematic of the shift in Nietzsche's thinking I am attempting to trace.

The point of departure for Nietzsche's early writing was that of skepticism and the nihilism that is its handmaiden. As Daniel Breazeale puts it:

> The prevailing epistemological mood of the notebooks of the early
> 1870s is one of profound nihilism, with respect both to the possibil-
> ity of genuine knowledge and the value of seeking it. But in these
> writings, Nietzsche not only gave eloquent expression to his doubts

on the subject of knowledge, he connected these doubts with their
theoretical presuppositions and consequences. That is to say, he developed an *analysis* of the nature of knowledge, which he conjoined
with an *argument* designed to show how skepticism unavoidably follows from the naive pursuit of truth. (*PT*, xxviii)

Skepticism leads to nihilism because there are no grounds on the basis of
which to claim superiority for one set of values or beliefs against its competitors. Skepticism can also be seen to lead to tolerance: I can't prove that my
views are any better than yours, and, tu quoque, you can't prove that your
views are superior to mine. In my view, tolerance here is short-lived—just because it has no warrant. Why tolerate your view if it seriously threatens mine
in the political arena? If I have the power to subjugate you and obliterate the
view you advocate, then my aesthetic imperative calls upon me to do just that.

The issue of truth is not politically neutral. For absolutists, it allows for
the tyranny we know so well: we are justified by the truth of our cause. But
for skeptics, it also allows for tyranny: nobody can say we are wrong. To
abandon all epistemological and moral criteria as illusory is to forsake the
possibility of rational debate: competition defaults to exercise of political
power through any means available.

In these early works, Nietzsche advocates the use of illusion to gain political mastery. I have been arguing that the skepticism to which Nietzsche
appeals to justify this use of illusion centers around the conflation of perspectival appearances (that is, phenomena, perceptions) [*Erscheinung*] and
illusion [*Schein*]. I want now to take a deeper look at this skepticism, and try
to understand the larger epistemological framework within which Nietzsche
is working in this period of the early 1870s.

3. NIETZSCHE'S EARLY EPISTEMOLOGY

The classical model against which Kant, Schopenhauer, and Nietzsche all
argue is summarized in the opening paragraph of Aristotle's *On Interpretation*. The diagram is my interpretation.[10]

Spoken words are the symbols of mental experience and written
words are the symbols of spoken words. Just as all men have not

the same writing, so all men have not the same speech sounds, but the mental experiences, which these directly symbolize, are the same for all, as also are those things of which our experiences are the images.[11]

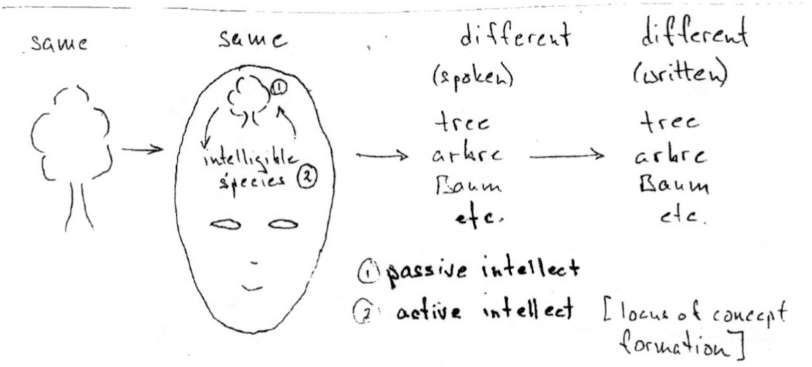

Figure 1

Now, let us look at the model Nietzsche sets out in the early texts before us:

> The various languages placed side by side show that with words it is never a question of truth, never a question of adequate expression; otherwise, there would not be so many languages. The "thing in itself" (which is precisely what the pure truth, apart from any of its consequences, would be) is likewise something quite incomprehensible to the creator of language and something not in the least worth striving for. This creator only designates the relations of things to men, and for expressing these relations he lays hold of the boldest metaphors.[12] To begin with, a nerve stimulus is transferred into an image: first metaphor. The image, in turn, is imitated in a sound: second metaphor. And each time there is a complete overleaping of one sphere, right into the middle of an entirely new and different one. . . . It is this way with all of us concerning language: we believe that we know something about the things themselves when we speak of trees, colors, snow, and flowers; and yet we possess nothing but metaphors for things—metaphors which correspond in no way to the original entities. (*TL*, 82–83)

Here is how I would diagram this:

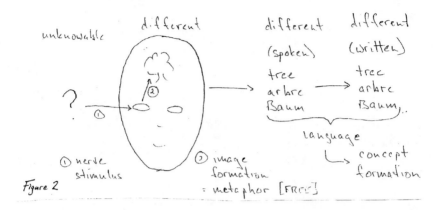

Figure 2

This is more or less the same schema as the one Aristotle sets forth, but with these two important differences:

1. The image/representation is not the same as the thing (but merely the effect of the nerve stimulus).[13]
2. The representation is not the same among all people.[14] "The relationship of a nerve stimulus to the generated image is not a necessary one" (*TL*, 87).

Artists generate the metaphors that govern how we see things. They establish conventions that vary from culture to culture. Hence, it is not the case that all humans have the same image when they look at a given thing.

The next point centers on the familiar distinction between categorial perception and seeing things in their ipseity or individual suchness. Nietzsche argues that concept formation proceeds by ignoring individual differences among things collected under a category or genus: "Every concept arises from the equation of unequal things" (*TL*, 83).[15]

In order to assert this in a self-referentially consistent way, Nietzsche would have to maintain that we can see the individuals as individuals and also note the difference between the single instance and the generic image or concept. Thus he has to assert that we both (a) do see things before the images are mediated by concepts, and (b) cannot see things except as mediated by concepts.[16] The very notion of an "individual"[17] or "original perceptual metaphor" (*TL*, 86) is an oxymoron on Nietzsche's own account—because

the metaphors of which language is constructed are *relational*; they depend
on perceiving things through the similarities among them as viewed from the
perspective of human interest.

Anticipating a doctrine later to be espoused by Derrida, Nietzsche argues
that the process of categorial cognition goes on at the unconscious level:
"Unconscious thinking must take place apart from concepts: it must therefore occur in perceptions (*Anschauungen*)" (*PT*, 41). Make the unconscious
history- and culture-dependent—that is, language-dependent—and the conclusion is that sensory stimuli, Nietzsche's "nerve impulses," produce different images or representations in different humans. And this leads to radical
skepticism:

> What then is truth? A movable host of metaphors, metonymies, and
> anthropomorphisms: in short, a sum of human relations which have
> been poetically and rhetorically intensified, transferred, and embel-
> lished, and which, after long usage, seem to a people to be fixed,
> canonical, and binding. Truths are illusions which we have forgotten
> are illusions; they are metaphors that have become worn out and
> have been drained of sensuous force. (*TL*, 84)

The ramifications of Nietzsche's early skepticism, the radical cognitive pessimism he adopts, are well known. It entails a denial of both Platonic idealism
and Aristotelian essentialism, the forerunners of contemporary transcendentalism and empiricism: there can be no type or genus known to exist in the
world independent of human classification; the world is carved up in as many
ways as there have been successful creators—and enforcers—of metaphorical
systems.[18] Another correlate of Nietzsche's radical skepticism is an equally
radical thesis of nominalism or conventionalism: the meanings of things are
determined by a sheer creative fiat of metaphor construction that cannot be
constrained by the demands of things to be seen in one way rather than another.[19] Truth becomes a matter of convention.[20]

These epistemological consequences of Nietzsche's early thinking have
been generally acknowledged, even widely affirmed, by contemporary
Nietzsche scholars, but the political consequences seem to have been overlooked. Perhaps they have been ignored because they are so noxious.
Nietzsche's early totalitarianism is couched in benign forms: "There can be
neither society nor culture without untruth. The tragic conflict. Everything

which is good and beautiful depends upon illusion" (*TL*, 92). And: "The truest things in this world are love, religion, and art" (*TL*, 95).

But, as we have seen, it is totalitarianism, nonetheless, and quite willing to enlist the philosopher of the future in the "police force . . . against all transgressions." And the art that generates the redeeming lie is "that art which rules over life" (*TL*, 12).

4. SUMMARY AND PROSPECT

The skepticism that produces Nietzsche's totalitarianism is itself grounded in the dualistic ontology that governs his thinking in the early writings. The aspect of this dualism at stake here is the binary opposition between Being and becoming. Being is the domain of immutable Truth, the domain of gods. Nietzsche's creator genius, his ideal artist, is an earthly god who creates the vision that serves the religious purpose of unifying culture, determining history, justifying existence, and redeeming it through the beautiful lie. "Only insofar as the genius in the act of artistic creation coalesces with [the] primordial artist of the world, does he know anything of the eternal essence of art" (*BT*, 52).

The artist, in creating gods, becomes god and supreme ruler through the vehicle of the beautiful illusion, the illusion whose "truth" is grounded in the absolute rule of the "aesthetic criterion," the "only criterion that counts" for Nietzsche in this phase of his thinking. The artist as creator-commander is benign, as Dostoyevsky's "Grand Inquisitor" was benign: he produces "metaphysical comfort."

The warrant for the rule of the creative genius is skepticism, the utter absence of veridical cognition.[21] The warrant for skepticism is perspectivalism: Truth is defined in terms of Being, of a divine view inaccessible to humankind. Only Being can justify beings, only Being can offer the divine wisdom capable of countering the worldly wisdom of Silenus—that it is best not to have been born at all—and redeem the tragedy of finitude, becoming, pain, and death. The inaccessibility of Being creates a void that the artist's beautiful lie fills. Such lies constitute the history of a people. As such, they are historical, but they are lived in the ahistorical mode, that is, they are lived as abiding Truth; that is, they are lived dishonestly.[22]

It is my view that Nietzsche abandons this standpoint in his later writings, indeed, that he argues against it and develops an antithetical philosophical orientation. I will set forth my case in subsequent chapters; here I can only offer a preliminary sketch of it.

The skepticism-aestheticism-totalitarianism of Nietzsche's early work is grounded in the logic of Being, in the binary opposition of finite perspectives or untruth and the infinite nonperspective of Truth. As early as *The Gay Science* and *Thus Spoke Zarathustra*, Nietzsche deliberately shifted to the logic of becoming, a logic incipient in the early work but in a privative or latent mode. The epistemological consequences of this shift take awhile to come to the surface, but they manifest themselves as a change from Nietzsche's early *identification* of finite perspective or appearance [*Erscheinung*] and untruth or illusion [*Schein*] to his later attempt to separate the two. This separation allows Nietzsche to acknowledge the finite truth of appearances, and that allows him to abandon the epistemological—and moral—nihilism of his early years.

Nietzsche remained a polemical thinker throughout his writing career. This had the negative effect of luring him into the very binary oppositions he later sought to resolve, and kept those resolutions from full conceptual realization. But his polemics also committed him to defend the truth of his own views and to expose the lies of antagonists such as Socrates, Kant, Schopenhauer, and the rest. Nietzsche needed to develop a theory of truth commensurate with the ontology of becoming, overcoming, and self-transcendence that drove his sense of historical purpose.

In order for there to be a difference between illusion [*Schein*] and appearance [*Erscheinung*]—that is, if the thesis of radical skepticism and the beautiful lie it enfranchises are to be ruled out—then appearances have to be regularly constrained or delimited or configured: our perspectives must both have a measure and provide a measure. This is the thought that begins to articulate itself through Nietzsche's writings of the 1880s.

CHAPTER TWO

NIETZSCHE'S METAMORPHOSIS

Every art, every philosophy may be viewed as a remedy and an aid in the service of growing and struggling life; they always presuppose suffering and sufferers. But there are two kinds of sufferers: first, those who suffer from the *over-fullness of life*—they want a Dionysian art and likewise a tragic view of life, a tragic insight— and then those who suffer from the *impoverishment of life* and seek rest, stillness, calm seas, redemption from themselves through art and knowledge, or intoxication, convulsions, anesthesia, and madness . . . revenge against life itself.

—Friedrich Nietzsche, *The Gay Science*[1]

I. THE CHANGELING IN 1876

Nietzsche's metamorphosis is a process of self-transcendence without finality. It terminates in decay and death. There is no otherworldly redemption, no reward in a hereafter. There is, and only is, life-unto-death, that eternally recurring organic cycle, celebrated in the agon of the Greek phallic plays, of birth-growth-decay-death. If one separates life and death into distinct abstract entities mutually excluding one another, as words encourage us to do, then one enters a dualistic mode of thought with a binary logic that forces a decision. That is, A and non-A, thesis and anti-thesis, life and its negation: they cannot both be true, cannot both be good; one has to choose between them. In 1876,[2] Nietzsche chose life—or thought he did—but actually chose life-death, the whole cycle. The unfolding of Nietzsche's thought from this time forward is the gradual and sporadic recognition that to affirm life is to affirm life-death, that the binary logic behind his polemics has to be overcome in order to reach the nobility of the truly tragic figure: the new

Dionysus, loving his fate full in the face of the wisdom of Silenus, the tragic thought that man's greatest good is to never have been born.

The Birth of Tragedy was a tribute to Wagner. In it, Nietzsche elevated Wagner to the plane of Sophocles and Aeschylus by attributing to him the same metaphysical structure that underlies the greatness of Greek tragedy and solves the Aristotelian conundrum of taking pleasure in witnessing pain. Dionysian passion is vindicated by Apollonian dream-work or illusion. The saga of the gods makes life meaningful, puts human suffering in the context of a benign order with promise of reward hereafter, and thereby provides metaphysical comfort. Art redeems life. The poet is an earthly god who creates a meaningful universe and presents it as a truer vision of Reality than the one merely apparent in quotidian lives filled with misery and boredom. Of course, the Reality generated by art is illusion, an Apollonian dream, but so is everyday life an illusion—for good, sound Kantian reasons—and a lesser illusion, because it lacks beauty and fails to meet Nietzsche's supreme aesthetic criterion.

The philosophical foundation upon which *The Birth of Tragedy* is built is the conflation of perception or phenomenal unfolding and illusion or dream. In Kantian terms, this is the conflation of *Erscheinung*, or perceptual appearance, and *Schein*, illusion. The relation between these terms is ambiguous and complex. They can be conflated because each is equally removed from the noumenal Reality of the thing in itself, but they have to be distinguished in order to preserve the differences between seeing and dreaming, dealing with the everyday world and hallucinating. The metaphysical comfort provided by the artist or poet trades on this ambiguity: we are to take the beautiful hallucination as the context for the mundane appearance, and live as though this narrative were true. The narrative is an eminently useful fiction because it brings meaning to lives that appear to terminate in decay, pain, and death.

Beyond that, the metaphysical structure of poetic narrative is an ultimately powerful political tool; it allows the poet-creator to generate a religion: an organizing principle capable of governing the state and commanding obedience among its people. Here is a myth to live by, here are the rules that you have to follow to get your reward in heaven. Conform to them on earth and that will generate the relative harmony of like-minded community and provide peace and tranquillity. To be followed by absolute peace and absence of strife in the world hereafter, where the messy effects of temporal unfolding do not apply.

By 1876, Nietzsche had succeeded in identifying this structure as a choice of death over life. He had also succeeded in identifying the figure of the dying god, Christ, as yet another of the many world-historic symbols for our all-too-human yearning for stillness, peace, and death. And he had learned to see Wagner as a Christian death-monger, feeding off the herd of conforming admirers.

2. WAGNER

> By the summer of 1876...I said farewell to Wagner in my heart.... He had condescended step by step to everything I despise. (Nietzsche, *PN*, 675–76)[3]

Nietzsche's break with Wagner marked a crisis, a turning point, in Nietzsche's personal and intellectual life. Wagner was the symbol for the philosophical standpoint Nietzsche occupied in his early writings, his time of metaphysical skepticism and aestheticism. When he repudiated Wagner, he repudiated that standpoint, and began a polemic against it that continued throughout his productive years. The sheer number of writings he devoted to Wagner is a beacon of excess: *Richard Wagner in Bayreuth* (1876); *The Wagner Case* (1888); and *Nietzsche Contra Wagner* (1895). When Nietzsche repeated the passage quoted above from *The Gay Science* in *Nietzsche Contra Wagner*, he put it under the title "We Antipodes." That is an apt statement of the oppositional thinking in which he was engaged at the time. Wagner became the symbol for everything Nietzsche hated: Christianity, anti-Semitism, romanticism, hedonism, popularity, and the comfortable life. Wagner was the poet laureate of the rising tide of German nationalism that Nietzsche abominated. Wagner wrote the narrative that provided the metaphysical comfort for German identity at the turn of the century.

When Nietzsche broke with Wagner, he took leave from the University of Basel, and resigned three years later. He also broke with the circle of friends he had cultivated during the time he enjoyed Wagner's patronage. His relationship with his sister, Elisabeth, shifted to a negative axis over the issue of anti-Semitism—now foregrounded as a guiding principle for Nietzsche's identity as a "free spirit" and "good European" in opposition to the emergent German ideology of Aryan racial superiority, modeled on Wagner's unique elision of Nordic gods and such Christian heroes as Parsifal.

What makes this personal history philosophically significant?

The core of Nietzsche's diatribe against Wagner is an accusation of dishonesty, a peculiar kind of dishonesty: the dishonesty of the actor. Actors are
people who deliberately and convincingly portray themselves as what they
are not. They earn their living and secure their reputations by being what
they are not, by playing roles: "falseness with a good conscience" (GS, 316).
Actors misrepresent themselves in order to please crowds: they put on the
guise that will ingratiate them to the lowest common denominator. To be an
actor is to be what the herd wants one to be. Nietzsche saw Wagner as the
consummate actor and regarded that dishonesty as the secret to his success:

> You will guess that I am essentially anti-theatrical[4]—but Wagner
> was, conversely, essentially a man of the theater and an actor, the
> most enthusiastic mimomaniac of all time. . . .
>
> I once made this clear to an upright Wagnerian . . . and I had rea-
> sons for adding: "Do be a little more honest with yourself! After all,
> we are not in the theater. . . . No one brings along the finest senses
> of his art to the theater, nor does the artist who works for the the-
> ater. There one is common people, audience, herd, female, pharisee,
> voting cattle, democrat, neighbor, fellow man; there even the most
> personal conscience is vanquished by the leveling magic of the great
> number." (GS, §368; pp. 325–26)

Nietzsche condemns Wagner on moral grounds for being an actor, that is,
for being inauthentic, for being false or dishonest both to himself and to the
herd whose favor he courts. The idea that it is somehow sleazy to be an actor,
immoral to be inauthentic, is not new; one can find it in Plato's Ion. What is
new is taking that thought to be the groundwork for an ethics of authenticity.
Nietzsche's attack on Wagner can be seen as a founding moment of the existentialist movement as it developed from Nietzsche to Heidegger to Sartre
and beyond.

Nietzsche turned away from his safe haven in Wagner's coterie with the
zeal of a convert, seeking higher ground in the ether of the austere mountain-
tops where, from a solitary perch, he could look down upon the tiny ant-size
figures scurrying about along well-worn paths in the valleys below. The theater is below, essentially low-down, because it is the place of the ignoble lie.
The lie, the self-esteem generating fantasy fed to the spiritually impoverished
masses, is the founding lie of communality itself: we, the members of this
community, this tribe, this clan, are better than you who belong to another;

we are number one. In the case of Wagner, the lie takes the specific form of the historical destiny of the German people, descended from pure-blooded Aryan spiritual warlords, marching onward as Christians to take possession of the grail that is rightfully their own. Nietzsche lavished contempt upon that lie, but he also took note of its underlying general structure, the spirit of rancor, revenge, or, preferring the ring of the French word, *ressentiment*.

Resentment is the prime mode in which inauthenticity manifests itself. The low-down herd animals of the valley know themselves to be lesser, feel bitter envy toward the rich and powerful, need balm for that gall, and find it in revolt: the revolution of the wheel that turns the lesser into the greater. This is the slave revolt in morality Nietzsche will analyze in *On the Genealogy of Morals* (1887), but it is well to note that Wagner in 1876 is Nietzsche's prototype of the priestly caste that emerges to mobilize the resentment of the masses in a world-historic power grab.

It is also well to note—if only as a suspicion for the moment—that Nietzsche's expressions of contempt for Wagner's immense success and popularity are somewhat shrill. Here, taken from the same passage in *The Gay Science* quoted above (§368), is what Nietzsche says about the music he exalts in *The Birth of Tragedy*:

> My objections to the music of Wagner are physiological objections; why should I trouble to dress them up in aesthetic formulas? My "fact" is that I no longer breathe easily once this music begins to affect me; that my foot soon resents it and rebels. . . .
>
> My melancholy wants to rest in the hiding places and abysses of *perfection*: that is why I need music. What is the drama to me? What, the convulsions of its moral ecstasies which give the common people satisfaction? What, the whole gesture hocus-pocus of the actor? . . .
>
> And, incidentally, if it was Wagner's theory that "the drama is the end, the music is always a mere means," his *practice* was always, from beginning to end, "the pose is the end; the drama, also the music, is always merely a means to *that*." (GS, 324–25)

Nietzsche condemns the music he once loved because now he sees that it is in service to imposture. Wagner is ensconced in Bayreuth as a monumental figure of German culture and Nietzsche's books do not sell. Nietzsche knew *ressentiment* from the inside out. The gratuitous misogyny permeating his writing cannot be understood in any other way. *Ressentiment* is the

counterforce to self-transcendence that this diminutive *Übermensch* strug-
gled with every step up and down his mountain.

3. ROMANTICISM AND *RESSENTIMENT*

Nietzsche's ethics of authenticity clearly influenced Heidegger's putatively
value-neutral descriptions of inauthenticity, but the difference between the
two thinkers is consequential. For Nietzsche, inauthenticity is a form of dishonesty, a manner of not telling the truth when there is a truth to be told.
For Heidegger, authenticity is facing the truth that there is no truth to be
told, that is, confronting the anxiety of the null basis for Dasein's existence,
thrownness, and being-unto-death.[5]

Nietzsche's moral condemnation of Wagner is grounded on an appeal to
truth. The truth he appeals to, however, is a new kind of truth: neither the
Truth grounded in the absolute of infinite knowledge, nor the "truth" of the
abyss of groundlessness, but the finite truth afforded by appearance [*Erscheinung*]. When, in the spirit of affirmation of life, Nietzsche abandons the ni-
hilistic skepticism underlying his early writing, he faces a metaphysical crisis.
God is dead. There is no Truth. But romanticism is a lie: Nietzsche's perspective is somehow better than Wagner's. How can it be better if all perspectives are equally removed from the impossible infinite perspective? How can
Nietzsche maintain the attitude of moral superiority implicit in everything
spoken by Zarathustra without some warrant, some ground he can defend?
If there is no afterworldly Truth, where is the truth to be found in this world?

I have cast the problem in Kantian terms because those are the terms in
which Nietzsche addressed it most directly. Schopenhauer's pessimistic aestheticism is the prime target of *The Birth of Tragedy*, but that rests squarely
on a variation of Kantian transcendental metaphysics, as does Nietzsche's
critique of Schopenhauer and his own vindication of the Apollonian dream
as situating the Dionysian pathos of becoming in a meaningful context. Kant
had argued that Reality in itself lies beyond the realm of possible human
cognition because all human cognition is mediated by the faculties that carry
it out. But since we are hardwired to view the world through structures, demonstrated by Newton to be universal and necessary for sentient, rational creatures like ourselves, we can lay claim to knowledge of the human world, the
phenomenal world, the world as it appears to us.

This world is Newton's dream formalized along categorial lines derived by

Kant from his revision of Aristotelian metaphysics. Schopenhauer's human world, equally removed from but dominated by his Reality, Nature, is driven by will and the categories of passion, appetite, and instinct. Nature drives us to will what it needs to be done to sustain itself, and deceives us in the process into believing that we are willing our own interests when, in fact, we are serving the interests of Nature, which are contrary to our own. Influenced by his study of Eastern philosophy, Schopenhauer advocates stilling the will, banishing the illusion of the ego and its attendant suffering for the sake of survival, and viewing the world objectively from the standpoint of aesthetic removal and dispassionate contemplation. In *The Birth of Tragedy*, Nietzsche re-indexes the will from negative to positive, puts it in service to life, and regards Art as the supreme human capacity to create a world of meaning. Kant was mistaken in privileging science; science is but one of the products of Art. Schopenhauer was mistaken in turning to Art as redemption *from* life; Art is the redemption *of* life: it manifests the human will, and its creativity is the ultimate source of our power.

In 1876, art in the hands of Wagner had collided with itself, put itself in service to death by creating a phenomenal domain structured by the will to the serenity and peace of non-being, non-life. Art had produced non-Art. The shadow of Art had eclipsed its own sun, its intrinsic values had gone awry and spawned a human world stifling to the spirit of affirmation: German nationalism, socialism, and the conformist hegemony of the common. Art must reassert itself against the undertow of afterworlds as will to life, will to power. To do this, art must be true to this world, the world in which humans live. Here is the ultimate agon, life versus death.

How to win this war? What would it mean to win this war? By what tokens would one be able to recognize the victor? Let us enter this question through a back door: What would it mean *not* to win the war? How would one recognize the vanquished?

If the mad ranting of a certified crazy, initially appropriated as propaganda by a political force generally acknowledged to be bent upon genocide, were to be vindicated by popular approval and pressed into service of progressive causes out to win the culture wars of its time . . . If copies of *Zarathustra* were to migrate out of the backpacks of the *Wehrmacht* into backpacks emblazoned with the symbols of peace and the slogans of vegetarianism . . . Would Nietzsche smile down from on high, contented that he had slain the dragon? Would it vindicate Art and "those who suffer from the *over-fullness of life*—[who] want a Dionysian art and likewise a tragic view of life, a tragic insight" to find that Nietzsche has outperformed Wagner at New Bayreuth, that his narrative is now in ascendance, that it has proven to be useful in the cause of social critique? Book sales are certainly up. And Nietzschean genealogy, as a philosophico-political tool for exposing and dismantling the hidden hierarchies of power responsible for oppressing large segments of humanity, is widely deployed in the intellectual capitals of democratic culture in Europe and points west. If Nietzsche is not number one, he is close to it, up there in front.

More is at stake here than Nietzsche's elitist attitude toward popularity. Nietzsche frequently wrote words to the effect that widely shared beliefs are to be viewed with suspicion, or even summarily dismissed, just because they are widely shared: herd thinking is, of itself, necessarily wrong. "Herd thinking" is an oxymoron. Kundera captures the spirit of Nietzsche when he writes that true statements, when they become slogans chanted by a mob, become false. Behind the rhetorical flourish is a philosophical thesis. The thesis is that truth emerges in a process of becoming, that the disclosure of every revelation, if it is taken to be final, obscures a further truth. A correlate of this thesis maintains that popular acceptance of a truth—accepting some view for oneself because it is generally accepted—falsifies it for the believer because he believes it for the wrong reasons. I believe it to be true, not because I can supply the warrant, point to the evidence, give the arguments, but because I dwell in a community of shared beliefs, where membership in community is predicated upon accepting what is commonly believed. If my beliefs are not lucid, if I do not examine and cannot supply the warrant for my belief, then I cannot take personal responsibility for the belief . . . or for the actions that flow from it. Herd animals stampede because there is a stampede, not because they saw the lion.

Transcendental philosophy, from Kant to Husserl and beyond, grounds itself by appealing to the limits of conceivability. Instants of time flow together to produce the experience of motion and duration. This synthesis presupposes an agency of synthesis that, itself, stands outside of time (otherwise it would require its own temporal synthesis). It is inconceivable that there could be temporal continuity without a transcendental unity of apperception. Husserl's eidetic methodology rests on the same appeal to the limits of conceivability: when free variation reaches a limit of conceivability [the essence at stake is defined].[6] Lived space is three-dimensional because a fourth spatial dimension is inconceivable.

What defines the limits of conceivability? Saint Anselm could not conceive God as nonexistent; apparently, Nietzsche could. Kant argued that the phenomenal world, the world in which we live, is defined by necessary and universal structures that control how we have to understand things, how they have to be for us. Husserl argues for an "innate a priori" that functions much the same way to define the limits of possible experience in the phenomenal domain. Schopenhauer argued that Nature implants in us a way of seeing, filtered through will or desire, that predisposes us to represent the world in certain ways, but that can be changed by a self-induced modification of the will to distance itself from desire.

Nietzsche argued in *The Birth of Tragedy* that poets can establish a whole new a priori, a dreamscape with its own *eidos*, its own way of looking at things that is capable of framing a new conceptuality and a new sentience. That is what those who named the gods did. That is what the metaphysicians did when they renamed the gods. It can be done again and again, each successful naming founding a community of believers, people who find themselves bound together by having been born into a set of beliefs generated, ultimately, by the Art of the poetic saga, the naming of the gods.

Art can create a human world and populate it by manipulating desire, ultimately, the desire for meaningful lives. Lives are made meaningful by providing metaphysical comfort, and that, in turn, is ensured by feeding self-esteem and holding out the promise of reward. In his early writings of the 1870s, Nietzsche called for an Artist-king to generate a new religion of Art that would bind the state into a community designed to support cultural production under the supreme principle of the aesthetic criterion. The aesthetic criterion at work is beauty defined as the object of desire. The object of desire, Nietzsche thought then, was metaphysical comfort.

Then, in the microcosm of Bayreuth, governed by the monumental figure of Wagner, Nietzsche began to discern beneath the metaphysical comfort of German romanticism the fuel that fed both its fire and the fire of German nationalism: rancor, envy, *ressentiment*—the very essence of the ignoble.

In the Germany emergent in his day, Nietzsche saw community bonded by the inconceivability of the contrary of their shared belief system, their religion. Their illusion. Their mass hysteria. Their flight from lucidity and personal responsibility. Their participation in someone else's dream, a dream contrived to satisfy their deepest desire. Beauty, as the object of desire, reaches its culmination in vengeance against all that is noble.

4. REVALUATION OF ALL VALUES

Nietzsche turned away from Wagner and his own former self on moral grounds. He did not abandon the aesthetic criterion; he subordinated it to a moral criterion, the criterion of nobility. That left him with the life-project of defining, defending, and becoming genuine nobility. The themes that will define nobility—overman, will to power, *amor fati*, and the new truly tragic figure of Dionysus—begin to surface in *The Gay Science*, reach crescendo in *Zarathustra*, and are defended in the later works, notably *Beyond Good and Evil*.

Interpretations of these major themes in Nietzsche abound and collide. Nietzsche has been seen as everything from a proto-Nazi to a harbinger of postmodern thought. Bad philosophy at its worst; creative genius at its best. The one point upon which most agree is that his writing style—being fragmentary, laced with irony, changing with mood, delivered in metaphor, and delighting in contradiction—makes it near impossible to reduce his thought to a coherent standpoint. Nietzsche is just not consistent, and it is wrong-headed to try to force his free spirit into a straitjacket of logic: Nietzsche's truth lies in verve, zest, tempo, and shadow play. Nietzsche, the preacher of freedom and self-transcendence, is also the herald of eternal recurrence, a teaching that commits him to strict determinism. Go to Nietzsche for inspiration, not for doctrine. No matter what he thought at that passing moment, what does he awaken in you? Pick your quotes ad lib and fly.

Nietzsche, the symbol, is truly overdetermined and irreducible to formula. Nietzsche, the mirror for the philosophical Narcissus, has inspired a feast of great writing, Milan Kundera being the latest to pique my fancy; and I deem it sheer foolishness to search for the algorithm that could package his thought neatly.

Nonetheless, Nietzsche did have something to say. What he had to say excludes what he thought was wrong. Nietzsche is a thinker of right and wrong. If you care about what he thought was right and what he thought was wrong, it is important to try to get that right. Reductio ad absurdum is still a viable critique: if you attribute contradictory standpoints to a given thinker, you just do not know where that thinker stands on that issue. Eternal recurrence and freedom, for example.

Nietzsche did contradict himself. He did, and he said he did. He said that he got it wrong in *The Birth of Tragedy*. He changed his way of thinking in 1876 (or thereabout), did an "about-face," and struck out in new directions.

He abandoned metaphysical comfortizing as a philosophical goal and took its critique as a philosophical goal. The face of Dionysus took on a new, stern cast: without forgetting how to dance, he became truly tragic. In fact, *amor fati* made Dionysus a better dancer, put him in sync with a deeper beat.

Nietzsche had style. I take that to be indisputable. Nietzsche's style cannot be reduced to a set of attributes. Also indisputable. Style is adverbial, a modality, but is nonetheless recognizable; indeed, is eminently recognizable. Style is eminently recognizable because style confers unity. There is unity in [Nietzsche's][7] style, and that unity provides a measure and a guide in the attempt to work out what he thought was right from what he thought was wrong, that is, in the attempt to understand what he had to say.

How to name Nietzsche's style? Honestly. Nobly. For Nietzsche, the two adverbs are synonyms. Honesty, named in *Zarathustra* as "that youngest among the virtues,"[8] is the modality of thought that unifies Nietzsche's thought from 1876 on. Honestly is how Nietzsche wanted to do things. He wanted to be Wagner's antipode. He wanted to be noble. And, in his own way, he was.

I have been describing Nietzsche as a moral philosopher. Now that characterization has more content: Nietzsche argues for a morality of honesty and nobility, pointed toward self-transcendence, aimed at identifying and eradicating *ressentiment* as he finds it without and within. That is the measure that he applied to himself and others. In the context of a philosophy of self-transcendence, one never finally measures up to one's own measure, and I have already acknowledged that I think Nietzsche never managed to surpass his own rancor. But it was a mighty agon, worthy of being retold, and Nietzsche acquitted himself well. Nobly. Nietzsche took on an adversary stronger than himself: to suffer defeat was no dishonor, the important thing was to fight.

The project of the revaluation of all values can be stated in simple terms: it is the attempt to identify and label the dishonesty informing the values at work in the rancorous herd. What is not simple is to see that it is not so much the values themselves as the *manner* in which they are deployed that Nietzsche condemns. There is deceit in Truth-telling, will to ascendancy among the preachers of equality, and so forth. As I argued in the preceding section, Nietzsche's mightiest foe is the darkness of self-deceit, the lack of lucidity that constitutes the herd animal as such, the acting-out of an assigned role as though it were one's own with little awareness of the meaning of the role, hence with no capacity to take responsibility for it. Honesty requires lucidity.

Lucidity is incompatible with community insofar as community entails acceptance of a common set of values just because they are foundational to the community. The principle of lucidity drives the *Übermensch* out of the community, makes him an outcast and a pariah. That was the fate Nietzsche chose for himself in 1876. The facts at the level of personal history are well known; the philosophical portent of lucidity, however, remains somewhat obscure.

Zarathustra regularly sends his disciples packing, telling them to go their own way and not to follow him. That is the principle of lucidity at work: Nietzsche does not want to grow his own herd; he wants disciples disciplined to identify the values informing their own behavior, hence to be able to take responsibility for what they do. Beyond that, however, the principle of lucidity precludes the project of creating a transcendental narrative designed to generate a communal system of belief. Nietzsche is deliberately opposed, from 1876 on, to the construction of an ideality that would displace the reality of life. He is in mortal combat—life versus death—against all forms of transcendental philosophy that would displace life with a narrative of life, that would constitute a life-world filtered through an ideality constructed of metaphors. It is clear to all that Nietzsche is opposed to all afterworlds constructed of rancor and wistful, wishful thinking; and that he advocates being true to this world, the one in which we eat carefully, try in vain to get a good night's sleep, and look for pain medications that offer some hope of relief. What does not seem clear to all is that his honest confrontation with this world commits Nietzsche to a kind of realism for which there is as yet no name. Or too many vague and misleading names. For the moment, I shall designate it as the "commitment to this world," and try to avoid premature triggering of ontological alarm systems.

Nietzsche's commitment to this world is the phase in his metamorphosis that takes him from a transcendental projection of ideality in *The Birth of Tragedy* predicated on undermining the distinction between appearance and illusion to a growing awareness that the distinction has to be *honestly* maintained. Here is a clear and forthright statement of the position Nietzsche takes in *The Birth of Tragedy*:

> Though it is certain that of the two halves of our existence, the waking and the dreaming states, the former appeals to us as infinitely preferable, more important, excellent, and worthy of being lived, indeed, as that which alone is lived—yet in relation to that

mysterious ground of our being of which we are the phenomena, I should, paradoxical as it may seem, maintain the very opposite estimate of the value of dreams. For the more clearly I perceive in nature those omnipotent art impulses, and in them an ardent longing for illusion, for redemption through illusion, the more I feel myself impelled to the metaphysical assumption that the truly existent primal unity, eternally suffering and contradictory, also needs the rapturous vision, the pleasurable illusion, for its continuous redemption. And we, completely wrapped up in this illusion and composed of it, are compelled to consider this illusion as the truly nonexistent—i.e., as a perpetual becoming in time, space, and causality—in other words, as empirical reality. (*BT*, 44–45)

"We . . . are compelled to consider this illusion . . . as empirical reality." That statement is dishonest. It is a forthright instance of self-deceit. It contradicts itself: the denial cannot be maintained without the affirmation of what it denies. It says I will live as though I cannot tell the difference between dreaming and perceiving, and I will do that to redeem my waking life. I will live a pretense.

It is one thing to commit oneself to dropping all pretensions and becoming an honest person, but it takes something beyond the commitment to carry it out. Kant cannot be summarily dismissed. His argument is too strong. To honor his commitment to this world, Nietzsche has to do justice to Kant's truth, to the epistemological problems associated with appeals to empirical reality. Nietzsche's commitment to this world has to be reconciled with the perspectivalism, drawn directly from Kant, which continues to inform his philosophy to the end. Nietzsche's philosophy from 1876 can and should be read as a recurrent quest to find grounds for that reconciliation, as a continuously renewed effort to understand—and deal honestly with—the epistemological problems associated with maintaining the distinction between *Schein* and *Erscheinung* as well as the problems associated with denying it.

. . . .

CHAPTER THREE

ILLUSION, APPEARANCE, AND PERSPECTIVE: NIETZSCHE'S HONEST TRUTH

To the realists.— You sober people who feel well armed against passion and fantasies and would like to turn your emptiness into a matter of pride and an ornament: you call yourselves realists and hint
that the world really is the way it appears to you. . . . You are still
burdened with those estimates of things that have their origin in the
passions and loves of former centuries. Your sobriety still contains a
secret and inextinguishable drunkenness. Your love of "reality," for
example—oh, that is a primeval "love." Every feeling and sensation
contains a piece of this old love; and some fantasy, some prejudice,
some unreason, some ignorance, some fear, and ever so much else
has contributed to it and worked on it. . . . There is no "reality" for
us—not for you either, my sober friends.
—Friedrich Nietzsche, *The Gay Science*

I. THE QUESTION

Are we in touch with reality? That may be the question that initiates philosophy, one of the ways of articulating the initial doubt that gives rise to reflection, inquiry, and critique of human knowing. Philosophy begins in the mode
of cognitive insecurity. And that is where it will stay indefinitely, as long as we
remain finite and embodied. We know, then, from the start, that any answer
given to the question—including the one to be presented here—will be insufficient, tentative, subject to change. We also know that how we respond to
the question, how we live through the experience of cognitive insecurity, is
existentially portentous: a life structured around anxiety and doubt is different from a life of complacent acceptance of a given understanding of what
is real. Given that portent, it is well to choose carefully among the answers
competing for our credibility. Our latent ontologies—the prethematic sense

of what is real each of us has—set global horizons that influence all our thinking and doing.

2. ILLUSION AND APPEARANCE

Are we in touch with reality? Kant formulated this question around three key terms: "illusion" (*Schein*), "appearance" (*Erscheinung*), and "thing in itself" (*Ding an sicht*). Nietzsche initially adopted Kant's terms—and their attendant philosophical baggage—and worked within and upon the paradigms of Kant's Cartesian ontology and epistemology.[1] That is, Nietzsche accepted Kant's manner of framing the question, but his manner of answering it evolved into an ontology that displaced the initial Cartesian framework. Nietzsche begins with an ontology of Being and moves toward an ontology of becoming.

In the "Transcendental Aesthetic," Kant takes the phrase "thing in itself" not to require elaborate definition. Later, notably in the "Transcendental Dialectic," he will define it in explicitly theological terms: the thing in itself is the thing as known by the infinite and perfect mind of God. "Appearance" is the thing in relation to the finite subject, the thing as it is given to us, mediated by our "mode of intuition," that is, mediated by the "representations" (*Vorstellungen*) constituting our "sensible intuitions." "Illusion" is rather narrowly defined as that which results when we "ascribe *objective reality*" to appearances, that is, when we take what we see to be identical to what God sees. Kant also says that appearances are not illusions in the additional sense that "objects . . . are always regarded as something actually given."[2]

In *The Birth of Tragedy*, Nietzsche calls upon us to ascribe objective reality to the representations offered in the Apollonian dream created by the artist. In the straightforward Kantian terms just defined, he advocates transforming everything into "mere illusion." Later, he recants, and under the moral rubric of honesty, makes a commitment to this world: we are now to treat illusions as what they truly are, the result of mistaking our representations for the objective reality knowable only by a defunct god. Illusion being thereby dispelled and the thing in itself remaining beyond our finite grasp, we are left with appearances: we are left with the world as it is given to us, mediated by our forms of intuition, space and time, and the categories of the faculty of understanding. How are we to think of appearances?

Space, time, and categorial functions are *forms* of intuition in the specific

sense that they provide formal grounds for synthesis and constitution of relations. In Kant's ontology, all relation is "transcendental" in the specific sense
of being grounded exclusively in human faculties. The relations we ascribe
to things are relations they have for us and cannot, under penalty of illusion,
be ascribed to things as they are apart from us. Relations are ideal, human,
not real. Relations are also the only source of meaning: chaos is the name
for matter lacking all organization and structure. Chaos is no threat to Kant
because the relations among things in the phenomenal world of human experience are grounded in the universal and necessary categories of human
understanding. We can have true understanding of how things must be structured in the only world we will ever encounter.

This is not the case for early Nietzsche. For Nietzsche in 1872, relations
among things are human creations. The power to create relations and generate meaning is Art. That is why he, unlike Kant, subsumes science, as a
specific set of relations created by humans, under Art, as the general ability
to create relations. There is no necessity, as there is in Kant, to privilege one
way of relating things over any other. That was Nietzsche's warrant for living
the beautiful illusion.

After 1876, Nietzsche faces a dilemma. Either honest acknowledgment
that relations are ideal and groundless, that all meaning is fabrication, which
has no ground other than the power of artists to generate fantasy. Or rever-
sion to self-deceit. There is no way out of this dilemma in the context of the
Kantian ontology initially adopted by Nietzsche once the formal necessities
imposed by space, time, and the categories have been relativized to contingent products of artistic creation.

Nietzsche has but one alternative: he has to abandon or modify Kantian
ontology. And he has to do this in a specific way. He has to assert, against his
early nominalism, that the appearances given to us in sensible intuitions are
bound by relations that transcend human intervention and artistic creation,
that the form of experience is given along with its sensible matter, that the
world in which we live has meaning for us that does not derive from us. Only
if Nietzsche were to have modified his thought in exactly this way could he
write, as he did, that "I want to learn more and more to see as beautiful what
is *necessary* in things; then I shall be one of those who make things beautiful.
Amor fati: let that be my love henceforth!"

The logic here is inexorable and its consequences for Nietzsche's thought
are clear. Art is no longer the product of a sublunary god creating meaning
ex nihilo by Apollonian wish fulfillment and dream fiat. Great art is to be

produced by a truly tragic Dionysian figure who contends with the realities of human life as they demand to be seen, be they pleasant or not. In the texts following 1876, one finds that the pleasure principle informing the early aesthetic criterion—seeing beauty as the object of desire—has been suspended, indeed, placed in the domain of suspicion and mistrust, and a reality principle now governs a new aesthetic criterion—seeing transcendent necessity as beautiful.

In this movement away from Kantian transcendental idealism, Nietzsche once again does what Kant forbade: once again, he ascribes objective reality to appearances. This generates ambiguity for those who would interpret his work. In *The Birth of Tragedy*, he deliberately entered the sphere of illusion as Kant defined it. In the texts after 1876, he deliberately removed himself from that sphere of willful self-delusion. The motivations underlying these two movements are different and conflicting, but the result is the same: the ascription of reality to appearances. The ambiguity that results for his interpreters is the illusion/appearance ambiguity: if we read Nietzsche as remaining within Kantian ontology, we must conclude that he persists in the illusion of ascribing reality to appearance; if we read him as moving beyond Kantian ontology, we will see him seeking to dispel illusion in a demystifying search for transcendent reality. The question is whether Nietzsche remains a transcendental philosopher or becomes a philosopher of transcendence.

Let me say here that the question poses a false dichotomy: try as one may, one cannot consistently be a transcendental philosopher without at the same time being a philosopher of transcendence. That is what Nietzsche had to learn in order to teach. That is what this book has to show.[3]

3. PERSPECTIVE

Appearances are representations. Appearances are real. Appearances are reality as mediated through the cognitive faculties of a subject. Appearances are reality perceived from within a perspective. What is a perspective? What is the understanding of "perspective" that informs the "perspectivism" widely attributed to Nietzsche?

Kant teaches in the "Transcendental Aesthetic" that it is a formal condition of sensible intuition to be situated in space and time. To perceive from a spatio-temporal perspective, broadly speaking, is to be geographically and historically delimited in one's outlook upon things: to be present to reality at a given place and time. Is it the case that to ascribe reality to what presents itself to me at a given place and time is to enter the sphere of illusion? Or is it the case that this experience is definitive of the primordial and ultimately undeniable sense of reality that gives meaning to the term? What position does Nietzsche occupy on this issue? How one answers this question will determine how one resolves the ambiguity described above and whether one will regard Nietzsche as locked within a transcendentalist viewpoint or not.

One crucial point is clear. If one takes the reality that is present during a given moment of worldly unfolding as eternally Real for an infinite intellect, one has made exactly the mistake that Kant warned against: one has confused presence to a finite intellect with Presence to an infinite intellect. That confusion is what Kant correctly identified as the essential feature of dogmatic metaphysics or transcendental dialectic. The most famous proponent of dogmatic metaphysics is Parmenides, and his Eleatic manner of thinking has informed Western thought in one way or another from his day to ours: it is the will to atemporal knowledge in the midst of temporal unfolding. We know two things about Nietzsche's position with regard to this will: we know that he embraced it in 1872 in *The Birth of Tragedy*, that this illusion of Eternal Reality was the source of the metaphysical comfort to be provided by the Apollonian dream of the sublunary Artist; and we know that he explicitly repudiated it after 1876:

> Those exceptional thinkers, like the Eleatics, who nevertheless posited and clung to the opposites of the natural errors, believed that it was possible to *live* in accordance with these opposites: they invented the sage as the man who was unchangeable and impersonal, the man of the universality of intuition who was One and All at the same time, with a special capacity for his inverted knowledge: they had the faith that their knowledge was also the principle of *life*. But in order to claim all of this, they had to *deceive* themselves about their own state: they had to attribute to themselves, fictitiously, impersonality and changeless duration; they had to misapprehend the nature of the knower. (*GS*, 169–70)

It is dishonest, a form of self-deceit, to indulge in the will to atemporal knowledge, and Nietzsche is explicitly *en garde* against doing so himself.

Nietzsche's reality is located in the unfolding presence of worldly history and is perspectival in that sense. To take what appears to me here and now as emblematic of reality is far from "privileging" presence—that is the Eleatic mistake—it is to be honest about being historically and geographically situated in a perspective. That honest recognition then functions to release the good European, the free spirit who would transcend his simple location by moving about *in the world*.

Space and time are not the only formal conditions for sensible intuition; there are also the categories of understanding. We know what Kant's categories were. What were Nietzsche's? Kant's categories were universal, necessary, and atemporal. Nietzsche's categories, generated by human art, were particular, contingent, and temporally evolving. One could look at the world as Homer did, or as Sophocles did, or even as Wagner did. In fact, if one wants to be the artist who generates the categories of understanding for a given historically situated community, Nietzsche tells you how to do it. You found a religion:

> *On the origin of religions.*— The distinctive invention of the founders of religion is, first: to posit a particular kind of life and everyday customs that have the effect of a *disciplina voluntatis* [discipline of the will] and at the same time abolish boredom—and then: to bestow on this life style an *interpretation* that makes it appear to be illuminated by the highest value so that this life style becomes something for which one fights and under certain circumstances sacrifices one's life. Actually, the second of these two inventions is more essential. The first, the way of life, was usually there before, but alongside other ways of life and without any sense of its special value. The significance and originality of the founder of a religion usually consists of his *seeing* it, *selecting* it, and *guessing* for the first time to what use it can be put, how it can be interpreted. . . .
>
> To become the founder of a religion one must be psychologically infallible in one's knowledge of a certain average type of souls who have not yet *recognized* that they belong together. It is he that brings them together. The founding of a religion therefore always becomes a long festival of recognition. (GS, 296–97)

The categories of understanding of a given historically situated perspective are grounded in the lifestyle of a given herd interpreted in such a way as to give it the force of an identity-conferring religion for which one will fight and die.

A perspective is an interpretation elevated to a religious belief system: more Eleaticism, an atemporality of inertia, based on fear of change.[4] The categories of understanding constitutive of the perspective of herd animals are herd-specific, historically situated, and contingent—but taken by the animals themselves to be what religious belief systems always are: universal, necessary, and atemporal. More dishonesty. And another violation of the principle of lucidity. The herd animal dwells in a perspective that it must fail to recognize as such at peril of losing his identity, the meaning that it confers upon his life, and his place in the herd.

Nietzsche's perspectivism is hardly an affirmation of transcendental myopia. To contend that we are situated in finite perspectives, even to affirm that inevitable human situatedness, as Nietzsche's doctrine of *amor fati* clearly commits him to do, is not to celebrate any particular situation and turn its perspective into a personal a priori. Nietzsche's perspectivism is, rather, an entreaty to move on in space, time, and categories of understanding, the latter now conceived as culture, lifestyle, applied interpretation of patterns of existence, ways of contending with the necessities imposed by life. It is a transcendental condition for the possibility of choosing a better lifestyle that one be aware of more than one possibility or modus vivendi.

Nietzsche's recommendation to the would-be free spirit is, at first blush, startling: he argues for unity of personal style, aimed at a finality that incorporates personal weakness and ugliness concealed by reinterpretation and thereby rendered sublime. This might well give us pause: Finality in the project of self-transcendence? Tolerance of personal weakness? Here is what Nietzsche says:

> *One thing is needful.*— To "give style" to one's character—a great and rare art! It is practiced by those who survey all the strengths and weaknesses of their nature and then fit them into an artistic plan until every one of them appears as art and reason and even weaknesses delight the eye. . . . Here the ugly that could not be removed is concealed; there it has been reinterpreted and made sublime. . . . In the end, when the work is finished, it becomes evident how the constraint of a single taste governed and formed everything large and small. Whether this taste was good or bad is less important than one might suppose, if only it was a single taste! . . . For one thing is needful: that a human being should *attain* satisfaction with himself, whether it be by means of this or that poetry and art; only then is a

human being at all tolerable to behold. Whoever is dissatisfied with himself is continually ready for revenge, and we others will be his victims, if only by having to endure his ugly sight. For the sight of what is ugly makes one bad and gloomy. (*GS*, 232–33)

A self-satisfied *Übermensch* who has *finished* the creative process of self-transformation? Can this be Nietzsche? There is, I am sorry to report, no trace of irony in this passage.

The Gay Science is a transitional work, as are all Nietzsche's writings. It announces many of the themes that will be developed in *Zarathustra*: the death of God, eternal recurrence, will to power, even the self-overcoming that will be the prime characteristic of the overman. It does not develop these themes, however, remaining deliberately epigrammatic, skipping from topic to topic, guided by little in the way of architectonic, and resulting in a mosaic that does not resolve into a discernible pattern. It also contains a lot of very awful poetry, lavish self-indulgence that transgresses the border of banality. Sometimes, as all his readers know, Nietzsche just does that. Sometimes these lapses are significant; sometimes they are not. This lapse is significant.

There is an unresolved tension in the passage just cited between two major themes in Nietzsche's thought: Art and self-transcendence. Nietzsche's early aestheticism did not die an easy death, but lingered on to confound him— *and* to inspire him. What we witness here is Nietzsche, the classicist, conceiving the artwork as embodying perfection, finality, and closure. The project of self-transformation is a creative process: the artist making himself into the artwork he wants to be able to affirm. He, thus, strives for perfection. And, as artist, creator of himself, he wants to leave the herd and achieve singularity, uniqueness, ipseity: that kind of unity. But notice the how and the why.

The how is seeing the necessary character of things as beautiful, taking transcendent reality for what it is and affirming it. Nietzsche believed that all things were driven by will to power; he took it as a personal project to develop the spirit of a warrior in the agon of life, but he was a small, sickly man. That was something he had to come to terms with, and did. This is a topic for later discussion, but now it can be said that Nietzsche managed to find a way to affirm his infirmity. "Sublime" is perhaps too big a word; "sublimation" might have been more apt.

The why is to free himself from the spirit of revenge. The spirit of revenge is the engine of *ressentiment*, and *ressentiment* is Nietzsche's indwelling evil genius, his resident slime ever ready to erupt. The self-acceptance, affirmation of self, warts and all, that is taken as a goal in this passage is not pointed toward complacency; it is pointed away from revenge.

We know where this thought is headed. It is on the way to Zarathustra, the bridge of self-overcoming with no finality, just termination. It just has not reached that point yet.

4. NIETZSCHE'S PERSPECTIVISM AND THE REALITY OF APPEARANCE

> We do not "know" nearly enough to be entitled to any such dis-
> tinction [as that which opposes] "thing-in-itself" and appearance.
> (GS, 300)

The concept of "thing-in-itself" is a limiting concept; it points to a limit to knowledge; it names something we know we cannot know. Only God, whose knowledge of the "thing-in-itself" is definitive of it, could distinguish it from the appearances that constitute the everyday experience of humanity. Is it not twisted logic, then, to regard everyday experience as illusory, somehow less than real, because it fails to measure up to an ideal we cannot conceive? It is the logic—the onto-logic—of Eleaticism, the ontology of Being: posit an infinite knower, take that knower's vantage to be definitive of ultimate Reality, timeless and unchanging, and then use that as a measure of our finitude and ignorance. The grain of truth in this Eleatic logic is the cognitive insecurity it expresses. Being finite, knowing that we are subject to error and know less than we need to know to make infallible decisions, we measure ourselves against an imaginary being, an infinite knower, we cannot conceive much less emulate. This is the onto-logic that Nietzsche repudiates in his announcement of the death of God; this is the ontology of Being that he seeks to purge from his thinking after 1876.

The passage quoted above is taken from book 5 of *The Gay Science*, added in the second edition published in 1887. I cite it here to indicate the direction in which Nietzsche's thinking was headed on the subject matter of this chapter, appearance and reality. The idea expressed may have only been a premonition in 1882, but it was latent in the thoughts he did articulate at that time.

At stake here is the question of whether Nietzsche's perspectivism is compatible with the attribution of reality to appearances [*Erscheinungen*]. My answer is that it is not only possible to regard one's perspectival view of the world as just that, a perspective *on the world*, but that the perspectival limitation is a measure of the reality of what is seen: it is the nature of the real to reveal itself only partially in space and time; we see things one side at a time, and that is a measure of their transcendence, their reality. Can this thought be attributed to Nietzsche? Yes and no. It is not fully articulated until later, but it informs what he does say in 1882, although countercurrents remain in his thinking at that time.

Nietzsche's perspectivism, as we have just seen, includes not only the formal constraints of spatio-temporal unfolding, but also the formal constraints of understanding and interpretation. If all our perspectives upon things can be reduced to interpretations, how can they be held to be openings onto reality?

If the interpretation is tantamount to a religion, a belief system enforced by the herd, then its reality consists in being a shared myth, an illusion necessary to sustain the herd identity. Nietzsche's prescription here is honesty: leave the herd. The question is: Where to go? And his answer to that question in 1882 is to undertake an experiment in truth-seeking.

In §110 of *The Gay Science*, titled "Origin of Knowledge," Nietzsche argues that "over immense periods of time the intellect produced nothing but errors, [and that] a few of these proved to be useful and helped to preserve the species" (169). Among "such erroneous articles of faith," Nietzsche lists the belief "that a thing is what it appears to be." He goes on to say that "it was only very late that truth emerged—as the weakest form of knowledge" and one that our organism was "unable to live with," having been attuned for so long to the erroneous but useful articles of faith.

It is at this point that Nietzsche sets forth the critique of the Eleatic sage discussed above. The Eleatic sage is the one who attempts to live with the timeless truths behind the passing "natural errors," but in order to do this, has to deceive himself into believing that he is a knower capable of holding himself aloof from prejudice, passion, impulse, and all the subterfuges that would prevent him from coinciding with the eternal. This is patently self-deception, because the will to such coincidence is itself driven by "a desire for tranquility . . . or for dominion." "The subtler development of honesty and skepticism eventually made these people . . . impossible":

> This subtler honesty and skepticism came into being wherever two
> contradictory sentences appeared to be *applicable* to life because
> *both* were compatible with the basic errors, and it was therefore

> possible to argue about the higher or lower degree of *utility* for life;
> also wherever new propositions, though not useful for life, were also
> evidently not harmful to life: in such cases there was room for the
> expression of an intellectual play impulse, and honesty and skepti-
> cism were innocent and happy like all play. (*GS*, 170)

From such play, specifically the agon, the power match, between contestants
in this argument, there developed a new need, a need for truth, sparked by
all sorts of impulse, including but not limited to utility and delight. This
sets the stage for a new fight, the fight between "the impulse for truth"—
which, grounded in this new need, is now "proved to be also a life-preserving
power"—and the "life-preserving errors."

No matter what degree of plausibility one assigns to this genealogy of
knowledge, the conclusion Nietzsche draws is portentous. If both truth and
error can be life-preserving, then utility for life cannot be a measure of truth
and error: truth cannot be reduced to useful fiction.

What, then, of Nietzsche's assertion, cited above, that the belief that a
thing is what it appears to be is a useful fiction? The statement—a thing is
what it appears to be—is ambiguous. The ambiguity lies in the copula "is"—
it is the ontological ambiguity identified above. If one understands this statement to mean that the thing's eternal being is fully revealed in the moment
of its present appearance, one has made the Eleatic mistake: the thing is not
fully disclosed, its past and future unfolding are not apparent. But what is
disclosed may be, and usually is, enough to know how to deal with the thing,
whether or not to eat it, for example.

Let the thing be the egg of a hen. We know enough to take it as nutritious,
but we do not know it sub specie aeternitatis, the course of the development
of DNA that evolved to produce this object. Actually, we are now a bit uncertain, given the cholesterol content of egg yolks, whether it is as nutritious as
we once thought. There is room for debate: Are eggs really and truly good to
eat? Truth becomes an issue. This example is apt insofar as it relates to diet,
a matter of no little concern to Nietzsche, as is evident in his latest writings,
and something about which he expressed strong opinions.[5] When it is a matter of eggs—or water or beer or coffee or tea—when to consume them, if at
all, how much to consume, and whether to take a walk afterward, Nietzsche
wants to know the truth because he is truly concerned about his health.

Are such concerns genuinely philosophical? Relevant to the question of
Nietzsche's underlying ontology? He wrote about them. But perhaps we

should apply Hume's commonsense advice here: it is one thing to be a phenomenalist in one's study, but when one goes out into the street, it is well to believe that the carriage bearing down on you is real. Put one thing in your books, live another.

The question with which Nietzsche ends his discourse on the "Origin of Knowledge" presages his conclusion to the 1882 edition of *The Gay Science*: *Incipit tragoedia*. The tragedy begins when Zarathustra decides to leave his mountain retreat and go under:

> Thus knowledge became a piece of life itself, and hence a continually growing power—until eventually knowledge collided with those primeval basic errors: two lives, two powers, both in the same human being. A thinker is now that being in whom the impulse for truth and those life-preserving errors clash for their first fight, after the impulse for truth has proved to be also a life-preserving power. Compared to the significance of this fight, everything else is a matter of indifference: the ultimate question about the conditions of life has been posed here, and we confront the first attempt to answer this question by experiment. To what extent can truth endure incorporation?[6] That is the question; that is the experiment. (GS, 171)

Incipit tragoedia: Zarathustra is the experiment.

· ·

CHAPTER FOUR

ZARATHUSTRA: TRANSCENDENCE HERE AND HEREAFTER

I. TRAGEDY: GOD, FREEDOM, AND IMMORTALITY

Nietzsche announces the coming of Zarathustra in *The Gay Science* and says two things about it: it is an experiment, and in that experiment tragedy begins. What is tragedy?

Nietzsche set forth an account of tragedy in *The Birth of Tragedy* and then repudiated it. The account he repudiated justified human existence by means of deliberately living in accordance with an illusion that would provide metaphysical comfort. The content of the illusion was, thus, metaphysics, but metaphysics specified in different ways according to the subject matters Nietzsche addressed from Greek tragedy to Wagnerian opera. By 1876, however, it became clear that the metaphysics Nietzsche repudiated was a generic metaphysics he found informing world religion as such and its philosophical underpinnings. His touchstone remained the Judeo-Christian tradition into which he was born and its ancient Greek heritage, but his attack on metaphysics extended into Eastern religions as well. What, for Nietzsche, is the essence of the metaphysics underlying world religion as such?

The essence of religion is faith in God, freedom, and immortality insofar as the unity named in that triad holds out the hope for eternal happiness.[1] That is what Kant argued in *The Critique of Pure Reason*, and that is the cleanest statement of the metaphysical viewpoint Zarathustra contests in his saga.

The constellation of ideas at the core of Zarathustra's teachings centers on the famous themes of the death of God, eternal recurrence, *amor fati*, and will to power, but there are two other sustained lines of thought intertwined with these themes that must be considered as integral to them. The first is the nobility thesis, which takes honesty or authenticity as its key value and revenge, *ressentiment*, or systems of reward and punishment as the focus of its critique. The second is a set of paradoxes or antinomies that emerge as the famous themes are developed: the symbol of the dead god that lives on, the symbol of eternal recurrence lived in the overman's freedom of self-transcendence, and the symbol of the self to be affirmed beyond the grammatical fiction of the ego. God, freedom, and immortality, coupled with the promise of eternal reward: whether Nietzsche consciously chose to center his attack of metaphysics on Kant's Ideal of Pure Reason is a matter of little concern to me here; my hypothesis is simply that Kant's Ideal is the best expression of the metaphysics Zarathustra defines himself against.[2]

The thought of tragedy is inseparable from the thought of life and death. Zarathustra is a saga of life and death. The beings who are destined to live and die in this saga are gods and humans. They come ceaselessly into being and they pass ceaselessly away. What makes this truly tragic is that they do not live on. The challenge posed by this truly tragic view of human existence is the question of its value, whether it can be honestly confronted and affirmed. That is the experiment Nietzsche takes up with his alter ego in *Thus Spoke Zarathustra*.

In his preface to the second edition of *The Critique of Pure Reason*, Kant simply states that he has "found it necessary to deny *knowledge* in order to make room for *faith*."[3] Why necessary? Kant's answer is, once again, simple. It is necessary to have faith in order to be happy. This looks like a hypothetical imperative because it *is* a hypothetical imperative, and that might make us pause because it seems like flimsy ground on which to construct an absolute deontology, but that is what Kant does. Here is what Kant writes in "The Canon of Pure Reason":

> Happiness, taken by itself, is, for our reason, far from being the complete good. Reason does not approve happiness (however inclination may desire it) except insofar as it is united with worthiness to be happy, that is, with moral conduct. Morality, taken by itself, and with it, the mere *worthiness* to be happy, is also far from being the complete good. To make the good complete, he who behaves in such a manner as not to be unworthy of happiness must be able to hope that he will participate in happiness. Even the reason that is free from all private purposes, should it put itself in the place of a being that had to distribute all happiness to others, cannot judge otherwise; for in the practical idea both elements are essentially

connected, though in such a manner that it is the moral disposition which conditions and makes possible the participation in happiness, and not conversely the prospect of happiness that makes
possible the moral disposition. For in the latter case the disposition would not be moral, and therefore would not be worthy of
complete happiness—happiness which in the view of reason allows of no limitation save that which arises from our own immoral
conduct.

Happiness, therefore, in exact proportion with the morality of
the rational beings who are thereby rendered worthy of it, alone
constitutes the supreme good of that world wherein, in accordance
with the commands of a pure by practical reason, we are under obligation to place ourselves.[4]

We have to posit God, freedom, and immortality on grounds of faith, even
though they cannot be demonstrated on grounds of knowledge, because,
otherwise, we could not hope to participate in happiness. Without freedom,
no morality. Without immortal souls, no reward. Without God, no promise, no hope. Only if we accept the "Ideal of Pure Reason" as a regulative
ideal, can we justify human existence. Without this justification, life would
be empty of value and meaning: one comes into being, does what one does,
and regardless of what one does, one passes out of existence, one simply
ceases to be.

The standpoint taken up by Kant is predicated on an ontology of Being,
an Eleatic ontology that posits an eternal sphere of Reality beyond the
appearances constituting our experience of this world. To repudiate the
Kantian position, Nietzsche's own position in *The Birth of Tragedy*, one must
repudiate the underlying metaphysics. The movement of Nietzsche's thought
is from an ontology of Being toward an ontology of becoming. If one interprets the famous themes of Zarathustra within the context of Kant's Eleaticism, they generate paradoxes: there is no enduring self endowed with
a noumenal faculty of free will, but Zarathustra is a self that makes free
choices. If one interprets the themes within the context of an ontology of
becoming, the paradoxes admit of resolution: Zarathustra is subject to the
necessities governing organic life, but within that context has the freedom
to move his body up the mountain or down. At the beginning of the book,
he is headed down.

2. GOING DOWN AND UNDER

> Verily, a polluted stream is man. One must be a sea to be able to receive
> a polluted stream without becoming unclean. Behold, I teach you the
> overman: he is this sea; in him your great contempt can go under.
>
> What is the greatest experience you can have? It is the hour of
> the great contempt. The hour in which your happiness, too, arouses
> your disgust, and even your reason and your virtue. . . .
>
> The hour when you say, "What matters my reason?" (Z, 125)

Zarathustra's prologue is an expression of contempt. He meets an old man,
a saint, in the woods. This old saint, like Kant, loves the god that promises
happiness, but has no pathological affection for humankind, although he is
willing to give men alms and help them bear their burden. Zarathustra does
not tell him the truth that his god is dead. He sees the saint as incapable of
bearing that truth.

Zarathustra descends from his mountain in the mode of condescension.
He has a message for the people down under, the people he compares to a
polluted stream; he wants to teach them the overman, the man that is superior to them, before the hour of the last man, when it will be too late to be redeemed from the happiness they have invented with their eyes blinking shut.
He preaches his sermon of contempt and receives contempt and a threat in
response. The jester who had leaped over the tightrope walker and sent him
to his death warns Zarathustra that he will deliver the same fate to him if he
does not leave town before the next day, that the only thing that saved his life
that day was stooping to the dead man, lowering himself, making himself
contemptible. Zarathustra does leave town, having abandoned, after just one
try, his quest to spread his teaching of overman to the human-polluted stream
flowing through the valleys. "Never again shall I speak to the people: for the
last time have I spoken to the dead" (Z, 136). Now he will seek a few followers: "Living companions I need, who follow me because they want to follow
themselves—wherever I want" (Z, 135).

Zarathustra descends in a mode of contempt for people, finds it mirrored
back at him, and absolutely forsakes his quest for universal redemption: he
will not be the scapegoat that bears the pollution. He will form an elite
corps, a few good men, who follow themselves in following him—wherever
he wants. This is what Zarathustra says he needs. Why does Zarathustra

need living companions who follow him in a mode of ambivalent autonomy? "I love him whose soul squanders itself, who wants no thanks and returns none: for he always gives away and does not want to preserve himself"
(Z, 127).

Zarathustra esteems the excess of giving without expectation of return: he
explicitly repudiates the reciprocity that defines friendship, purports to have
freed himself even of the motive of personal survival, but says that he needs
this odd group of followers. Why?

The *Untergehen* cannot be read as an act of grace and generosity. It does
not belong in the bag of metaphors with scapegoats and savior figures, bod-
hisattvas and returners to the cave. The difference between Zarathustra and
these familiar figures of redemption is that they have been redeemed and
Zarathustra is still seeking: They have seen a light that Zarathustra knows is
out. They have been afforded a glimpse of the other side and have postponed
their voyage to it long enough to spread the word to fellow beings still suffering from human existence. Zarathustra knows that there is no other side;
his truth is that there is no redemption from human existence, that it does
not stand in need of redemption. It needs only affirmation. And that is what
Zarathustra needs from his living companions: affirmation. Affirmation of
his truth.

The *Untergehen* is an initial step in Nietzsche's redefinition of his relations to others. It is clearly an about-face from his former totalitarian
politics. Zarathustra is not the poet-creator that will generate the myth
capable of unifying a culture—and policing it—in such a way as to maximize the production of great art and high culture. That elitist project has
been left behind with Wagner and Eleatic metaphysics, repudiated once
and for all.

The project that takes its place is a new elitism, an elitism of a new kind
of nobility, a new kind of contempt: a contempt that flows outwardly toward
the herd and inwardly toward the self, a scorn of the lowly that is, at the same
time, an affirmation of self-transcendence. Note that self-transcendence presupposes an ambivalence with regard to the self: contempt for the lowly aspects of oneself that one seeks to overcome, but admiration for the nobility
that one seeks to attain. Overman is the symbol of the need that links Zarathustra to the odd group of followers he wants, and it defines a new modality
of human relations, a new *ethos*. This new ethos is a new way of being with
others based on Nietzsche's youngest virtue, honesty, and his oldest ally, art,

both taken as essentially related to truth. The clearest exposition of this new creative noble contempt is to be found in Zarathustra's opening speech, "On the Three Metamorphoses."

3. THE CAMEL, THE LION, AND THE CHILD

This speech, little more than two pages long, has received more critical commentary than its length would seem to warrant. I attribute this to its architectonic value: it provides a synopsis of the principles of construction of *Thus Spoke Zarathustra*. I read it as the prelude to an attack on traditional metaphysics, what has latterly and properly come to be known as onto-theology, coupled with an enigmatic gesture toward what might be sought beyond metaphysics. As noted earlier, I take Kant to have condensed traditional metaphysics into the themes of God, freedom, and immortality, and will link those themes to the figures of camel, lion, and child.

A. The Camel

The camel is Nietzsche's symbol of strength, specifically the strength to carry the burden of difficult truth. Nietzsche writes of "suffering hunger in one's soul . . . for the sake of truth," and of "stepping into filthy waters when they are the waters of truth" (Z, 138). He characterizes the strength of the camel as including both the arrogance of exulting in strength and the humility of wounding one's haughtiness. Be the irony intended or not, Nietzsche is appealing to the classical Christian virtue of humble fortitude as that which is required to bear the truth about the dead god who lives on.

Just as it was difficult for Nietzsche to leave the comfortable security he enjoyed as a favored member of Wagner's coterie, so it is difficult to leave the security of the metaphysical comfort conferred by the promise of Christian redemption in the hereafter. When that comfort includes the pleasure of *ressentiment*, the reassurance that the lords of this world who trample one's self-esteem will be brought low in the world to follow, it is especially difficult to leave behind. Difficult, but necessary, for the sake of genuine nobility: the strength to endure and affirm the truth of worldly becoming, the truly tragic nature of human existence expressed in the wisdom of Silenus. We who have been born into the cycle of birth, growth, decay, and death cannot honestly vindicate our suffering by the promise of a return to everlasting peace in the beatitude from which we fell at birth. To exist, to have been born, eliminates the option of not having been born, and to seek release from the contradictions of coming into being and passing away by dwelling in the illusion of a return—or in a Schopenhauerian desire to transcend desire—is to wallow in self-deception. The camel bears the difficult truth, the truth that we have always known, that the dead god is truly dead. Resurrection is dishonesty.

B. The Lion

The lion symbolizes defiance, freedom from the oppressive weight of commandments delivered from on high in the form of a canon of "thou shalts." Freedom is a condition for self-transcendence. If, as Leibniz argued, all predicates attributable to a subject are contained within the subject from the start, then self-transcendence can be no more than an illusion: what I will become is already determined within what I am now. This creates an antinomic collision between freedom and determinism in Nietzsche's thought that replicates the antinomy in Kant discussed above: if freedom is a condition for self-transcendence, but eternal recurrence predelineates all events, including human actions, then these two main theses of *Zarathustra* collide and Nietzsche's thought is rendered absurd through inconsistency.

The antinomy also poses a serious challenge to the thesis being developed throughout this book, the thesis that Nietzsche's thought traces the process of breaking free from the onto-theological metaphysics of Being and moving toward an ontology of becoming. The doctrine of eternal recurrence, taken literally, presupposes the cyclical model of time announced by the dwarf in the chapter "On the Vision and the Riddle": "Time itself is a circle" (Z, 270). This conception of time is wedded to Eleaticism, to the ontology of Being, to the idea that becoming is no more than an illusion. Time is an illusion taken as real only by those finite beings who live within it and experience change; seen sub specie aeternitatis alpha and omega coincide, the return of the Absolute unto itself coincides with its fall into time, and Being is conjugated only in the present perfect: everything is already finished.

What could eternal recurrence mean in the context of an ontology of becoming? I have two hypotheses.

The first is that eternal recurrence is a metaphor Nietzsche draws upon to articulate the thesis of *amor fati*. One thinks of the whole of one's life repeating itself over and over for eternity, and like the young shepherd, one is threatened by disgust to the point of nausea: life is disgusting because it is going nowhere, but merely recapitulates the contradictions of human existence, birth and death, joy and pain, coming into being and passing away. If one can think that thought, and still affirm one's life in all its aspects, one has achieved the apex of affirmation, love of fate; one has developed the capacity "to see as beautiful what is *necessary* in things."

The second hypothesis is that the cyclicality of becoming, as portrayed in the Greek phallic plays, the everlasting cycle from birth through agon to death, the spring-summer-fall-winter drama of repetition, prefigures the tragedy of recapitulation apparent in human suffering. Cronos fights with his father, Ouranos, and wins, but only to lose to his own son, Zeus. As it is with the gods, so it is with us: to become a man, one must slay the father-rival, only to be slain by one's son. Such has it always been, and so will it always be . . . unless one breaks the cycle of repetition of the same. When the shepherd bites through the ouroboros,[5] he breaks the temporal circle of recapitulation.

Zarathustra is a book about breaking cyclical patterns and transcending the herd mentality that contents itself by running in circles, living life as it has always been lived, looking back over its shoulder to glimpse its end, the goal of returning to the beatific peace from which it fell at birth. Zarathustra defies the conservative belief that human finitude is a disgrace, a fall from oneness with godhead of God-Brahman-Atman-Tao, into the freedom that, by its very nature, contests what divinity has preordained. The self-loathing of human finitude, expressed by Nietzsche's archfoes from Buddha to Schopenhauer, from Socrates to the pied piper, the scapegoat from Nazareth, is what Zarathustra seeks to defy and transcend.

Hence the lion, who meets the No to freedom implicit in the "thou shalt" of obedience with its more powerful No, which affirms freedom and the finitude that is its correlate. The young shepherd bites off the head of the nauseating snake of eternal recurrence and jumps up. "No longer shepherd, no longer human—one changed, radiant, *laughing!*" (Z, 272). To become the shepherd, the human that transcends what humanity has been, to set out on the path overman, one must defy the eternity of gods and their commandments and set oneself free to become more than mortals have ever been.

The lion "seeks out his last master: he wants to fight him and his last god" (Z, 138). The figure of the great dragon with the golden scales leads the unwary reader to externalize the foe taken on in the agon of wills. The "thou shalt" does come from the elevated past, the reverence for all that has been pronounced holy, and indeed there are external authorities who enforce obedience. The would-be overman must contend with these enemies to his freedom, but that is not his hardest task. "He once loved 'thou shalt' as most sacred: now he must find illusion and caprice even in the most sacred, that freedom from his love may become his prey" (Z, 139).

The hardest challenge for the lion is the pale criminal, conscience, the enemy within. Conscience is the internalization of the values of the herd. Once internalized, these values are one's own, hence to challenge them is to challenge oneself. The herd values self-sameness and reacts negatively to exception and distinction; the herd values conservation of accepted ways and reacts negatively to challenge and change. Self-transcendence presup- poses change and departures from de facto norms; such departures consti- tute exceptions to the usual that call into question the easy familiarity of fulfilling the latent expectations associated with one's place and function within prevailing social structures. One is uneasy in making such changes, one feels that one is doing something wrong, and one feels that way because one has been feeding on the approval gained by acquiescence to the tacit expectations of the crowd. "Your love of the neighbor is your bad love of *yourselves*. You flee to your neighbor from yourselves and would like to make a virtue out of that. . . . The *you* is older than the *I*; the *you* has been pronounced holy, but not yet the *I*: so man crowds toward his neighbor" (Z, 172).

When the lion defiantly says no to the "thou shalt" of communal values, he evokes the wrath and enmity of the masses. Beyond that, he provokes con- demnation from that aspect of himself that bases its self-esteem upon the herd's acceptance and affirmation, that is, he feels guilty: he feels alone and unloved by that part of himself that wants the love of all. The defiance of the lion frees the spirit of self-transcendence from obedience to the customs of the herd, but at the expense of a bad conscience. "'He who seeks, easily gets lost. All loneliness is guilt'—thus speaks the herd. And you have long belonged to the herd. The voice of the herd will still be audible in you. And when you will say, 'I no longer have a common conscience with you,' it will be a lament and an agony" (Z, 174). To stay within the herd, however, also entails bad conscience, the guilt of failing to win freedom from arbitrary constraint upon which human dignity depends.

The question that remains unanswered is what to do with the freedom won by the lion. "Free *from* what? As if that mattered to Zarathustra! But your eyes should tell me brightly: free *for* what?" (Z, 175). The metamorphosis is not complete; the lion must become a child.

C. The Child

The child is Nietzsche's symbol for creativity and affirmation.[6] But what does the child create? Art is the generic name for human creation. The creators of art are the ones who give us new ways of looking at things, not only individual things, but things taken in sum, as a whole. The supreme artist, identified by Nietzsche in *The Birth of Tragedy*, is the one who gives birth to divinities, the figures through which we think the whole.[7] Hitherto, the function of the artist has been to provide metaphysical comfort. But metaphysical comfort has been repudiated on the grounds of its dishonesty, its all-too-human motivation in *ressentiment*. It promulgates the lie of the afterworld to satisfy its longing for vindication of weakness and revenge against the powerful. The self-deceptive lie is protected by the herd: belief is sustained by universal acceptance.

The lion has left the herd. Building on the strength of the camel to bear the burden of truth, the lion defies the oppression of the external "thou shalt" and seeks freedom from conscience, the values internalized from the community in which he has dwelled. The challenge of self-transcendence is the motive that drives *Zarathustra*. "The worst enemy you can encounter will always be you, yourself. . . . Lonely one, you are going the way of the lover: yourself you love, and therefore you despise yourself, as only lovers despise. The lover would create because he despises. What does he know of love who did not have to despise precisely what he loved!" (Z, 176–77).

The child has to create himself. The child has to create a self he can honestly esteem. The child has to purge himself of his old love by creating love anew. Only then will he begin to be capable of loving himself. In more literal terms, what the child is challenged to create is value. "To esteem is to create: hear this, you creators! Esteeming itself is of all esteemed things the most estimable treasure. Through esteeming alone is there value: and without esteeming, the nut of existence would be hollow. Hear this, you creators!" (Z, 171).

The task of the child is to create values, but what are the values that are to be created? And are these values to be valued simply because they are new?

"Can you give yourself your own evil and your own good and hang your own will over yourself as a law?" (Z, 175). Furthermore, are the values created by the child to be valued simply because they are his own, because they are the new laws he has given to himself? Is autonomy its own warrant? Is every genuinely free act to be affirmed simply virtue of being free?

These questions of selfhood and autonomy—and the language in which Nietzsche frames them—bring us back to the Kantian triad of God, Freedom, and Immortality. The challenge put to the child is a Kantian challenge: Can you create your own values and will them autonomously? The etymology of "autonomy" defines it as giving the law (nomos) unto oneself (auto), and this is conceived as freedom and independence.[8] The challenge for Kant lies in what he calls the "antinomy of practical reason."[9] Freedom is a necessary condition for the possibility of morality, but, as creatures of nature, we are bound by the category of causality: "The freedom attributed to the will seems incompatible with the necessity of nature."[10]

Kant disposes of this antinomy by arguing that morality is inconceivable unless one posits a noumenal self, a self beyond the phenomenal sphere governed by causality, as the ground of the freedom required for moral agency. As shown above, this free noumenal self must also be presupposed to be immortal to provide the finality required for morality, that is, the promise of happiness.

For Kant, freedom is duty-bound to the universality predelineated by its essential rationality. The categorical imperative commands action in accordance with the a priori precept that defines freedom, rationality, and universality as coincidental. Our duty in the sublunary sphere is to transcend pathological interest, releasing ourselves to thereby obey the dictate of reason always to "act as if the maxim of your action were to become through your will a universal law of nature."[11] Here are the seeds of Hegel's equation of divinity, reason, and the universal, and Schopenhauer's telos of stilling desire, the Will of nature, in a movement toward aesthetic objectivity.

To understand the figure of the child, one need only transpose the postulate, wisely accepted by Nietzsche, that freedom is a necessary condition for moral assessment, take it out of the noumenal sphere of Being, and place it in the worldly realm of phenomenal becoming. This entails rejecting Kant's idea that unconditioned freedom must be *presupposed* as fully realized in a noumenal self and replacing it with the thought that freedom has to be *won* through the lion's unending struggle with the forces that constrain it from within and without.

What freedom presupposes, for Nietzsche, is finitude and particularity. If the noumenal sphere is a lie posited in the desire for metaphysical comfort and the self-deception of wishful thinking, then all moral assessment, including Kant's, is driven by a will bound to desire. Moral deliberation in all cases turns out to be a matter of adjudicating among competing desires, and doing so within the finite context of particular perspectives. One can be honest about this and assume the burden of individual responsibility that follows from the truth of finite freedom. Or one can take the law from the "Thou shalt" originating in the noumenal sphere posited in the lie one tells oneself about the promise of everlasting happiness granted to the obedient.

Nietzsche's truth is that the universal does not lie in an antecedent noumenal Reality, but is rather an ideal projected in the desire to have one's own free will prevail. I do not tap into a preestablished Reason that ordains a universal "thou shalt" to which we are all bound by duty; instead, I use my own finite reason to determine the law worthy of obedience by myself and all others capable of understanding its validity. I want to be the exception to the false universal of herd conformity, an exemplar of genuine personal responsibility. Here is the ground of the will to power that drives all finite esteeming. But that phrase is a redundancy: esteeming and willing presuppose a lack seeking fulfillment and hence are intrinsically finite. Here also is the truth of the categorical imperative hidden by Kant's onto-theological deontology: the values capable of commanding universal assent cannot be presupposed as already given, but must be won in the struggle for lucid moral assessment.

4. LUCIDITY AND NOBILITY

By way of transition to the final question remaining to be addressed in this chapter, the question about what is to be willed in the creation of the child and the warrant for that choice, it might be well to note here that the preceding discussion of desire and will sheds light on another dominant theme in *Zarathustra* and the works to follow: the theme of affirming instinct and celebrating the passions.

The onto-theological metaphysics of Being necessarily invokes a dualism of appearance and Reality. It is manifestly the case that things come into being and pass away in the world in which we dwell, the world of appearances. Hence, to posit a sphere of immutability, modeled upon the atemporality and perfection of numbers and essences, requires an ontological disjunction between the world of changing appearances and the world of immutable Reality. Permanence in time, that is, timelessness, remains the criterion for Reality from Parmenides through Kant and beyond. The correlation of desire with transience and peace or absence of desire with immutability is but another adumbration of this traditional dualism. In repudiating the dualism and the self-deceptive longing for Being, Nietzsche's affirmation of this world of becoming commits him to an affirmation of all the categories of becoming: passion, desire, the senses, appearances, agon/conflict, willing, and of course, the ultimate passion, death. Transience is now the criterion for finite reality.

The sections of *Zarathustra* devoted to these themes are too numerous to be reviewed here, but it is well to note that the thesis being argued here illumines their rationale. One must not forget that Nietzsche is by disposition an enthusiast, an iconoclast, an oppositional thinker, and an ironist intent on exposing fraudulent thinking wherever he found it. His writing is driven more by inspiration and the mood of the moment than it is by a carefully planned and systematically structured strategy. Nonetheless, inchoate, horizontal, and murky as it may have been in his thinking, a principle was at work in his selection of targets and diatribes: Zarathustra is making war against the demons that urge acquiescence to the surviving values of the dead god. And Kant was a privileged vehicle for the articulation of those values.

Just as freedom from is inseparable from freedom for, as there is a "Yes" lurking within every "No," the child is prefigured in the lion. For every value condemned by Nietzsche as contaminated by self-deceit, there lurks on the horizon an inarticulate affirmation struggling to reach lucid expression. Indeed, this lucidity is itself one of the two values that prevail in Nietzsche's ontology. The other is nobility.

Nietzsche left relativism behind when he departed from the absolutes of onto-theology having seen both absolutism and relativism as two sides of the same counterfeit coin, the dualism of appearance and Reality. Nietzsche espouses a host of finite values, of which some have already been identified—such as truth and honesty, strength and power, freedom and creativity—and others that remain to be explored—among them the warrior spirit, physical

health, and genuine selfhood. Lucidity and nobility, however, are the superordinate values that generate the warrant for the values just listed. Lucidity
and nobility, in turn, are unified by their common opposition to the spirit of
ressentiment that subtends the impotence and self-deception Nietzsche takes
as his archfoes.

Lucidity is the value that informs the truth and honesty symbolized in the
camel: one cannot be honest if one is mystified by lies, if one's motivations
are driven by values assimilated from the herd without prior critical scrutiny.
Coupled with the will to truth is the need for the strength to confront the
voices within that urge to return to the comfort of the herd and punish the errant spirit with guilt. The defiance of the lion augments the camel's strength
with the power to negate the commands of authority and conscience, to
stand alone against those whose self-preservation depends upon obliterating
exceptions to their rule. The affirmation of the child depends upon creativity.
To impose a new order within the sphere of personal becoming, to will the
will that is one's own only to the extent that it is lucid, to augment personal
freedom by opening new options, all this requires nobility. There is no dignity without freedom, no freedom without lucidity, and no lucidity without
a vision of the better. Nobility defines itself against the low-down spirit of
impotence and revenge; its quest is for transcendence in *this* world.

· ·

CHAPTER FIVE

BODY AND SOUL: NIETZSCHE'S SELF

The task for the years that followed [*Zarathustra*] was indicated as clearly as possible. After the Yes-saying part of my task had been solved, the turn had come for the No-saying, *No-doing* part: the revaluation of our values so far, the great war.

—Friedrich Nietzsche, *Ecce Homo*

In his ruminations on *Beyond Good and Evil* in *Ecce Homo*, Nietzsche suggests a comparison between himself and God. On the seventh day following creation, God becomes a serpent lying down beneath the tree of knowledge. In his leisure, he reflects that he has made everything too beautiful, and recuperates from being God by becoming the devil. After the affirmation of *Zarathustra*, Nietzsche decides to mount an attack on modernity. His primary target is Kant.

I. CONVENTIONAL FICTIONS

It is popular today to find in Nietzsche the precursor of the postmodern thesis that meaning is reducible to signifiers, that we always and only see the world through the mediation of language, and that, for this reason, the strongest claim for truth that can be found is one that regards truth merely as a useful or conventional fiction: what we take to be true is merely a way of talking about the world that has been found to be of some use to the community and therefore has been adopted as a convention.

There is significant support for this interpretation in the texts of Nietzsche, and the interpretation itself is not without merit. I will argue, however, that this view is superficial, and that when the relevant texts are put into context, one finds a rich and complex pattern of thought that is far superior to the interpretation now enjoying so much popularity. "I shall repeat a hundred times; we really ought to free ourselves from the seduction of words!" (*BGE*, 23).

How do words seduce? Nietzsche offers an extended analysis of this query: thought is historical; history sediments linguistic structures; those structures are the basis for conceptual systems; and philosophy is largely the articulation of the conceptual systems embedded within the language of the time.[1]

This standpoint is an extension of the earlier view, articulated in *On Truth and Lies in a Nonmoral Sense* (PT, 82–83), that we think in metaphors and that those metaphors, once adopted, form the basis of convention.[2] Art is the genesis of metaphor. Art thus underlies science and philosophy insofar as the latter two are pointed toward the exploration of conceptual schemas, that is, insofar as they are language-dependent.

If this were the end of the story Nietzsche tells, the postmodern interpretation would be sufficient. But there is more to think about. Why does Nietzsche talk of the seduction of words? How do words seduce? How could we free ourselves from their seduction? Why would we want to?

Nietzsche takes up the question of causality in a discernibly Kantian way: "One should not wrongly reify 'cause' and 'effect,' as the natural scientists do . . . ; one should use 'cause' and 'effect' only as pure concepts, that is to say, as conventional fictions for the purpose of designation and communication—*not* for explanation. In the 'in-itself' there is nothing of 'causal connections'" (*BGE*, 29). Kant could have written that passage. But what Nietzsche makes of this is not what Kant makes of it. The difference is that Kant thought the pure concepts or categories were universal and necessary and Nietzsche thought that they were historical accumulations from the poets, those who create metaphors.

What is it to reify? It is to turn a word into a thing. As Hume pointed out, there are no things, no phenomena that are impressions of cause and effect or will or ego. These are words we use to form relations between impressions. Kant grounded these relations in the understanding, ultimately in the noumenal self, the transcendental ego, the transcendental unity of apperception: that is, in the immanent agencies responsible for organizing the world.

In Nietzsche's view, Kant made a logical mistake: he did exactly what he inveighed against. He took a word used to designate relations among things—and made it into a thing or agency that does the relating. "'How are synthetic judgments *a priori possible?*' Kant asked himself— and what really is his answer? '*By virtue of a faculty.*' . . . But is that—an answer? An explanation? Or is it not rather merely a repetition of the question?" (*BGE*, 18–19). The Kantian faculty is just the sort of reification Nietzsche repudiates.

Nietzsche poses the question in a different way—"Why is belief in such judgments *necessary?*"—and gives his own answer: "Such judgments must be *believed* to be true, for the sake of the preservation of creatures like ourselves; though they might, of course, be *false* judgments for all that!" (*BGE*, 19). Now this is not entirely incompatible with Kantian transcendental argumentation. Why must we take this to be true a priori? Because the contrary is inconceivable. What must be presupposed to think of the world in the way we do? The structures of thinking that produce this way of experiencing the world.

The profound difference between Kant and Nietzsche is the difference between (a) grounding things in logical necessity and taking the world as we find it to be the way the world has to be for us, and (b) grounding things in historically (that is, contingently) evolving psychology and taking the world as we find it as subject to becoming, growth or decay, in any case, change.

2. EGO AND WILL

> There are still harmless self-observers who believe that there are "immediate certainties"; for example, "I think," or as the superstition of Schopenhauer put it, "I will"; as though knowledge here got hold of its object purely and nakedly as "the thing in itself," without [the possibility of] any falsification on the part of either the subject or the object. But that "immediate certainty," as well as "absolute knowledge" and the "thing in itself," involve a *contradictio in adjecto*, I shall repeat a hundred times; we really ought to free ourselves from the seduction of words! (*BGE*, 23)

The two examples of reification Nietzsche stresses in the first part of *Beyond Good and Evil*—"On the Prejudices of Philosophers"—are the ego and the free/unfree will. The context is a critique of Kant. Kant posits these entities—the immortal soul substance and freedom of the will—as necessary presuppositions, as two of the three Ideas of Pure Reason. Why are they necessary?

A. Ego

Kant requires a free and enduring soul substance for several reasons: it accounts for the unity of experience through the synthesis of temporal moments, and it is the condition for the possibility for morality. Without freedom, no responsibility, no dignity; without immortality, no possibility of reward in the hereafter.[3] Furthermore, Kant subscribes to the Cartesian thesis of the indubitableness of the ego as an immediate certainty achieved in the cogito.

Nietzsche contests both the unity ascribed to the soul or the ego and the immediate certainty also ascribed to it:

> When I analyze the process that is expressed in the sentence, "I think," I find a whole series of daring assertions that would be difficult, perhaps impossible, to prove: for example, that it is *I* who think, that there must necessarily be something that thinks, that thinking is an activity and operation on the part of a being who is thought of as a cause, that there is an "ego," and, finally, that it is already determined what is to be designated by thinking—that I *know* what thinking is. (*BGE*, 23)

Here and in the passages that surround this one (*BGE*, §§16–18), Nietzsche predelineates Sartre's famous critique of the Husserlian transcendental ego, which, in turn, led Lacan and MacIntyre to designate the ego as a fabrication, as a false reification (*méconnaissance*) or a narrative that constructs an identity mistakenly conceived as its own origin. And, as the thinkers just mentioned, Nietzsche attributes this fabrication to a grammatical habit; he conceives it as an instance of our proclivity to attribute worldly reality to some unitary agency that generates our words or concepts: "'Thinking is an activity; every activity requires an agent; consequently—'" (*BGE*, 24).

You are now reading a book I have written on Nietzsche's thought: True or false? Nietzsche's thought is complex, difficult, provocative, full of insight and portent, creative, and unique. I am the person now trying to compose my thoughts on Nietzsche's writings and to articulate those thoughts as best I can. Are these two statements true or false? In the binary logic of Parmenides and Zeno, that is, the logic that dominates the ontology of Being, true and false are the only choices here. If the ego is the ground of personal identity, and if the persons referred to in the pronouns "you" and "I" and in the proper noun "Nietzsche" are fabrications grounded in nothing more than the habitual structures of the Indo-European languages we speak, that is, if no such persons exist in the world, then the answers to my questions cannot be "true" and hence must be "false." Is it false that you are now reading these words?

If it is true that you are now reading these words, then we confront a problem. The problem is that of understanding what such terms as "ego" and "will" should be taken to mean in the context of Nietzsche's critique, and the correlative problem of generating a viable interpretation of the truth-value of "conventional fictions" or "useful fictions." We need to know more about judgments that "must be believed to be true, for the sake of the preservation of creatures like ourselves; though they might, of course, be *false* judgments." Believing something to be true for convenience or utility or self-preservation even though one knows it to be false—say, for example, the proposition "God exists"—sounds a bit like self-deceit, and not at all compatible with the honesty Nietzsche takes to be essential to nobility.

We shall return to this issue shortly, but should keep it in mind as we take up Nietzsche's critique of the free/unfree will.

B. Will

Nietzsche's critique of the will is explicitly directed toward Schopenhauer, but also applies to Kant insofar as the latter depends heavily on a faculty of willing as a foundation for morality. Nietzsche's critique of the will is analogous to his critique of the ego insofar as the will is also taken to be an immediate certainty, something "absolutely and completely known" (*BGE*, 25). As in the case of the ego, Nietzsche attributes this spurious apodicticity to prejudice grounded in habit, another case of reifying a word or concept.

In opposition to these traditional conceptions of the will as a unitary faculty, Nietzsche proposes to think of willing as: (a) "something *complicated*, something that is a unit only as a word"; (b) something that involves "a plurality of sensations, namely, the sensation of the state '*away from which*,' the sensation of the state '*towards which*,' the sensations of this '*from*' and '*towards*' themselves,[4] and then also an accompanying muscular sensation"; (c) an act in which "there is a ruling thought"; and (d) "an *affect* [*ein Affekt*],[5] and specifically the affect of the command" (*BGE*, 25). He goes on to say that "what is strangest about the will [is that] we are at the same time the commanding *and* the obeying parties" (*BGE*, 26).

What allows us to comprehend this complex set of characteristics is the idea that "our body is but a social structure composed of many souls" (*BGE*, 26). There is an agon going on in the case of willing: many competing demands speak within, each driven by its own desire/affect, each seeking to supervene over the others and move the body toward its own goal. Freud, himself a serious reader of Nietzsche, said that the ego is the battleground on which this agon among conflicting emotions welling up out of the unconscious is played out. This might be close to the mark, but, as we shall see, for Nietzsche, the borders between conscious and unconscious are not so starkly drawn, and there are cases in which we become conscious of the decisions we have made only after we have acted on them. Nietzsche is critical of Kant's insistence on privileging intentions, and in a later section (§32) argues that "the decisive value of an action lies precisely in what is *unintentional* in it" (*BGE*, 44). The point here is that the "social structure" of our body is far from a democracy based on rational decision making, but rather more like Hobbes's state of nature where warring elements fight to dominate.

In the ontology of becoming working itself out through Nietzsche, the unifying principle is change: agon, strife, conflict. Each resolution breeds a new competition, a new struggle for domination. Nietzsche's term for this is "will to power" (about which much more remains to be taken up), and reason is but one of the forces competing to dominate the organism. In fact, reason is a late entry in the competition, and does not always prevail when pitted against such primitive agonists as fear, desire, and bloodlust.

Schopenhauer, under the influence of Buddhist writings, regarded human will as a form of self-mystification and the source of human misery. Will originates in desire, and desire, particularly the desires to perpetuate our own individual being (that is, survival instincts) and maximize bodily pleasures (that is, the various forms of appetite including the sexual instincts), generates the system of illusion we take to be the world. If we can still our desires, we can liberate ourselves from the miseries of fearing death and longing for an impossible satisfaction of all desires. Enlightenment and release consist in realizing the illusory nature of all that we take to be real, especially the self and the worldly appearances that promise pleasure or threaten pain, and thereby free ourselves from thralldom. Freed from the false discriminations [which are][6] driven by desire that generate our illusions of individuated things that entice or threaten us, we enter a state of peace, beatitude, and reunification with the One undifferentiated continuum of Being.

Schopenhauer conceives the idea of an autonomous human will as a mystification implanted in us by Nature in order to satisfy its own goals. The will of Nature is brute will to self-perpetuation. When we reproduce ourselves, when we conjugate and perpetuate our species, we do so under the illusion that we are fulfilling our own desires (which we are) and satisfying our own interests (which we are not). Child bearing and rearing are self-sacrificial acts of altruism, and humans are not characteristically altruistic or given to self-sacrifice; we are rather more inclined to be egoistic, more inclined to be driven by our own pursuit to maximize personal pleasure and minimize pain. Nature therefore implants in us the sexual desire that uses short-term pleasure to drive us to fulfill its long-term and unwavering goal to perpetuate itself, contrary to our own individual interests.

The path to Schopenhauer's version of nirvana or release or enlightenment is marked by a strange conjunction of asceticism and aestheticism. Aestheticism is usually conceived in terms of *aisthesis* [aisqesis], that is, sensation or sensual pleasure, but Schopenhauer conceives it, along Kantian lines, as consisting in suspension of all pathological interest: the aesthete, for Schopenhauer, is one who distances himself from desire and views representations as such, as objects of contemplation, not as things we want to possess or avoid. Just as it is a mistake to want to possess the nude figure in a painting or to want to eat the fruit represented in a still-life, so is it a mistake to desire or fear any thing represented in everyday perceptual appearances. Aestheticism thus becomes asceticism, the foreswearing of desire, hence the suspension of will. Through the *ascesis* [askhsis] or rigorous exercise of reflective removal that suspends willing, one achieves a state of objectivity, a dispassionate spectatorial attitude unmoved by desire. One achieves peace and relief from the strife of becoming.

Schopenhauer educated Nietzsche into the ontology of becoming by providing a negative example. Nietzsche's will to power is the antipode of Schopenhauer's will to transcend willing. Nietzsche's joyful affirmation of the agon of life is the antithesis of Schopenhauer's pessimistic abjuration of change, ceaseless struggling into being, augmenting one's own being, and then passing out of being. In saying no to the incessant becoming of life, in the self-deceptive will to deny its own willing, Schopenhauer taught Nietzsche to ask what it would take to say yes with resolution and unremitting honesty. Nietzsche's philosophy is a rejection of quietism, be it the quietism of Buddhism or the quietism of Schopenhauer's aestheticism that it inspired.

As it is with Kant's "I think," so it is with Schopenhauer's "I will": neither ego nor will is a unity, given to intuition as an immediate certainty. There are no transcendental unities, no immanent faculties corresponding to the words "ego" and "will." To infer from this that there is nothing corresponding to these words, as Sartre, Lacan, and some of their followers have, however, would be both logically inept and a manifest misinterpretation of Nietzsche. If *Zarathustra* is a book about self-transcendence, there must be room for something like selfhood in Nietzsche's thought. If will to power is Nietzsche's characterization of the life-process itself, then there must be room for something like willing in Nietzsche's thought. And if self-transcendence involves willing, then selfhood and willing must be intimately related in Nietzsche's thought.

3. EGO AND WILL, BEING AND BECOMING

As it was with Truth and truth, so it is with Ego and ego, Will and will: the terms change meaning within different ontologies. In the framework of Kant's transcendental idealism, one must posit two egos and two wills, and each of these two pairs involves, as Nietzsche said, a *contradictio in adjecto*.

The transcendental ego, or transcendental unity of apperception, is a noumenal faculty, which must stand outside of time since it constitutes time. The empirical ego, the historical person taken to be the ground of my personal identity in all its particularity and contingency, must be a temporal entity. They must be united insofar as the unity of the first is the condition for the possibility of the unity of the second. But they cannot be united insofar as the first is atemporal and the second is temporal, and insofar as the first is universal, selfsame in all instantiations, and the second is particular, continuously emergent, bearer of incompatible attributes, and hence never selfsame over time. The self that is more myself than I, that is, my noumenal self, cannot be I, myself. Yet it must be I, myself. *Contradictio in adjecto*.

Why must the transcendental ego, the noumenal self, be coterminous with my empirical ego, the person I experience myself to be in everyday life? Two reasons, one epistemological, the other axiological.

The "I think" must be able to accompany all sensuous representations. All moments of conscious experience must be able to be identifiable as moments of *my* experience; otherwise, there would be no unity of experience, and conscious life would be reduced to a Humean bundle of impressions with no principle of cohesion. The condition for the possibility of the "I think" to accompany all my sensuous representations is satisfied by the transcendental unity of apperception as the ground of the unification of experience over time. In short, the oneness of experience stands in a relation of co-implication with the mineness of experience: oneness implies mineness, and mineness implies oneness, hence oneness and mineness stand in a relation of identity.[7] Hence the noumenal ego must be identical with the empirical ego.

The empirical self, my particular self, is the self that acts in the world, the self that behaves in a moral or immoral way. Freedom is a condition for moral assessment. Everything I experience in the phenomenal world must, as a condition for being experienced, fall under the categories of the understanding, including the category of causality. Hence the empirical ego is experienced as causally determined. Hence the freedom that is necessary for moral assessment must be ascribed to the noumenal self. But that noumenal self must be identical with my empirical self; otherwise, my empirical self would not be subject to moral assessment. Also, the self that is subject to moral assessment, the individuated empirical self, must be identical with the immortal or noumenal self if it is to have the promise of reward in the hereafter for its moral behavior in the phenomenal sphere, a promise that cannot be held out toward individuals who fail to behave in a moral way.

The concepts of ego and will, understood within the ontology of Being, involve the absurdity of bearing contradictory attributes. They are instances of what Kant himself called "the antinomy of pure reason." According to Kant, transcendental dialectic, or transcendental illusion, has its seat in pure reason. When pure reason applies the categories that structure the phenomenal world to the noumenal world, it goes astray. Kant was committed to positing a noumenal world, a world as perceived by the *Ens Perfectissimum*. Hence he was doomed to commit the fallacies he himself identified.

In announcing the death of God, Nietzsche took a path that led out of the sphere of Being, the sphere of God, freedom, and immortality in the direction of an ontology of becoming. The question he posed, the experiment he undertook in heralding Zarathustra at the end of *The Gay Science*, asked whether there could be values robust enough to sustain morality in a God-forsaken world, a morality beyond that of good and evil defined in theological terms.

Accepting the premises that morality of any kind, be it theological, crypto-theological, or atheological, presupposes agency and freedom of some description, and that agency and freedom require some sense of selfhood and will, we confront the question of how Nietzsche attempts to conceive selfhood and willing within the context of an atheological ontology of becoming. Framed in a different way, the question asks how Nietzsche's critique of ego and will in Schopenhauer and Kant leads him to redefine those terms.

We have already seen, in passages quoted above, that Nietzsche regards will and ego as complex, rather than unitary, and, far from being given as immediate certainties, as evolving over time through processes that are largely opaque to us. The "who" of my identity is not an agency antecedent to my actions that prefigures them; it emerges through actions in which a host of dissonant motivations of which I am at best marginally aware compete for ascendancy. In the morning I get up, splash water on my face, brew a cup of coffee, and sit down at the computer determined to finish the chapter I am working on. Then it is noon, and I have written nothing but responses to e-mail, paid some bills, and researched the cost of a getaway to Jamaica. What I was doing was not writing. It was not clearing the decks for action; it was searching for obstacles to put in the way of what I had willed to do, of what I thought I wanted to do. Lunch, nap, fresh start, and here I am writing these words, feeling a bit more in charge of myself and renewed in my purpose.

This is not the first time I have danced this dance, nor will it be the last. Is this a matter of weakness of will? Or, rather, is it not a negotiation among conflicting desires, all of which are my desires, the desires of a self that is not unitary, not transparent to itself, but could be more lucid, given a bit of resolution?

> No people could live without first esteeming; but if they want to preserve themselves, then they must not esteem as the neighbor

> esteems. . . . A tablet of the good hangs over every people. Behold, it
> is the tablet of their overcomings; behold it is the voice of their will
> to power. . . . The delight in the herd is more ancient than the delight
> in the ego; and as long as the good conscience is identified with the
> herd, only the bad conscience says: I. (Z, 170–72)

These excerpts from "On the Thousand and One Goals" affirm the ego,
but the ego affirmed is one that has a bad conscience. Conscience is the
voice of the internalized values of the herd. We are all herd animals and are
bred to feel good about ourselves when we earn the praise of our neighbors
by fulfilling their expectations and acting in consonance with the values
on which the community is founded. But the lucid and creative spirit tests
communal values and discards, even violates those values that cannot withstand scrutiny. The minister delivers a sermon on honesty, and then says
to each communicant as he delivers the wafer of bread, "This is the flesh
of Christ." It would be irreverent and impolite to stand up and say, "No,
in truth, it is a piece of bread and not the flesh of Christ." One would not
feel good about doing such a thing. Stand up in defiance or remain seated
and silent, one would not feel good either way. The point is that the ego is
not unitary; what it is to be an ego is to struggle with the dissonant voices
within. Will to power, mentioned in this passage for the first time in Nietzsche's published writings, is manifested by overcoming the part of the
self driven by internalized values that cannot withstand lucid evaluation.
The delight [Lust][8] in the ego is not carefree joy; it is fulfillment of the longing to be more than one is.

Nietzsche says that willing is "an affect and specifically the affect of command." Who then issues the command? Where does agency lie? It cannot
be in a unitary ego, for "we are at the same time the commanding and the
obeying parties":

> "Freedom of the will"—that is the expression for the complex
> state of delight [Lust-Zustand] of the person exercising volition,
> who commands and at the same time identifies himself with the
> executor of the order—who, as such, enjoys also the triumph over
> obstacles, but thinks within himself that it was really his will itself
> that overcame them. In this way the person exercising volition adds
> the feelings of delight [Lustgefühle] of his successful executive

> instruments, the useful "under-wills" or under-souls—indeed, our
> body is but a social structure composed of many souls—to his
> feelings of delight [*Lustgefühle*] as a commander. . . . In all will-
> ing it is absolutely a question of commanding and obeying, on the
> basis . . . of a social structure composed of many "souls." (*BGE*,
> 26–27; W2, 583)

We identify with the part of ourselves that triumphs, with the one of the
many souls that was obeyed by the others. But how then do we account for
the shame we feel when the wrong soul wins? And how do we know which
soul is the right one to obey? Lacking this judgment, there could never be
remorse for any of our actions because we would always identify with the
winner of the agon, no matter what action was undertaken.

The answer lies in the triad of values that underlies Nietzsche's esteemings: lucidity, honesty, and nobility. If, upon reflection, the under-soul that
prevailed was a voice of the herd speaking in us, that is warrant for suspicion.
If, upon inspection, we find that the voice that prevailed did so because we
feared the reaction of the herd, then that is warrant for doubt. But if, on the
other hand, we are lucid about the reason for choosing to listen to this voice
rather than that—be that voice dissonant or consonant with the values of the
herd—then that lucidity vindicates the choice.

We identify with the commanding voice whether or not it withstands scrutiny. If it does not, we feel shame. Perhaps the shame of dishonesty: I obeyed
that voice, not because I affirmed the value it expressed, but because I feared
disapproval. Or the shame of ignobility: I let that voice prevail, not because
it spurred me to greater heights, but because it was more comfortable to sub-
merge myself in the warm bath of communal approval. No morality without
freedom, no freedom without personal responsibility. Lucidity and honesty
are conditions for personal responsibility. Nobility is the open-ended quest
for higher ground that drives self-transcendence. Will to power, in this context, is the will to command oneself.

But who is the oneself? How does one know who one really is? One
identifies with the self, the under-soul, whose voice prevailed, but reflection
opens the possibility of shame and disavowal; in any case, it necessarily involves a distancing of oneself from the commanding self with whom one
has identified. Self-transcendence is the quest that defines the *Übermensch*.
And self-transcendence is self-estrangement, self-overcoming. The opposite

of oneness with oneself, the opposite of coincidence with oneself, the opposite of the stasis of a fixed and enduring identity, the opposite of an abiding
core or matrix of properties that reliably determines behavior. Is its being
then, as Sartre argued, to be what it is not and not to be what it is; that is,
to be nothing?

Without attempting to read anything into Nietzsche's thought that does
not have a home there, I will refer again to Nietzsche's statement that "our
body is but a social structure composed of many souls":

> "Body am I, and soul"—thus speaks the child. . . .
>
> But the awakened and knowing say: body am I entirely, and noth-
> ing else; and soul is only a word for something about the body.
>
> The body is a great reason, a plurality with one sense, a war and
> a peace, a herd and a shepherd. . . .
>
> Behind your thoughts and feelings, my brother, there stands a
> mighty ruler, an unknown sage—whose name is self. In your body
> he dwells; he is your body. (Z, 146)

The substratum of personal identity is not an eternal soul; it is the aging
body, a living-unto-death organism caught up ineluctably in the strife of becoming. We are palpably not nothing. We are bodies with histories; we are
entities whose identities are conferred, not by abiding properties, but by be-
havioral style. "*One thing is needful.*— To 'give style' to one's character—a
great and rare art! It is practiced by those who survey all the strengths and
weaknesses of their nature and then fit them into an artistic plan until every
one of them appears as art and reason" (*GS*, 232).

The self is not a unitary ego; it is one's body. The self is not self-
transparent; it is an "unknown sage," a source of wisdom that has to be
plumbed. The body does not say "I," but does "I," and its rationale for doing
what it does may never be fully apparent. Hence, the quest for lucidity has no
stopping point, no point at which we are fully aware of why we think and act
as we do. To the extent to which we are aware of the reasons and motives that
drive us, we can take personal responsibility for our actions, and know that
we are willing our own will rather than obeying the will implanted in us by
the common conscience of the herd.

Ego and will are grammatical fictions in the sense that they designate agencies of behavior required by grammar: every action presupposes an actor;

every verb requires a subject. The mistake here lies in reifying the grammatical presupposition and then attributing to it self-certainty and agency. They are not merely grammatical fictions, however, insofar as lucidity, personal awareness, is a condition for freedom: only insofar as I know what I am doing and why I am doing it can I act deliberately and take responsibility for what I do. It is a mistake to presuppose, as Kant does, that we are free in some domain beyond the sphere of worldly experience; the truth is that freedom and personal responsibility are commensurate with lucidity, and the struggle for lucidity is a never-ending task.

God did not endow us with a faculty of free will in order to render us subject to judgment, reward and punishment. Freedom is proportional to the number of options open to our bodies in moving about in the world. Our bodies, the bodies that we ourselves are, are constricted by the laws of physics, to be sure, but also by the laws of psychology: if we are not aware of an option, we cannot exercise that option in a deliberate way; if we are not aware of our motives, we cannot choose among them.

Reflection is a capacity human bodies develop—we, as a species, have learned to objectify ourselves and alienate ourselves from ourselves the better to understand ourselves—the I or the self recognized in reflection is an incarnate self, not a soul substance, to be sure, but not nothing, either. What we recognize ourselves to be, including the idealizations we want ourselves to be, is not an apodictic finding, not an immediate certainty, but rather a conjecture: at best an honest self-assessment, at worst a self-deceptive narcissistic fantasy (although such idealizations have positive functions, as well). As a conjecture, it may well be and probably always is subject to doubt—truth being as elusive and hard to grasp as Nietzsche continually says—but conjectures subjected to tests of corroborating or disconfirming evidence command varying degrees of confidence over time.

The sense of personal identity that emerges through reflection is contingent, evolving, becoming. And so is the degree of autonomy each organism is able to gain for itself. *Übermenschlichkeit* is a project, an undertaking with no finality other than death, and not all who undertake it achieve the same degree of success. Yet differences in self-mastery and self-awareness among different human beings are palpably real.

The self posited by Kant as the locus of morality and freedom was a grammatical fiction, a transcendental presupposition grounded in the seduction of words to reify abstractions and ramified by antecedent commitments to

Christian moral precepts conceived within the context of an ontology of Being. The worldly self that Nietzsche affirmed and sought to develop is not a useful convention—if only because it tends to subvert what is common, what draws humans together to form a herd—but rather a fleshly reality seeking to augment its power to be better than it is within the turmoil of becoming. One thing that the self affirmed by Nietzsche assuredly is not is a fabrication deliberately constructed to delude itself about itself. It is of such fabrications that herd animals construct their identities.

The portrait of self-overcoming Nietzsche painted in *Zarathustra* had to be accompanied by a treatise that exposed the presuppositions and values of the philosophical substructures he was contesting. *Beyond Good and Evil* delivers such a critique; but at the same time, it must also articulate and defend the philosophical tenets underlying his affirmations: there is no way to do one without doing the other.

Nietzsche claims that moral considerations underlie all the ontological, epistemological, and metaphysical a prioris of Kantian philosophy and transcendental philosophy in general. What are these moral considerations? For Nietzsche, they represent the values of the philosophers in question, their esteemings, their commitments. "In the philosopher . . . there is nothing whatever that is impersonal; and above all, his morality bears decided and decisive witness to *who he is*—that is, in what order of rank the innermost drives of his nature stand in relation to one another" (*BGE*, 14).

If philosophy is driven by moral considerations, and moral considerations depend on the innermost drives of philosophers, then our exegesis is not yet complete. Much remains to explore in the moral dimensions of Nietzsche's agon with Kant.

• •

CHAPTER SIX

MORALITY IN A GOD-FORSAKEN WORLD

> We believe that morality in the traditional sense . . . was a preju-
> dice . . . something that must be overcome. The overcoming of mo-
> rality . . . let this be the name for that long secret work which has
> been saved up for the finest and most honest, also the most mali-
> cious, consciences of today, as living touchstones of the soul.
> —Friedrich Nietzsche, *Beyond Good and Evil*

I. TRUTH REVISITED

The triad that subtends Nietzsche's morality is the intersection of lucidity, honesty, and nobility, and the value that brings these three terms into unity is truth. The locus of the problem of truth remains the issue of Nietzsche's evolving treatment of the distinction between illusion [*Schein*] and appearance [*Erscheinung*].[1] If these are indistinguishable, then there is no ground for assigning greater truth-value to the one rather than the other. This is the standpoint Nietzsche occupies until 1876. I have argued that Nietzsche does a turnabout in 1876 in which he acknowledges that treating the wish fulfillment of illusion as having an equal or even stronger claim to our credibility than the harsh realities of everyday perceptual experience is dishonest, a form of romantic self-deception. In this context, I argued that Nietzsche's notorious ambivalence with regard to truth could be resolved by distinguishing between Truth as eternal verity within the ontology of Being (which Nietzsche clearly does repudiate) and truth as perspectival and subject to modification within an ontology of becoming.

What can be known about the perceptual world of becoming? What kinds of truth claims can legitimately be defended? "You know that no philosopher so far has been proved right, and that there might be a more laudable truthfulness in every little question mark that you place after your special words and favorite doctrines (and occasionally after yourselves)" (BGE, 36).

In the world in which we dwell, all truth is provisional; every truth will be overcome by a stronger truth—including this one. This is far from the reflexively self-defeating statement that all truths are relative, because the very idea of one finite truth being overcome by another, stronger one presupposes that there are grounds for differentiating between greater and lesser claims to truth about a given subject. This is the point of Zarathustra's admonitions to his disciples not to accept what he says merely because he says it, but to determine for themselves and by their own means the merit of his pronouncements. Healthy skepticism suspends belief pending examination of evidence, in contrast to abject skepticism, which determines ahead of time that all truth claims are equally groundless, hence all are equal, hence there are no legitimate grounds for preferring one point of view to another. Abject skepticism is abject relativism, a position Nietzsche had abandoned by 1876.

Note the implicit appeal to the value of lucidity here. To accept a viewpoint as true without being able to cite the reasons for the acceptance is, in Nietzsche's assessment, a manifestation of herd behavior: I hold a given belief because this belief is commonly held and sanctioned within my community. Religious belief is almost universally of this nature: one is born into a community of believers, and ostracized from the community if it is found that one has departed in significant ways from the tenets of that faith. Nietzsche goes so far as to say truths become lies when they are unthinkingly accepted:

> A new species of philosophers is coming up. . . . Are these coming philosophers new friends of "truth"? . . . They will certainly not be dogmatists. It must offend their pride, also their taste, if their truth is supposed to be a truth for everyman—which has so far been the secret wish and hidden meaning of all dogmatic aspirations. "My judgment is *my* judgment": no one else is easily entitled to it—that is what such a philosopher of the future may perhaps say of himself.
>
> One must shed the bad taste of wanting to agree with many. "Good" is no longer good when one's neighbor mouths it. And how should there be a "common good"! The term contradicts itself: whatever can be common always has little value. (BGE, 52–53)

This is patent hyperbole: the value of Boyle's law or the distaste for deceit is not diminished by common acceptance. Beneath the hyperbole, however, there is a philosophical gauntlet being thrown down, one that warrants serious consideration. Nietzsche here is challenging the traditional equation of truth and universality. I have addressed this issue earlier,[2] but it is well to revisit it and consider it in a different light.

The distinction I have drawn between the de facto universal and the universal as regulative ideal,[3] points to a dark aspect of the correlation between truth and universality: a principle of conservation of ordinarily taken-for-granted beliefs, a potentially despotic reluctance to change the way we think about things, even when there is compelling evidence that we should. Think of Copernicus and geocentricity. Coherence with the body of accepted belief remains valid as one criterion for truth, but when, in practice if not in principle, it supervenes all others, it becomes an obstacle in the growth of ideas: the martyrdom of creators is a recurrent abomination in the history of our fatuous species. If the longest-standing operational definition of madness is seeing things differently from most of us (as I believe it is), then it takes genuine discernment to separate the psychopaths from the seers. Nietzsche still stands as a case in point: "Whatever philosophical standpoint one may adopt today, from every point of view the *erroneousness* of the world in which we think we live is the surest and firmest fact that we can lay eyes on" (*BGE*, 45).

How can there be this worldly truth if the world in which we think we live is erroneous? Heidegger is indebted to Nietzsche for the idea that *erring* means "errant or wandering or becoming; stumbling along through trial and error." Truth and untruth are intertwined; whatever reveals also conceals. This takes truth out of the domain of the unconditional yes or no, true or false, out of the domain of binary opposition, and acknowledges the finitude of perspective. Nietzsche characterizes youth's proclivity for the yes and no, "the taste for the unconditional" as "the worst of tastes" (*BGE*, 43), and speaks of the philosopher's duty to look "beyond the bourgeois world and its Yes and No" (*BGE*, 46).

Error is intrinsic to becoming, and becoming is the nature of life.[4] But . . . what about truth in this domain?:

> It is no more than a moral prejudice that truth is worth more than mere appearance [*Schein*]; it is even the worst proved assumption there is in the world. Let at least this much be admitted: there would be no life at all if not on the basis of perspective estimates and appearances [*perspektivischer Schätzungen und Scheinbarkeiten*]; and if, with the virtuous enthusiasm of some philosophers, one wanted

to abolish the "apparent world" [*die >>scheinbare Welt<<*] altogether—well, supposing *you* could do that, at least nothing would
be left of your "truth" either. Indeed, what forces us at all to suppose that there is an essential opposition of "true" and "false"? Is it
not sufficient to assume degrees of apparentness [*Stufen der Schein-
barkeit*] and, as it were, lighter and darker shadows and shades of
appearance [*Gesamttöne des Scheins*]—different "values," to use
the language of painters? Why couldn't the world *that concerns
us*—be a fiction [*Fiktion*]? (*BGE*, 46–47; W2, 599–600)

This passage condenses a host of ideas and paradoxes into one enigmatic ut-
terance. It also consolidates several themes set forth in earlier phases of my
argument and affords the opportunity to demonstrate their interdependency.
Here are the themes that have to be correlated. The elaboration that follows
is perforce of the need for brevity couched in dogmatic terms, that is, without
supporting argumentation. The arguments have already been presented in
preceding chapters.

- Denial of the binary opposition of truth and falsity
- Equation of "True" with "moral" in the ontology of Being
- Assertion of the apparent world as the only real world in the ontology
  of becoming
- Necessity of working with degrees of apparentness, that is, conditional
  truths and corrigible judgments
- Intersection of art and truth (concept and percept, imagination and
  perception)

If Truth is defined as adequacy to the object, then it requires an omniscient
and atemporal knower. For finite humans, this adequacy is not only not
achievable, it is unimaginable. Divine omniscience has no correlate in human
experience because absolute transcendence transcends us absolutely, and
there can be no mediation. Finite truth is then necessarily imperfect, lacking in adequacy, circumscribed, and in that sense, tainted with falsity. Nevertheless, it is truer to say the earth is a sphere than to say it is a flat plane
(although the latter is a useful hypothesis for builders).

Being is the universe viewed sub specie aeternitatis. That is a necessarily
empty or unfulfillable intuition for finite creatures. If time is real, Being is also
an unfulfillable intention for any being. If morality is to be unconditional, it

must be apprehended from a standpoint that has no correlation with finite experience.

To take our measure of truth and goodness from a standpoint that is, by definition, absolutely inaccessible and incomprehensible to us is absurd, necessarily without meaning for us.

It is equally absurd to conclude from the above that there is no truth or goodness in the finite realm of human cognition. That is to say, there are viable means of judging the relative merits of competing claims to truth and value. Such judgments are corrigible or subject to modification, but they are not arbitrary.

The apparent world of becoming, the world of human experience, is the only world for humans. The noumenal world itself is a human world devised by human intellect, and, as Kant himself acknowledged, ascription of any content to this world is nonsensical and absurd, a sacrifice of reason to wish fulfillment. There is, in fact, a world that transcends us; it is the phenomenal world in which we live, but about which we know relatively little.

Given this general context, what concretely does it mean to assert that it should be sufficient "to assume degrees of apparentness, . . . lighter and darker shadows and shades of appearance, . . . different 'values' [in the] language of painters"? Some light may be shed on this by recalling Nietzsche's characterization of youth as indulging in "the worst of tastes, the taste for the unconditional." The section in which this appears (*BGE*, §31) begins as follows: "When one is young, one venerates and despises without *that art of nuances which constitutes the best gain of life*" (*BGE*, 43; emphasis added). The "best gain of life" is the "art of nuances." Art offers us the means of fine discrimination. How so?

Consider the thought that imagination illumines perception in a manner that is analogous to the way in which concepts illumine things. Concepts allow us to see things in relation to each other. They do so by the distortion, often cited by Nietzsche, of overlooking differences.[5] Art or creative imagination enables the qualitative aspects of things to become more apparent. Caricature reveals character better than photography (unless, of course, the photographer is a Man Ray): alter a line and a quality vanishes. Art is both allusive and revelatory: it shows you a way of seeing the world you might have missed had the artist not guided you with the "coherent deformation" [Maritain] of his emphases. Art is a distortion that reveals a truth. If you have read Melville and Conrad you will understand the sea better, actually see it in a richer way, than you might otherwise have.[6]

When Nietzsche poses the rhetorical question—"Why couldn't the world *that concerns us*—be a fiction?"—he is asserting the critical truth he learned from Kant that our perceptions are necessarily *our* perceptions and could not be otherwise. But he departs radically from Kant in holding that our perceptual world, far from being absolutely discontinuous from Reality, is reality as best it can be conceived by finite [beings].[7]

The array of concepts a scientist brings to the world allows him to see the world more accurately than those who lack the conceptual matrix afforded by his training. The art of nuances developed by artists allows them to see things the rest of us miss—like that speck of reflected light on the eye that brings a face to life in a painting—until they show it to us. The world that concerns us is a fiction in the hyperbolic sense that it is not the world as it is in itself. But, as we have just seen, there is no world in itself. Literally: no such world exists; the concept is empty. The point is critical, worth the bother of repetition in order to be sure it is clear.

"Why couldn't the world that concerns us—be a fiction?" That is Nietzsche's rhetorical question. The answer is that it could be seen as a fiction in comparison to the world as it is in itself. But the world as it is in itself is a world defined in relation to an infinite perspective. Such a world does not exist. Especially within the context of an ontology of becoming: it would entail encompassing the entirety of time when time has no terminal points. It is then ludicrous to regard our world as a fiction because it does not meet the criterion of adequacy to a world that cannot be conceived by us, that is, the world in itself.

The ideas just reviewed allow us to develop our understanding of Nietzsche's aesthetic criterion and its relation to truth. The aesthetic criterion no longer functions, as it did in *The Birth of Tragedy*, as the source of self-deceptive metaphysical comfort, but rather as a refined attunement to the world that lets us see it in a better, more nuanced, richer, more accurate way. Prior to 1876, Nietzsche granted the aesthetic criterion supremacy over what might be called the epistemological criterion, the claim to knowledge of truth. The dream world of illusion was aesthetically more gratifying than the perceptual world of appearances, and hence was held to be superior because it provided the metaphysical comfort we want but cannot obtain within the waking world where we see people die and simply cease to be. Now, after the turnabout in 1876, when the world of immutable Being has been repudiated as a deceit, the aesthetic criterion is no longer at odds with the epistemological criterion; rather, the two are complementary. Art, as the domain of imagination and creativity, coincides with truth because imagination and creativity are required to see the relations among worldly things in a richer, therefore truer, way. And a more satisfying way.

How so? Consider the implications of taking its elegance as a measure of the validity of a scientific theory. Kepler's explanation of elliptical planetary motion was no better at predicting the positions of planets than the Copernican idea of epicyclical motion, but it was simpler, more elegant, *and* it was later found to cohere with Newton's idea of gravitational force. The ideal of a unified field theory, which drives much of contemporary physics, is also motivated by the aesthetic criterion and its preference for simplicity and elegance. One could also mention the beauty of fractal geometry depicted by Mandelbrot, the elegance of the Fibonacci sequence to be found in such natural occurrences as the chambered nautilus and rows of seeds in pineapples, pinecones, sunflowers, and the like, and the astounding pictures of cosmogenesis—the becoming of the universe—beamed back to us from the Hubble telescope. Art was wedded to truth by Pythagorean theories of harmonics, and the marriage is stronger now than it was then.

Beyond such considerations as these is the solid truth that imagination and creativity are required to break old paradigms and replace them with new ones that turn out to be more illuminating of the world that concerns us. Nietzsche's early claim that art rules science is stronger post-1876 than it was when he originally formulated it: one has to *see* new patterns, that is, new relations among things, before one can formulate the new patterns in quantifiable terms, before one can take the next step in understanding the inextricability of quantity and quality, matter and form, worldly things and how they are organized. The agon between art and science is a fecund source of human awareness. Nietzsche saw that, and so, in some degree, did his student Heidegger.

The thought I am following here culminates—or at least, reaches a point of compression—in the idea that finitude and knowledge are inseparable. No knowledge except as a response to ignorance acknowledged, no growth in ideas so long as we remain complacent with comfortable paradigms, no breakthroughs without violating established beliefs, no creation without destruction, no life without struggle, no meaning without confronting the awesome and terrible face of the sublime. This clash with idols is an adumbration of the will to power we shall have to revisit. The point here is that finitude and ignorance are essential to knowing, that the leap of faith to an afterworld where all is at peace, where we can place our hope in the promise of serene coincidence with Being, is not the ideal of pure reason, but the forsaking of the greatest power we have. "Only on this now solid, granite foundation of ignorance could knowledge rise so far—the will to knowledge on the foundation of a far more powerful will: the will to ignorance, to the uncertain, to the untrue! Not as its opposite, but—as its refinement!" (BGE, 35).

God used to be the name of Truth. Nietzsche says that that Truth has become a lie. The house of God used to be a place where knowledge grew. Now it is a place where knowledge is killed. The word of God has lied reward and punishment into the nature of things. The promise of eternal reward is being taken as the meaning of life for the huge preponderance of mortals now walking on earth. No eternal reward, no meaning in life. No obedience to God's absolute will, no ground for morality.

We have seen Nietzsche's argument that God does not function well as a ground for truth. It is now time to take up his argument that God does not function well as a ground for morality, either.

2. MORALITY

> With a stiff seriousness that inspires laughter, all our philosophers demanded something . . . exalted, presumptuous, and solemn from themselves as soon as they approached the study of morality: they wanted to supply a *rational foundation* for morality—and every philosopher so far has believed that he has provided such a foundation. Morality itself, however, was accepted as "given." (BGE, 97)

What Nietzsche said of his own time is not entirely true of the time in which I am writing. Only one part of contemporary moral philosophy is given over to the quest to provide foundations for morality. There is another part that has given itself over to the quest to undermine or deconstruct the foundations of morality. Both parts, however, have done what Nietzsche accused his contemporaries of doing; that is, they have accepted the idea of morality as given. One may find redefinitions of "good" and "evil" in contemporary moral philosophizing, but one will have to look in places I have not seen for the kind of thinking that challenges itself to find values that are beyond good and evil.

What does the phrase "beyond good and evil" mean for Nietzsche? A hypothesis: "beyond good and evil" means beyond finality. Specifically, beyond the finality that subtends the various forms of morality informing the great world religions, beyond the intentions attributed to the deities and cosmological structures of the universe, beyond the sense of purpose attributed to Being, either overtly or covertly modeled on the (necessarily anthropomorphic) principle of sufficient reason. To put this thought in different terms: I have looked in vain for a search for values within the context of an ontology of becoming, that is, within an ontology that rules out any notion of cosmic destiny, purpose, or atemporal end.

That, I think, is where Nietzsche was going. How far he was able to proceed along that path remains to be seen.

Let me begin, as usual, by putting my cards on the table—divulging my own position and making it available for scrutiny and criticism—right from the start. I think that Nietzsche's revaluation of all values is many things: a breath of fresh air; an attempt to think through a radical position honestly and to follow the thought wherever it leads even if it leads to unpalatable conclusions; a much-needed critique of contemporary ethics and morality; and maybe even partly right (which is to say probably partly wrong).

In my view, value theory in the domain of morality is driven by a tension between self and others, private interest and public welfare, the particular and the universal. Theories of political and distributive justice must balance these two forces when they take up such questions as those of rights and property.

At the metatheoretical level, there are at least two ways of regarding the relationship between self and others, particularity and universality.

1. *Binary opposition.* Under this view, the interest of the self is intrinsically in opposition to the interest of the collective. With regard to power and wealth, each of us wants it all, hence we are reluctant to relegate any of it to other persons. This is the model presupposed by social contract theory. In order to avoid the state of overt warfare, what Hobbes called the state of nature, we relinquish our natural right to fight for the goods of the world, give up some of our freedom to compete, in order to secure freedom from the ability of others to do the same.

2. *Ecological model.* Under this view, the welfare of each is bound up with the welfare of the whole, not only other humans, but every element of the ecosystem. In order for the individual to prosper, the whole system has to be in balance. If some identifiable element threatens the whole, we have to

band together to remove the threat, be it a virus, a hurricane, or a sociopath. If some identifiable element enhances the whole, we have to band together to work for that enhancement, be it clean air, education, or safe highways.

In my view, the truth lies between these two models. There are ways in which self and others will always be in tension, just because variations in perspective are inevitable. Universal accord will never be reached, and there is some question in my mind as to whether such accord should be assumed to be the supreme goal or regulative ideal that drives political and moral theorizing. On the other side, some degree of harmony, based on acknowledgment of our interdependency, is necessary for the survival of each of us just because many of our interests are common.

In my view, Nietzsche clearly adopts the binary opposition model and rejects the ecological (or communitarian) model because he treats the tension between self and others = collective = herd as an irremediable conflict, one in which the individual is always oppressed by the herd and has little or nothing to gain from communality.

I think that Nietzsche is right insofar as the balance between individual freedom and collective pressure to conform has been weighted too far on the side of the herd. The collective is necessarily conservative and intrinsically resists change, even though change is inevitable and occasionally beneficial to all.

The other half of the story, in my view, lies in Nietzsche's failure to think beyond his polemics, to recognize the implications of his own errant thoughts on Zarathustra's *Untergehen* and the need of the *Übermensch* for social contact. The "choice human being" is unable to remain in the citadel of loneliness—he needs to "go *down*, and . . . 'inside'" (*BGE*, 37). Here Nietzsche acknowledges the tension I advocate, but in his writings on morality his polemic against the herd tends to lead him to ignore the interdependency of all living things. More remains to be said about the deficits that follow from Nietzsche's proclivity to adopt a polemical attitude, but I will defer that critique and turn directly to his theorizing about morality.

Nietzsche begins his "Natural History of Morals" (*BGE*, part 5) by analyzing the values constitutive of the system of morality in which he finds himself in an attempt "to prepare a *typology* of morals" (*BGE*, 97).[8] The notion of morality that he regards his contemporaries as having taken for granted as given is based on something like a principle of altruism, which he quotes Schopenhauer as articulating. "'Hurt no one; rather, help all as much as you can.'— That is really the proposition for which all moralists endeavor to find the rational foundation" (*BGE*, 99).⁹

Nietzsche goes on to argue that the grounds for this common sentiment are *psychological* rather than axiological or deontological: "Moralities are . . . merely a *sign language of the affects*" (*BGE*, 100). The portent of this little phrase is immense: it signals a profound shift in thinking about the foundations of morality. Although psychology has been a serious consideration in moral philosophy from the time of Aristotle forward and acquired even greater influence in the writings of such philosophical heavyweights as Hume and Freud, this influence has for the most part been subsumed under an overriding commitment to reason. Hume's famous assertion that "reason is and ought only to be the slave of the passions" notwithstanding, reason has traditionally been held to be the arbiter in discerning good from evil. The moral exemplar has been held to be the person whose passions (instincts, desires, pathological inclinations, etc.) are held in check by reason.

The erosion of the supremacy of reason has been apparent across the spectrum of the humanities since the nineteenth century, to be sure, but Nietzsche's proclamation of the death of God introduced a qualitative change whose effects are only now beginning to become apparent. Heidegger asserted that Western philosophy since the time of Socrates has been dominated by "onto-theology"; that is, that appeals to reason have been implicitly, even unintentionally, appeals to the ground of divine Reason. Derrida and the school of postmodern thought capitalized on Heidegger's insight, and Continental philosophy undertook the project of the deconstruction of Western philosophy with a vengeance. Deconstruction is essentially the project of revealing the theological presuppositions underlying the metaphysical foundations of Western culture. Those theological presuppositions are themselves traceable to an ideal of reason that consists in the absolute coincidence of thought with its object, and that is clearly an impossibility for finite minds, but also demonstrably an impossibility *simpliciter*.

If the ideal of reason is philosophically untenable, then a fortiori reason cannot provide the foundation of morality. That is the portent of Nietzsche's little phrase. Or part of it, the recognized part. What remains unrecognized can be stated in two assertions:

1. The death of absolute Reason does not entail the death of finite reason.
2. Finite reason is intertwined with passion and cannot be divorced from it.

The deconstructionist movement failed to consider (1),[10] and, Freud notwith-standing, mainstream philosophy continues to treat passion and reason as standing in binary opposition. I attribute the latter to the failure of main-stream philosophy to relinquish its nostalgia for the ontology of Being and replace it with the project of thinking through the possibilities that open up within the context of an ontology of becoming. Nietzsche, I think, offers the most fecund source for this project, and that is why I am writing yet another book on him.

Returning now to that source, we should not be surprised to find Ni-etzsche arguing that the foundations of the psychology of morality rest on an innate proclivity to obey. "'You shall obey—someone and for a long time: *else* you will perish and lose the last respect for yourself'—this appears to me to be the moral imperative of nature" (*BGE*, 102). This is not a surprise be-cause, as we have seen, morality is a matter of willing, and willing entails the agon of mastery and obedience. What may be a surprise is that Nietzsche's attitude toward obedience is bivalent. On one hand, he says, with contempt, that moralities are "but counsels for [individual] behavior in relation to the degree of *dangerousness* in which the individual lives with himself . . . , [that such counsels] measured intellectually [are] worth very little . . . but rather, to say it once more, three times more, [they amount to nothing more than] prudence, prudence, prudence, mixed with stupidity, stupidity, stupid-ity. . . . This, too, for the chapter 'Morality as Timidity'" (*BGE*, 109–10).

On the other hand, however, obedience is good training. "What is essential 'in heaven and on earth' seems to be . . . that there should be *obedience* over a long period of time and in a *single* direction: given that, something always develops . . . for whose sake it is worth while to live on earth; for example, virtue, art, music, dance, reason, spirituality—something transfiguring, sub-tle, mad, and divine" (*BGE*, 101). Obedience to a governing paradigm, it will be recalled,[11] was what Nietzsche sought to bring about for the sake of the political unity that would produce high cultural achievement in his pre-1876 totalitarian essays, but subsequently repudiated because it involved deceit and led to a host of consequences toward which he took a very dim view: Pla-tonism, Christianity, utilitarianism, German nationalism, Wagnerian theater, and so forth. Now, however, a new thought emerges: despite these distasteful consequences, the rigor of sustained obedience—the training in discipline involved in such obedience—could also produce higher types of humans, cre-ators who could generate the things that make life worth living: virtue, art, music, dance, and so forth.

Sustained and focused obedience can—and has—produced the morality of timidity, but it can also lead to the creativity of the child Nietzsche calls for in the third metamorphosis of the spirit on its path of self-transcendence. This bivalence toward obedience requires a means of distinguishing between the obedience that produces timidity and the obedience that produces creativity. That means is ready to hand: it is the difference between obeying the herd instincts or obeying the higher instincts; that is, the difference between obeying the internalized "thou shalt" of other commanders and taking command of oneself, becoming a *self*-propelled wheel, choosing *in a lucid way* what to esteem and what not to esteem.

Nietzsche clearly distinguishes these two forms of obedience in two crucial passages:

> Inasmuch as at all times, as long as there have been human beings, there have also been herds of men (clans, communities, tribes, peoples, states, churches) and always a great many people who obeyed, compared with the small number of those commanding—considering, then, that nothing has been exercised and cultivated better and longer among men so far than obedience—it may fairly be assumed that the need for it is now innate in the average man, as a kind of *formal conscience* that commands: "thou shalt unconditionally do something, unconditionally not do something else," in short, "thou shalt." . . .
>
> The strange limits of human development . . . is due to the fact that the herd instinct of obedience is inherited best, and at the expense of the art of commanding. (*BGE*, 110)

Few command, many obey; the obedience of the many, passed down from generation to generation since the dawn of humankind, has now become our heritage: "the herd instinct of obedience."

What about the other form of obedience? The commanding type obeys itself, but who is the self that does the commanding? It is the self that self-transcendence wants to actualize: not so much the self that *is* now, but the self that it wants to *become*. The creative spirit, the self that wants to "give style to his character," is the self that makes or creates itself in an act of poiesis:

> Every artist knows how far from any feeling of letting himself go his "most natural" state is—the free ordering, placing, disposing,

giving form in the moment of "inspiration"—and how strictly and
subtly he obeys thousandfold laws precisely then, laws that precisely on account of their hardness and determination defy all formulation through concepts (even the firmest concept is, compared
with them, not free of fluctuation, multiplicity, and ambiguity).
(BGE, 100–101)

Self-transcendence, the creative becoming of the self poetically dramatized
in the persona of Zarathustra, is a prime instance of will to power as art.
This assertion requires—and will receive—further elaboration and textual
substantiation, but for the moment the persona of the artist will suffice as a
paradigm of the obedience required to take command of oneself. The elaboration required must examine the nature of the "hardness and determination" of the "thousandfold laws" that defy conceptualization, and broach
the question of how such laws can be lucid to the artist in his "moment of
'inspiration.'" But to prepare the way for this, we must return to the issue of
the psychological grounding for Nietzsche's typology of morality.

The psychological ground of Nietzsche's typology of morality is fear:
"Fear is . . . the mother of morals" (BGE, 113). "Whoever examines the
conscience of the European today will have to pull the same imperative out
of a thousand moral folds and hideouts—the imperative of herd timidity:
'we want that some day there should be *nothing any more to be afraid of!*'"
(BGE, 114).

What is the source of this fear? Nietzsche mentions several themes here:

1. We fear what threatens to disrupt our tranquillity. This is the basis for
utilitarian morality, and Nietzsche traces it to Platonic eudaemonism. The
Platonism consists of an "inference [that] smells of the *rabble* that sees nothing in bad actions but the unpleasant consequences and really judges, 'it is
stupid to do what is bad,' while 'good' is taken without further ado to be
identical with 'useful and agreeable'" (BGE, 103). Nietzsche, as we know,
yearns for something higher than comfort, and is willing to suffer pain to get
there. He associates utilitarianism with leveling out or reduction to the lowest common denominator, and regards it as grounded in the project to avoid
pain and achieve comfort by refraining from threatening one another.

2. We fear the "man of prey" (BGE, 108), the healthy beast who stands
outside the herd and threatens to impose his will on it. "High and independent
spirituality, the will to stand alone, even a powerful reason are experienced

as dangers; everything that elevates an individual above the herd and intimi-
dates the neighbor is henceforth called *evil*" (*BGE*, 113–14).

3. We fear the neighbor. When the social entity has been secured from
external dangers, we then begin to fear the neighbor when he begins to show
signs of independence and power. The very ones we needed to protect the
herd now become objects of fear insofar as their power to protect against
external threats can be turned against the herd itself. "'Love of the neighbor'
is always something secondary, partly conventional and arbitrary-illusory in
relation to *fear of the neighbor*" (*BGE*, 113).

4. We fear ourselves; specifically we fear our passions and experience them
as dangerous. The individual's fear of himself leads him to generate "recipes
against his passions, his good and bad inclinations insofar as they have the
will to power and want to play the master" (*BGE*, 109).

5. We fear novelty. "What is new finds our senses . . . hostile and reluctant;
and even in the 'simplest' processes of sensation the affects dominate, such as
fear, love, [and] hatred" (*BGE*, 105).

This catalog of fears could be expanded, but the point has been made. In
the psychological typology of the morality of good and evil, fear is the governing motive. We herd together to protect ourselves from external threats,
and then develop systems of obedience to protect the herd from internal
threats. Our highest form of dignity, being a moral person worthy of reward
in heaven, is based on our most ignoble passion: fear. If life is will to power,
but power is fearsome, then life turns against itself and affirms docility, humility, and timidity. The first commandment of all religion, the command to
obey the figure of the divine, when subjected to Nietzschean decryption, is
the commandment to be meek.

There is a paradox, maybe even a contradiction, here that needs to be
addressed. Life is will to power and life has generated a pervasive system of
values that negates power. To say that life has turned against itself in creating the morality of good and evil: Is this not to say that the will to power has
turned against itself?

This is not an easy question to answer. Facile responses are inadequate. To
let the paradox stand as such is to duck the question of profound inconsistency at the root of Nietzsche's thinking. And to say that self-emasculation
is itself an instance of the will to power operating in the deficient mode is to
read Nietzsche as adopting the very strategy of Schopenhauer that he set out
to challenge.

Readers familiar with Nietzsche will recognize the problem just identified as the problem or paradox of *ressentiment*. *Ressentiment*—the rancor of
the herd against those who stand above it—is, on Nietzsche's own terms, a
world-historic form of power that brought an end to the feudal system in Europe; toppled the warlords, barons, and kings; and established the ecclesiasti-
cal hierarchy. Beyond that, it is the force that in Nietzsche's own time showed
every sign of bringing down the very hierarchy it generated and establishing
another even more strongly bent on the goal of leveling out under the heading of socialism.[12] The most powerful force in organizing human life is the
will to power, life itself, turned against itself.

This paradox pervades *On the Genealogy of Morals*, the book to be addressed in the next chapter, and that is the context in which I will address it.
The point of raising it now is to demonstrate the continuity of Nietzsche's
thought at this time in his career. The problem structure of *On the Genealogy of Morals* is prefigured in *Beyond Good and Evil*, just as the agenda for
the latter grew out of *Thus Spoke Zarathustra*. Before going on to the next
chapter, however, there are two issues that need to be addressed in the work
at hand.

The first is the question of the roles of reason and passion in Nietzsche's
psychological account of the typology (or nascent genealogy) of morality. I
put forward the claim that Nietzsche departed from traditional morality by
repudiating the standard practice of setting reason apart from and above passion or emotion, and regarding the two as intertwined. Nor is it simply an
inversion that would elevate passion above reason. The point is that there is
a rationale to the passions that needs to be understood. Psychology purports
to uncover the *logos* of the *psyche*. In his typology Nietzsche does a masterful job of showing how the primordial affect of fear—what some might call
the survival instinct—gives rise to social forms such as morality and law. But
as Nietzsche also demonstrates, those social forms feed back into the psyche
and restructure it.

The specific case is Nietzsche's account of how obedience becomes a habi-
tus for the species that has acquired the force of instinct. This is an instance
of self-transformation on the part of the species. Dubious as it might now
appear, this is a genuine instance of self-transcendence: humanity changing
itself for the sake of a value, in this case, the value of survival and life-
enhancement. Nor is this idle philosophical speculation and rationalization,
but is rather bulwarked by research in anthropology and evolutionary biology.

Fear generated the fight-or-flight structure that dominated the species in the Pleistocene era. That structure is not propitious for survival in the polis, and has gradually receded with the increasing complexity of civilization and the emergence of *homo politicus* (that is, the contemporary herd animal designated *das Man* by Heidegger).

Nietzsche rails against the Christian project to extirpate the passions, but points to the paradox that "it was precisely during the most Christian period of Europe and altogether only under the pressure of Christian value judgments that the sex drive sublimated [*sublimiert*] itself into love (amour-passion)" (*BGE*, 102). In general, Nietzsche's attitude toward the passions is that they have to be refined, or in the terms I have been using, brought under the aesthetic criterion. These two instances will have to suffice to make the point that Nietzsche's psychology is not based on a reduction to base instincts, not the simple inversion of the traditional subordination of passion to reason. Values intervene in the process of sublimation, values that are not reducible either to passion or to reason as traditionally defined. The values that intervene have their source in the aesthetic criterion, that is, in art.

One consequence of this account of human self-transformation or self-transcendence that remains to be explored in the next chapter is that the Nietzschean project of the revaluation of values accommodates the historical reality that the force of values Nietzsche generally condemns can lead to new values that he affirms. The Platonic-Christian animus against passion can have the effect—under the propitious influence of art—of producing forms of eros that Nietzsche more or less embraces. Similarly, we will find him arguing that it is only when man develops the capacity for evil that he becomes truly interesting.

The second issue remaining to be taken up here is the passage quoted at the beginning of this chapter. Nietzsche introduces the portion I quoted with a cryptic and provocative survey of the history of morals in which he says that we stand at the end of the second of three epochs: the pre-moral, the moral, and the extra-moral (*BGE*, §32; pp. 43–45). "During the longest part of human history—so-called prehistorical times—the value or disvalue of an action was derived from its consequences" (43). This is the pre-moral phase; it corresponds to what Nietzsche will subsequently designate as "master morality" (51). Then, "in the last ten thousand years . . . one has reached the point . . . where it is no longer the consequences but the origin of an action that one allows to decide its value [and] involves the first attempt at self-knowledge" (44). In this phase the origin and value of an action "lay in the value of the intention" (44). Although Nietzsche does not name him, it is clear that Kant is the culmination of this "calamitous new superstition" (44).

It is the third phase, the phase that Nietzsche sees himself as ushering in, that provokes thought. Here is what Nietzsche writes:

> Don't we stand at the threshold of a period which should be desig-
> nated negatively, to begin with, as *extra-moral*? After all, today at
> least we immoralists have the suspicion that the decisive value of an
> action lies precisely in what is *unintentional* in it, while everything
> about it that is intentional, everything about it that can be seen,
> known, "conscious," still belongs to its surface and skin—which,
> like every skin, betrays something but *conceals* even more. In short,
> we believe that the intention is merely a sign and symptom that still
> requires interpretation—moreover, a sign that means too much and
> therefore, taken by itself alone, almost nothing. (*BGE*, 44)

"The value of an action lies . . . in what is unintentional in it": What could this possibly mean? When I think of unintentional acts, I think of such things as autonomic aspects of bodily functions like breathing and digesting. Or, perhaps, physical reflexes. Maybe even Freudian slips, unwilled disclosures of attitudes, prejudices, dislikes, enmities, and so forth that one would prefer to keep private. One might also think of conditioned reflexes, the sorts of things that athletes train themselves and their bodies to do automatically, like block-ing a punch, overriding the impulse to flinch when firing a weapon, keeping one's eye on the ball, anticipating an opponent's move, and so on. In what sense are these actions the locus or substrate of "decisive value"?

And what about the superordinate value of lucidity: How can an action in which consciousness conceals more than it reveals be the basis for "decisive value"?

Once again, I will have to defer the question, and respond rather with a gesture in the direction of an answer that will be articulated later. Think, again, of the artist "giving form in the moment of inspiration—and how strictly and subtly he obeys thousandfold laws then, laws that on account of their hardness and determination defy all formulation through concepts." Think, in broader terms, of creative acts as such in which a self transforms itself into a self it gropingly yearns to be. Think of the training and disci-pline that are required to act without deliberation in a manner that is only subsequently recognized as elegantly appropriate to the unique situation. Think of acts in which the self discovers itself, becomes itself, realizes itself. And prepares itself for the next step in the process of self-transcendence. Think, in short, of the aesthetic criterion and what it takes to give style to one's character. Ponder the more prosaic, but perhaps more revealing, moment in which the decision is made whether to leap spontaneously or stop to gain reflective distance. Could there be a sense in which that crucial decision could be called intentional? It might be exquisitely lucid, but it could not be reflective.

· ·

TEMPLATE FOR CHAPTER SEVEN

Editor's note: This appendix is the third, typed draft of notes that would have served Dillon as the template for chapter 7. Indeed, Dillon finished each chapter of the Nietzsche book by fleshing out and expanding a template such as this one. Thus, this template for chapter 7 is the penultimate draft of Dillon's intended chapter. While it is obviously incomplete and, in places, schematic, I have decided to include it because it is clear and cogent enough to convey a substantial sense of Dillon's intended content. There is no record in any of Dillon's notes or drafts of his intended title. Also, the template is titled "Art, Truth, and Illusion X," signifying that early on Dillon imagined his Nietzsche book to have at least ten chapters. However, there is no doubt from his final notes and curriculum vitae that this was to be chapter 7. Because of this text's unique character, I have made virtually no adjustments to it for grammar or format. For one important example, all the bracketed material is Dillon's own insertions, not mine—a practice Dillon used in his templates to make notes to himself.

Art, Truth, and Illusion X:

The Genealogy of Morals (1887)

1. Genealogical explanation and truth

First a word about the project of genealogical explanation in contemporary Continental thought. The word is ambivalence.

Foucault's histories of sexuality are genealogical narratives in that they purport to describe how we arrived where we are with respect to sexual norms and values on the basis of a retrieval of (mostly) documentary (as opposed, for example, biological) evidence regarding the evolution of sexuality as a social construct. The (not so) latent subtext is that the genealogy of sexual morals is driven by culture, which, in turn, is driven by language and power.

The ultimate term, I think, is power, but power manifesting itself primarily (though not exclusively) through language.

[I contest this view on basis of the cultural relativism underlying it. Foucault considers disease, but only as a social phenomenon. Although I do not hold that biology is destiny, I do believe that reproduction, disease, mating strategies, etc. establish a context to which different cultures respond in different, but assessable, ways. Contemporary research in brain structure, neurological components to sexual behavior, genetics, etc. has demonstrated to my satisfaction that biology cannot be overlooked in the project of developing a genealogy of sexuality. I reject natural law theory, but also reject purely constructivist accounts based entirely on conventionalism.]

Derrida deconstructs the notion of origin and the conception of empirical history that depends on it. The basic argument is that history depends on the language function—which means that events are always mediated by language, which gives them the significance they have. This, in turn, means that there can be no historical origin, because the vehicle of history is language, and language presupposes itself.[1] Derrideans claim that deconstructionism allows for a modified version of genealogy. I contest this: history turns out to be a *pas de marche* for Derrida. I don't think he has conceptual room to accommodate anything like a process of evolution, be it social or biological.

Genealogy as practiced by Nietzsche is, therefore, heavily contested in contemporary Continental thought—even though he is arguably the single most influential factor in the development of this tradition. Something has been lost in contemporary responses to Nietzsche that I think it is worthwhile to attempt to retrieve. The general thrust of my position should be familiar: I think Nietzsche points the way toward a third alternative not subject to the prima facie flaws of relativistic constructionism and absolutistic natural law theory. Without this third approach, one is left with the (prevalent) view that the denial of absolutism results necessarily in relativism: this is the binary logic of dualistic thinking.

I attribute to Nietzsche the strategy of understanding contemporary praxis in a diachronic or genealogical way. The attempt here is to generate a historical reconstruction, a narrative, a likely story in much the same way that all civilizations have generated cosmogonies and theogonies. These narratives are certainly narratives—they are creations of language and heavily endowed with symbolic meaning. But the symbolism includes natural causality—which may be a metaphor, but differs from other metaphors in that it is grounded in perceptual evidence and permits a degree of testing.

Biology is therefore relevant in the construction and testing of these narratives. As are physics, astronomy, chemistry, etc. My point is that narratives compete: some survive as conventions and some do not; the difference is the degree of success in accounting for events (or predicting, deciding, understanding, dealing appropriately, etc.), that is, in their relevance to the world in which we live.

The relevance of evidence makes genealogical narratives susceptible to testing and thus allows them a claim to truthfulness. If they can be proven to be wrong, then the absence of the demonstration of falsity provides a basis for claiming truth—although this is not the only basis for truth claims. Thus the choice among competing narratives need not be arbitrary. Indeed, I would assert in a general way that narratives of all sorts involve some kind of claim to truth (including literary as well as genealogical narratives).

> Preface, S4 (454)[2] Nietzsche's attempt "to replace the improbable with the more probable, possibly one error with another. . . . "
> Preface, S7 (457) Nietzsche's appeal to "what is documented, what can actually beconfirmed and has actually existed. . . . "

The assessment of the biblical book of genesis might provide a case in point.

What evidence is relevant? This, I think, is context dependent. Perceptual evidence counts. But so does historical evidence, psychological evidence, etc.

Nietzsche's academic posting at Basle was in philology. Much of what Nietzsche offers in support of his thesis in *On the Genealogy of Morals* is drawn from etymology. This is a research methodology that had profound influence on Heidegger—and the post-moderns who follow him. Note, however, that the etymological evidence does not stand on its own: it draws upon the context of historical reconstruction and on the idea of global typicality: what makes sense in this world.

2. Issues and tests
Reflexivity—Paradoxes of self-reference

> Preface, S3 (453) " . . . Under what conditions did man devise these value judgments good and evil? *and what value do they themselves possess?*"
> Preface, S6 (456) " . . . We need a *critique* or moral values, *the value of these values themselves must first be called in question*—and for

>that there is needed a knowledge of the conditions and circumstances
>in which they grew, under which they evolved and changed. . . . "

Self-referential questions tend to lead into circularity. "What is the value of
values?" The question presupposes an understanding of values—which is the
question it asks. Straightforward attempts to answer the question must beg
such questions as: what does "good" mean, what does it means to be good?
If one deems it good to be good because the promotion of goodness aids the
welfare of humankind—this presupposes a definition of "good" such that it
is good to aid the welfare of humankind.

There is the hermeneutic approach to these questions, which derives from
Heidegger's often-stated assertion that it is not a matter of getting out of the
circle, but of getting into it in the right way. My interpretation of this is that
to ask the question of truth or value in a critical = self-aware = self-referential
way is a propaedeutic to the project of thematizing the presuppositions constitutive of the understanding of the truth or value being questioned.

This interpretation opens (at least) two strategies.

A. The transcendental approach
To uncover the presuppositions of a given thesis regarding truth or value system is to uncover an a priori. Meno's paradox. We must have an inchoate
sense of X in order to inquire about it. The inquiry will result in a thematiza-
tion of that inchoate sense. In Kantian terms, it comes up with an a priori
regarded as universal and necessary. The operative presuppositions are held
to be necessary. In Kant's case, the necessity has to do with the unchanging
structure of the understanding.

In postmodern discourse, the a priori is grounded—not in the understanding's necessary structures—but in the structures of language. Nietzsche's version of this we have seen in *Beyond Good and Evil*, section 20. Language
dictates a way of looking at things that philosophers explore. But the results
are prefigured in the language. Heidegger's version is in *Being and Time* [in]
Vor-struktur or *vorhaben-sehen-greifen*, in *Rede* as existentiale, and the later
assertion that "language is the house of Being." The point is that language
contextualizes thought, establishes the presuppositions within which thinking takes place.

If one takes, as does Derrida, an extreme or one-sided version of the Heideggerian thesis that language masters us, then one is left in an immanence

of language—out of which it is inconceivable to break. This is a pure transcendentalism of language—even though the a priori may have no necessity or universality.

B. Transcendental-empirical approach [Merleau-Ponty's reversibility thesis.] This allows for both infra- and extra-referentiality. Here it is possible to assess competing language systems according to extra- or pre-linguistic evidence. Perceptual evidence. But also phenomena such as human misery, scientific-technological production, artistic creation.

Question: which of these models informs Nietzsche's thought?

As is clear, I think Nietzsche adopts the transcendental-empirical approach. That is, he clearly argues that language functions as a transcendental field, that language functions as did the Kantian categories to project a structure of thinking into the world. As evidence for this, we have all the talk about the I as "grammatical fiction"—and, at a different level, the passage in *Beyond Good and Evil* where Nietzsche attributes the common structure of thought in western philosophy to the common linguistic heritage.

But the empirical side also has representation in Nietzsche's thought. Here I have in mind the historical context he appeals to in the attempt to contextualize his appeals to linguistic usage. Nietzsche, as linguist, had to be aware of the empirical side of the language. Indeed, he appeals to this to make his case that value-laden words grew out of socio-economic conditions. Language cannot shed light on empirical reality unless it reflects that reality.

First Essay, S1 (461) Nietzsche calls for investigators who: "have trained themselves to sacrifice all the desirability to truth, every truth, even plain, harsh, ugly, repellent, unchristian, immoral truth. —For such truths do exist."

This argument, of course, has no force if one takes empirical reality to be constituted by language. But I would argue that Nietzsche appeals as much to psychology as to language: it may be that language conveys a system of thought, but it is emotion that drives language. Nietzsche's basic explanatory concept is *power*, and language is one of its manifestations. It is *ressentiment* that drives the shift in language that signals the shift in morality. And *ressentiment* is both a response to a power imbalance and an attempt to acquire power (First Essay, 10, 472-475).

Note, also, in this passage the appeal to factual circumstances in the "external world" (473), and later the appeal to what "really is true" (478).

3. Two issues in the content of N's genealogy

Let me start with a brief overview of the argument N presents in *On the Genealogy of Morals*. This will be review for most, so I'll go quickly.

A. *Slave revolt in morality*

This is the shift from the binary good versus bad in which good was the term used by the noble and powerful classes to describe themselves. Good here means strong, healthy, happy, capable, above all, powerful, able to exert one's will on the world and others. Bad means the opposite: weak, sick, unhappy, lowly, common, powerless, reluctantly obedient to the will of others. The story Nietzsche tells is that the priestly cast mobilizes the resentment of the lowly and deploys it politically by creating a new system of values based on a reversal for the earlier one. Good now means what bad used to mean, that is, humble, powerless, and poor; and evil now means what good used to mean, that is, strong, rich, adept, powerful. Nietzsche attributes this reversal historically to Jews whom he regards as the originators of the kind of hatred based on resentment. But this resentment has now grown into new forms: Christianity, democracy, socialism, etc. The common strain linking these is the demand for equality, what Nietzsche calls the leveling instinct: the mighty are to be brought down to size. To my knowledge, Nietzsche never addresses the interesting question as to whether the key notion of pride (hubris) as the cause of downfall in Greek tragedy also is a mobilization of *ressentiment*.

I'd like to stress the element of deceit in this reversal. "The slave revolt in morality begins when *ressentiment* itself becomes creative and gives birth to values: the *ressentiment* of natures that are denied the *true* reaction, that of deeds, and compensate themselves with an *imaginary* revenge" (First Essay, 10, 472, emphasis added). Nobles, when threatened or opposed, would react by deploying power, physical power. This is the "true reaction." The weak, denied this ability, tell themselves a story that feeds their illusions of revenge. The one who has bested me will be punished in another world, a better world beyond this one, where I will receive my reward. For Nietzsche, this is deceit: there is no such afterworld. More importantly, it is self-deceit: those who comfort themselves with this illusion, this "imaginary revenge," are lying, above all, to themselves. Thus, *ressentiment* and the ensuing reversal of values essentially depends on dishonesty and inauthenticity.

Lots of interesting questions come up, but I want to focus on two.

1. What about the "priestly caste" who create and market the illusion of afterworldly revenge, reward and punishment: are they also driven by *ressentiment*, or is there an important difference between the shepherds and the sheep? Historically, the shepherds have won the battle with the nobles, or at least the pen has become a worthy adversary to the sword. As winners in the political agon for power, are the shepherds the new nobility? If so, do they manifest any of the characteristics of the old nobility? Or are they burdened with self-deception at a higher level of lucidity?

2. If Nietzsche wants to reverse the reversal, if he wants to go beyond the good-evil axis around which contemporary morality is configured, what does he advocate? I think Kaufmann is correct in arguing that Nietzsche is not calling for a return to the old values: it is clear to me that Nietzsche sees evil as the source for human transcendence in the direction charted or exemplified by Zarathustra. But: what is this evil? Is it the evil of being powerful and adept? Is it the evil of the political power of the priestly caste, the use of reflexivity and artistic myth-creation to achieve mastery? (In what sense is this latter 'evil'?) Or is it some third thing not yet understood?

[These two questions are intertwined. I will address them first as commingled, then—time permitting (which it probably won't)—go on to try to separate them again.]

It is through the *ressentiment* of the priestly castes "that man first became an interesting animal, that only here did the human soul in a higher sense acquire depth and become evil" (469). Admittedly Nietzsche wants to move *beyond* good and evil, but that becomes possible only on the ground opened by the move to reflection and the power unleashed by the spiritual element. What is to be affirmed in this development? What elements are to be retained by the *Übermensch*?

Ressentiment allows the soul to become evil—which is a higher sort of soul, a deeper one, and one that is more interesting.

What is *ressentiment*? It is a response to the power of brute force which is based on developing the power of thought or reflection. This power of thought is not tied to *ressentiment*, but (factual claim) happened to be generated from the reaction to the worldly stimulus of oppressive power. *Ressentiment* exists without thought-power (that is, hatred of the powerful was not always creative, still exists without cunning), question is: can this power of thought exist, deploy itself in non-resentful ways? In artistic creation, for example.

The fact is that reflection, once awakened, found a source of power in the *ressentiment* of the down-trodden. It wasn't the down-trodden who deployed that power; it was the "priestly caste." They were filled with hatred inspired by impotence. But their response was to acquire power by mobilizing the *ressentiment* of the masses.

One might ask Marx whether all consciousness-raising is essentially driven by resentment or something like it. Could something else—say, problem solving in general or dealing with recalcitrant reality—lead to higher levels of reflective awareness? Perhaps it is relevant that the noble classes had to deal with the problems of recalcitrant reality, but that this was insufficient motivation to result in consciousness-raising. Is reflection always spurred by fear, threat, hatred? Or could something like Nietzschean overflowing produce similar results?

Interesting questions come up here about honesty and self-deception. The sheep were told that it was better to be sheep, but the priestly shepherds acquired their power, mastery, by not being sheep. There is deceit here, but is there self-deception?

The self-deceit of *ressentiment* lies in expressing hatred as love, wish for power into glorification of impotence. The herd was led into this self-deception, but how about the priestly shepherds? If they were Machiavellian in their deployment of power, they could not have been deceiving themselves about their intent.

Indeed, it seems as though the priests were power-brokers just like the nobles—but more effective. Because their source of power is stronger.

The original question, however, has still not been answered: can thought-power or spirituality be freed of its (accidental? *merely* historical?) ties to resentment?

Puzzling passage (First Essay, 10, 474-475). "The man of *ressentiment* is neither upright nor naïve nor honest and straightforward with himself. . . . A race of such men of *ressentiment* is bound to become eventually cleverer than any noble race. . . . [Among nobles, cleverness breeds respect for enemies, and is less favored than] the perfect functioning of the regulating unconscious instincts [Zen], and [what resentment there is] exhausts itself in an immediate reaction. . . . In contrast, picture 'the enemy' as the man of *ressentiment* conceives him—and here precisely is his deed, his creation: he has conceived 'the evil enemy,' 'the Evil One,' and this in fact is his basic concept, from which he then evolves, as an afterthought and pendant, a 'good one'— himself." This is puzzling because it does not seem to allow the distinction I have been trying to draw between sheep and shepherds, between the mob and its priestly leadership, between self-deception and deceiving others. It seems as though the priests have to internalize their own values of hatred.

Let this hang unresolved, for the moment, and go on to another basic question. Evil. What is evil? We have seen the term used in two senses so far.

A. The evil one is the enemy who fills us with resentment because he is noble and powerful. Above us.
B. The evil in the human soul is what makes it interesting, confers spirituality, creativity.

Now our question is a bit clearer. Can we be evil in sense B without adhering to a sense of evil in sense A? Or . . . is there a third sense of evil? Note that there is a clear difference between the two: the blond brutes, evil in sense A, were not evil in sense B.

Remember those passages in *Beyond Good and Evil* where Nietzsche writes about good flowing from evil. The idea seemed to be that something inherently valuable—line Nietzsche's own style of philosophizing—could grow out of the subtlety *beyond* good and evil, but necessarily related to that earlier phase. This is the way history actually unfolded, but might it have been otherwise? Might it now be otherwise? —Or is Nietzsche a crypto-resenter? Consider what he says about women. What Heidegger says about eternal recurrence being a product of Nietzsche's resentment against the passage of time.[3]

[In what follows I may or may not be departing from Nietzsche: will try to solve the problem posed, then look to see if I can find traces of it in Nietzsche's thought.]

The way the problem is cast pre-delineates its answer. The new kind of power, spiritual power, is contrasted with the old kind, physical power. Then the question is posed: is there a tie between spirituality, mentality, reflection—the capacities that make humans interesting—and *ressentiment*? Does the birth of reflection always follow from rancor, oppression, and self-deceit. I think not: my etiology of reflection stems from the self-alienation introduced by the internalization of the look of the other during the period of adolescence when secondary sexual characteristics make one publicly sexual.

There is a negativity here, but I don't see any intrinsic tie to *ressentiment*, although that connection is a possibility (for example, the conspiracy of the outcast ones, the search for group affirmation). [Follow this up.]

The thinking that generates the problem is polarized: dumb physically powerful brute versus smart physically weak connivers. Undercut the binary and one opens the possibility of a someone who is both smart and physically strong. Plenty of exemplars: Ulysses, Plato. Indeed, the connection between physical prowess in battle and statesmanship is long-standing: we usually want our political leaders to have experienced war—for one thing, it makes them circumspect about going to war. Socrates was noted for courage in battle, although Nietzsche doesn't seem to remember that.

I have stressed Zarathustra's vulnerability. Maybe I should have paid more attention to his acts of bravery. Martin Luther King preached a doctrine of non-violent confrontation, but faced violence with courage. And he was willing to acknowledge good qualities among his agonists.

For me, at least, this opens important space: the space for freedom fighters who were not motivated by a self-deceptive form of *ressentiment*.

The Ethics of Particularity
by
M. C. Dillon

· ·

CHAPTER ONE

SEXUAL ETHICS AND SHAME

I. CONTEXT

Merleau-Ponty's phenomenological account of the lived body and his non-dualistic ontology of flesh allow us to identify several pervasive errors in traditional accounts of normativity, especially as they apply to the value-laden domain of human sexuality. These errors have a common element: binary opposition or the bifurcation of phenomena into mutually exclusive domains such as body versus mind, fact versus value, nature versus nurture, biology versus psychology, and so forth. This chapter attempts to expose and rectify the errors resulting from ontological bifurcation.

Merleau-Ponty describes the lived body as incarnate intentionality. The cognitive dimension of incarnate intentionality is carnal knowledge, a way of knowing that grounds and sustains conceptual activity at the thematic and reflective levels. The body's pleasures and pains are forms of knowing and valuing, and they inform our responses to worldly events. Taboos and prohibitions, the phenomena associated with shame and guilt, have foundations in carnal knowledge. They also have foundations in the sediments of culture, language, and history inculcated through the rewards and punishments of early life and sustained through habit and the reinforcements of social approval and disapproval.

When these founding forces collide, the result is conflict, splitting, confusion, ambivalence, lability, and, hence, dysfunctionality. This chapter is premised on the hypothesis that the norms currently at work in guiding contemporary practice in the domain of sexlove are mystified and in need of critique.[1] The critique to be offered here is based on an attempt to uncover the ways in which the values and norms emergent from carnal knowledge collide with the values and norms institutionalized in contemporary culture.

2. NATURAL LAW AND SOCIAL CONSTRUCTION

The contemporary debate on normativity in sexlove polarizes under the opposed banners of natural law and social construction. It is a battle in the
musty old war of absolutism versus relativism. In this war, there can be no
victors, only casualties, because the ideological commitments of the antagonists are mutually exclusive: there are powerful arguments and solid half-
truths on both sides, but neither can acknowledge the strengths of the other.
The whole truth lies beneath the opposition: it is a mistake to believe that one
must conceive history and biology as disjuncts and cast one's lot on one side
or the other—when it is abundantly clear that history unfolds in a natural
setting that constrains it.

To regard nature and nurture as mutually exclusive is a profound mistake.
The key to resolving the fruitless debate that has been going on for centuries
lies in finding a conceptual scheme in which nature and nurture intertwine
and inform each other. In my view, Merleau-Ponty's conception of reversibility answers to this need. The natural body and the socially constructed body
coincide in my body. In the sphere of sexuality, the nature and disposition of
our organs of pleasure and reproduction circumscribe the possibilities for
sexual interaction, but those limits are broad, flexible, and vary historically
and geographically.

Merleau-Ponty writes that there is nothing accidental about the human
body and illustrates his claim with the opposed thumb: our tools and arti-
facts would be different if we had no thumb. Or if we had two. The whole
sphere of equipmentality—and therefore the ontological structure of
readiness-to-hand (*Zuhandenheit*), which Heidegger designates as the primary human reality—would not be the same. Suppose that we had one eye
or eyes on movable stalks. Or if male humans were configured like snakes, if
we carried our penises like deflated balloons inside our bodies, if they were
delicate and susceptible to separation from our bodies when inflated and extended, if we had to mate like snakes, carefully matching slits in our epi-
dermises up against one another so that the inflating penis could enter the
female's receptive organ, and if we had to do that without hands and without
being able to see what was going on down there . . . then what? Low incidence of rape, I think, and highly developed strategies for engendering complicity, cooperation, and consensuality. This is not mere speculation; ask a
herpetologist. Natural bodies and social forms intertwine within the species.
To view them as separable is to commit the fallacy of reifying abstractions.

3. SEXUAL BODIES

My body, as Merleau-Ponty (*VI*, 135) said, is an "exemplar sensible," "a sensible for itself," a thing that touches by being touched, a thing whose capacity to see is inextricable from its visibility to itself and others. Touching, I am touched; seeing, I am seen; speaking, I am spoken; hearing, I am heard. But there is always a difference between the two, a fission or *écart* that, as Robert Burns pointed out,[2] keeps a distance between the seeing and the being seen, a transcendence of the beloved beyond the loving regard. According to Merleau-Ponty (*VI*, 155), this reversibility of touching and seeing is the "fundamental phenomenon" that names "the ultimate truth" about the relations of words to things, minds to bodies, selves to others, visibles to invisibles, tangibles to intangibles, culture to nature, and time to itself and all things. Reversibility is the basis for carnal knowledge.

Carnal knowledge, the knowing of the flesh grounded in being flesh, transcends and informs discursive knowledge. When, in words clinical or poetic, I speak of the desire of my flesh, I know that I will never get it exactly right, but I also have a sense of what I want to say and choose my words on that basis. It is also true that my vocabulary limits and informs my experience. But sedimentation, the insinuation of language and cultural forms into experience, had to originate somewhere. Some poet or philosopher had to say something about the world that had not been said just that way before, and for it to be picked up and iterated, it had to make sense, it had to fit. It had to illumine something we all already knew in the mode of carnal knowledge, but had not quite grasped, like that fleck of reflected light on the surface of an eye that everybody had seen and overlooked until some cinquecento painter noticed it, which brought the painted eye to life and transformed the history of art. That painter had to *see* it before he could paint it.

Carnal knowledge. Poets and philosophers from Solomon to Plato to Hegel and beyond have written of love in the figures of union, knowing all the while that it was a flawed metaphor. As Hegel pointed out, if I *really* want to become one with the one I love, I would have to eat her, thereby losing her. There is something wistful in this mistaken figure, as though we could bring about union by invocation—by declaration, vow, and mystical transport. Our bodies cannot become one: matter differentiates, incarnation separates; "I am always on the same side of my body," stuck within the confines of my epidermis (*VI*, 148). But the flesh that individuates is the flesh that allows me to resonate with another sexually, to feel her desire feeling me and provoking

my response in the cycle of erotic intensification that is but one of the vicissitudes of reversibility. The figures and the *values* that flow from reversibility
are different from and better than those associated with union: resonance,
listening, attunement, wonder—all of which presuppose difference or nonco-
incidence. They give us better means of making love than do consummation,
engulfment, taking and having—all of which are aimed at obliteration of
difference. If one defines love in terms of possession, as Sartre did, then one
ends up as Sartre did, acknowledging that it is a vain pursuit that necessarily
culminates in an irremediable struggle of domination and submission. We
dallied with Sartre, as we now dally with Bataille, not really threatened by
their pessimism, knowing somehow that they had missed something, trust-
ing the affirmation of our own carnal experience, living in varying degrees of
adroitness through values we found it difficult to articulate, and troubled by
the discrepancies between our theories and our lives.

4. LIVED BODIES AND GLOBAL VALUES

In general, the values associated with sexlove are derivative from global values that attempt to address human life in a comprehensive way. There is an
intrinsic moment of universalization in all discourse about norms that is
apparent in such familiar structures as the golden rule and the categorical
imperative. Although we apply multiple standards as a matter of course—
treating children, the other gender(s), peoples of alien cultures, and different
organisms in the food chain according to precepts different from those we
apply to ourselves—we are not proud of that fact and find it hard to defend.
In theory, at least, we prefer laws to be conceived and applied on the basis of
equality.

Where did this emphasis on equality in ethical discourse originate? My
guess is that it is founded on humanism, and that humanism is founded on
what Merleau-Ponty calls "transfer of corporeal schema"—the proclivity of
human beings to recognize other beings like themselves and empathize or
identify with them. Animal rights advocates are not fond of humanism; they
want to extend recognition and empathy to other forms of life. The first philosopher I know to have been seriously troubled with this aspect of humanism was Descartes. Descartes practiced dissection, maybe even vivisection,
of animals, and it seems to have bothered him to do so. As a philosopher,
however, he found vindication in the distinction between humans and other

forms of life: we have souls, are made in God's likeness, and this is demonstrated in our exclusive possession of the divine light of reason. It is okay to
slaughter, cut up, and consume animals because they don't have souls. Our
souls are what make us valuable, absolutely valuable, and therefore equally
valuable. The bifurcation of body and soul is the essential presupposition of
humanism. It is a terribly convenient thought. It allows you to violate all bodies, even human ones, if they lack souls. Or have bad ones.

If one repudiates the binary opposition between mind or soul or spirit, on
the one hand, and body or flesh, on the other, then humanism and traditional
notions of equality lose their intellectual cogency. The value of another being
for me still depends upon my recognition and empathetic identification, but
that is no longer supported by the imperative for universal recognition of all
soul-bearing humans. What, then, does ethical recognition depend upon? It
rests upon carnal knowledge and the extension thereof in the abstract domain of discursive reason. People demand to be recognized. The demand may
be explicit and thematic or it may be horizonal, a shared assumption of mutual respect. The process of recognition begins early in life, reaches crisis in
adolescence, and may continue throughout life if one takes compassion as a
virtue to be developed. The crucial point here is that recognition is grounded
in the force and vivacity of concrete face-to-face encounters, that is, in the
present moment of carnal knowledge that takes place at the level of perception rather than thought. The thrust toward universalization operates at the
level of reflection and inductive inference. If I want respect, then so must
others like me. Anyone who has reared a child knows that the golden rule is
not an innate idea. It has to be learned. It is a cultural imperative, latent in
the idea of sociality.

The limits of universalization might be articulated through what I have
called the law of proximity: the value, positive or negative, of another being
is a function of distance. We love and hate those closest to us in psychic space;
we are relatively indifferent to those who exist only as abstract ideas; and the
spectrum between these limiting extremes is graduated in degrees of identification and removal. Degrees of psychic proximity are measures of intensity
of care; they also measure qualitative changes in ethical comportment.

This account of the ground and measure of ethical recognition tempers
the force of the universal and leaves room for individual judgment and dis-
cretion. It is more or less up to me how far to extend the scope of my compassion, to determine the extent of my response to the demand of the other
for recognition, to evaluate the circumstance and decide upon appropriate

demeanor. It is also up to me how to fashion my own demands for recognition and response from others. My style of relating to others at home, at work, in the community at large will reflect the values I find within—and the values I project upon—those locales and their denizens. This tempering of the universal is also a tempering of its correlate, the principle of equality. I may regard children as only potentially equal, and that may result in a qualitative difference in the nature and degree of the respect I accord them.

5. SEXUAL BODIES AND THE VALUES OF SEXLOVE

The transition from global values to the values of sexlove is not as smooth as I once thought it was. There is an edge that defines a difference between the thematic values of sexlove and their global horizons. The difference lies in embodiment and carnal knowledge. In sexlove, it is an affront to treat the other as an instance of the universal; one wants a kind of respect based more on one's ipseity than on one's membership in a class. As the tradition distinguishes *eros* from *philia, agape,* or *caritas,* so do I distinguish sexlove from friendship and communality. The bounds of these spheres necessarily overlap, hence the lines of demarcation are ambiguous, but there is a qualitative shift in modality as global values are brought to bear in the domain of sexlove.

Although there is a long history associating shame with illness, modern medicine has succeeded in abating this shame by attributing illness to transmission of germs and viruses rather than the will of a punitive god. But, in the case of AIDS and STDs in general, the stigma of illness has risen to the point where disclosure is a legal issue. There is a qualitative value shift in shame when it enters the sphere of sexuality.

The phenomenon of shame is founded upon reversibility: it is internalization of the other's negative regard. When I see myself through the eyes of an approving other, I feel pride; but if I internalize the condemnation of an alien look, I experience shame. The law of proximity applies to this domain of values as well: the carnal knowledge of shame is grounded in the face-to-face encounter, where it is most intense, but one can extrapolate from the concrete other to the community, even to the all-seeing gaze of divinity, and internalize the values they represent. This social pressure to conform to the values of the collective, known as conscience, is essential to the functioning of community.

One of the prime functions of gods is to instill conscience in us in order to maintain order within the state. And gods are notoriously ambivalent about sex. Sex is unruly, the cause of the disobedience and consequent fall of the first human being. Shame enforces obedience and order. But why is sexual shame qualitatively different from the shame associated with other unruly and disorderly human conduct that poses a threat to the collective? Why is it privileged as the *original* sin in holy texts as diverse as Genesis and *The Tibetan Book of the Dead*?

The catalog of threats posed by sexlove to social stability is long. Sexlove is destabilizing: the rule of exogamy requires sundering and reforming the most basic social grouping, the family or clan. Sexlove is essentially related to madness and irrationality. It is recalcitrant to order, essentially as defiant as Romeo, Juliet, and all the other teenagers the world has known. Sexual intercourse is the most efficient means designed by divinity or evolution to transmit the germs of death as well as the germ of life. And like the most virulent of viruses, sexlove changes form with every attempt to control it; indeed, it seeks out prohibitions in order to intensify the frisson of violating them.

The catalog is insufficient to account for the qualitative shift that takes place when one moves from global values to the values of sexlove. The plain fact is that there are greater threats to domestic tranquillity than those posed by sexlove: war, natural catastrophe, disease in general, and so on. Why, then, is sex primally shameful?

Sex is constituted as the original sin because it is the origin of shame. Children before the age of puberty are innocent; they are shameless because they have not developed the capacity to reflect, and shame is a phenomenon of reflexivity—the capacity to take up an alien perspective upon oneself. Adolescents experience shame in a peak of intensity that has no precedent in infancy and no equal in later life. Shame and defiance are the soul mates[3] that beget the turbulence and travail of adolescence. Why? Because adolescence is the phase in life in which we become sexual. The onslaught of sexuality coincides with that of shame: the two are united in the psychosocial ramifications that follow from the transformation of the lived body.

When the changeling's body develops conspicuous secondary sexual characteristics—conspicuous in the sense that they are socially visible in the way that the genitals are not—there is a change in the quality of the look it receives from significant others and the world at large. A new look intrudes, charged with a kind of interest that is different from the kinds of interest the child has learned to expect from its intimates and acquaintances. Through the structure of reversibility, the child sees itself through eyes that are no longer comfortably familiar, and its body image, its nascent and taken-for-granted identity, is cast into question. Be they prurient or protective, forthright or dissimulating, the desires of others begin to intrude in a novel and disquieting way. This change in the social atmosphere synergizes with the somatic changes induced by the flood of testosterone and estrogen coursing through the child's body and producing changes in its shape and moods that upset the equilibrium of the norms to which the child has become habituated. The result of this synergy of reversibility is global transformation and disorientation: the child's world has changed, and he or she is no longer at home in any part of it.

Adolescents can make babies and their bodies urge them to do just that and do it now, when they are at their baby-making prime. If your theology commits you to natural law, you are obliged on peril of inconsistency to acknowledge that your god wants girls to start bearing children shortly after menarche.[4] I suspect, however, that childhood pregnancy is increasingly stigmatized as cultures develop forms of civilization that require increasingly higher levels of maturation and economic independence as conditions for parenting. So gods and authorities had to invent delaying tactics and institutional controls. The taboos had to exceed in power the forces they were designed to oppose, and the forces they were designed to oppose are very powerful, indeed. The appeal to prudential reason seldom wins over the inducement of momentary pleasure in any case, especially among youth besotted with hormones, so strong measures must be taken. Shame, as we know, is a strong measure: it is the prime tool of law enforcement; it works even when nobody is looking.

Here, then, is the crux of the argument. We are looking for a ground for norms of sexlove in carnal knowledge and the sexual body. And we are now at the point where nature and culture are in outright opposition: the profligacy of nature defies the ordering principle of social regulation, but abets it by sowing the seeds of shame—the most powerful regulating force civilization has been able to harness. How might this dysfunctional structure be modified to reduce the splitting, confusion, ambivalence, and lability produced by the replication within ourselves of the conflict between the biological and the social dimensions that intertwine within our lived bodies?

6. PATHOLOGY AND NORMATIVITY

When the cultural context is sick, to adjust to it is to invite malaise. To be maladjusted to the cultural context is to suffer alienation and recrimination. That is the underlying dilemma that has to be addressed.

We are in the throes of the adolescence of civilization, a time marked by shame and defiance. Freud argued that human development is slowest in the sphere of sexuality. We grow up quickly economically and politically because our survival depends on dealing realistically with the need for food and the threats posed by aggressors. But in the sphere of sexlove, we can satisfy ourselves with fantasy and linger in the cradle of the pleasure principle. What we have to do, individually and collectively, is grow up.

In Freudian terms, maturation is the process of modulating the primary process by means of the secondary process, the reality principle. It is the process of measuring my immanent representation against the perceptual world in order to determine whether what I think is truly the case. There are some basic epistemological problems with this dualistic conception, given that what I think stands in a relationship of reversibility with what I see [and] that what I see is affected by what we—collectively—think, that is, by language and culture. But the operative distinction remains valid: with work I can distinguish what I *think* I see from what I *actually* see, and correct the one on the basis of the other. The big mistake of constructivism is to deny this important distinction, to construe perceptions as always mediated by cultural forms, and thereby to preclude the possibility of correcting widely shared misapprehensions by appeal to a perceptual reality that, with work, we all can see, a reality that can serve as the basis for nonviolent adjudication of conflicting viewpoints.

Adolescence is a time of shame and defiance, structures that are tempered by maturation. There can be no return to prelapsarian innocence—shame will exist so long as we have visible bodies and live in communities—but the reality principle allows us to distinguish between genuine shame, based on real violations of sound ethical principles, and mystified shame, shame grounded in shared misapprehension, cultural bias, unquestioned prejudice, and the structures of social enforcement. Mystified shame has the effect of infantilization, of prolonging the phase of life in which we are kept in order by a bible of good and evil written by another hand and enforced by external authority, an authority that relieves us of the burden of thinking for ourselves and becoming the authors of our own deeds.

Maturation is the passage from shame and defiance to self-control and resolution. It is a passage to freedom and autonomy, freedom from the internalization of false values and freedom to act upon those values one has tested and found to be truer. Maturation is taking up the burden of the responsibility we all have to judge for ourselves what is good and what is not. Adolescents test and challenge authority blindly and on the basis of passions they have not yet learned to control. Grown-ups reflect, decide, and act with resolution that comes from the confidence of measured judgment.

Falsity and mystification are counterproductive in all spheres, including that of sexlove. We have finally made condoms available to those who really need them, but are discovering that they are too ashamed to put them on. If we handled driver education the way we handle sex education, the roads would be slick with gore. If we handled sex education the way we handle driver education, we'd have fewer twelve-year-old mothers and might actually reduce the incidence of STDs among our youth. Difficult as it may be, the adult community is going to have to learn to affirm adolescent sexuality and nurture it with care.

The limits of the lived body are the limits of sexlove and the ground and measure of sexual morality. This is apparent in the relatively simple dimensions of childbirth and disease, but also discernible in the related sphere of psychopathology. The crucial phenomenon in the latter case is the mystification of shame that enters the *Gestalt* when we move from the context of global ethics to the theme of sexual morality. The remedy for mystification is truth: it is not the noble lies but the palpable truths about the genuine pleasures and perils of sexlove that will free us to assume the responsibility that is the source of human dignity.

. . . .

CHAPTER TWO

SEXLOVE AND ETHICS

I.

Sexlove is grounded in the transfer of corporeal schema that, through reversibility, allows me to recognize you as a fellow human being: it grants me the ability to see myself through your eyes and feel myself through your touch. This displaced experience of myself from the outside alienates me from myself, induces reflection, and establishes my self as a being-in-question. There is a hybrid collision and commingling of myself for myself and myself for you: the decentering induced by the impact of your look on me challenges my taken-for-granted familiar self in some ways and tacitly reinforces it in others. You confirm my existence, your recognition corroborates my identity, but do you see me as I want you to? Do you value me as I value myself?

Recognition of self and other is not abstract and value-neutral; it is permeated with the figures of desire: what self and other want, what self and other need—what we value, what we seek, what we fear and avoid. *This is the ground phenomenon of ethics.* In the collision and commingling of separate desires we confront the need to choose among the options available to us. In prereflective stages, we are vectored by the force of the desire whose power supervenes. In reflective stages, initiated and reinforced through the desire or demand of the other, we make more deliberate choices, complicated by the fact that my desire is mediated through my aboriginal need for your affirmation and my equally original fear of reprisal. Here is the root of the sociality to which we awaken through the development of the cogito.

The awakening of ethical consciousness subtends the nature-nurture binary. We could not see, much less recognize, each other were we not bodies. That is as much a natural fact as it is a contra-factual hypothetical. And the same might be said of the grounding of desire in bodily functions and needs. But as all consciousness already finds itself embodied, so is it the case that it finds itself already in a social milieu. Are these two aspects, separable only in language, then equi-primordial? Not if one subscribes to some theory of the evolution of the human from earlier forms of life. Not if one holds that hormonal processes prefigure the range of human desire, that diseases of the pituitary gland affect the development of sexuality during puberty and ado-lescence. To assert, however, that biological structures constitute necessary conditions for the development of human desire is not to render socialization epiphenomenal. It is, rather, to say that biology founds sociality as it founds consciousness, but also to say that the founded terms return to influence and contextualize their biological foundations through the structure Merleau-Ponty calls reversibility.

To seek the ground of ethical consciousness in the structures of the lived body, in the structures of reversibility that constitute the intertwining of na-ture and nurture, self and other, is to challenge the theories of normativity that seek foundations in a domain above the flesh, be it the heaven of ideas or the one in which deities reside. It is also to challenge the theories prevailing in some corners of the intellectual world wherein culture and its sign systems are taken to be autonomous and self-generating engines responsible for cre-ating the normative conventions in whose names we praise and condemn, reward and punish each other.

2.

We awaken to the tug of sexlove at the same phase in life that we begin to concern ourselves with the needs and demands of others in a reflective and deliberate way. When sexlove is not conditioned by the normative concerns that accompany desire, we invoke the categories of pathology and regard the act or agent as lacking in humanity. To fail to recognize another human as such is subhuman, abnormal, bad. Anger is transient, shot through with value, and presupposes recognition. We may assign negative predicates to those who commit violent acts in a moment of madness, hold them respon-sible, and even punish them, but there are different predicates and different treatments reserved for those who violate others in modes of indifference rather than in the passion of high emotion.

There is an essential lability to sexlove: the same structure generates cohe-sion and disruption. The course of sexlove is intrinsically bumpy: my affec-tion makes me vulnerable and that vulnerability constitutes my beloved as a threat. Threat is a prime source of anger and jealousy, and the intensity of sexlove magnifies a minor slight to an intent that is heavy with portent. I am not indifferent to those I love, and when the love is explicitly erotic, the sexual component raises the emotional stakes. Mate selection makes sexlove competitive in a way that parental and filial love are not.[1] There is always the chance that my beloved may find another more attractive than I, always the chance that the very stability of our relationship will induce a desire for novelty and greater intensity. The invocations of everlasting troth and the sanctions against promiscuity and infidelity testify to the essentially precarious nature of sexlove.

To form a new union is to disrupt several old ones. Sexlove begins with a violation of existing social structures. Everyone is always already spoken for, if not by a present lover, then by emotional bonds to family and friends. There are, of course, upheavals across the spectrum of social relations, but the primordial power of the taboos operative in sexlove makes a qualitative difference. Beneath this commonplace observation lies a paradox for traditional ethics.

Kierkegaard, following a line of thought developed by Kant and Hegel, designated the ethical as the universal. The categorical imperative is the correlate of a deontology based on universality and reason. One has a duty to all rational beings to act in accordance with the universal precepts of reason as the ultimate value. Moral error consists in acting as though one were an exception to these universal precepts. The threat to morality is exceptionality or, as Kierkegaard designated it, the particular. Insofar as I act as a unique individual, insofar as the nature of my action is informed by my particularity—by what sets me apart from others and constitutes a surd in the system of universal categories called rationality—my act is a departure from the domain of the ethical. From this there follows Kierkegaard's well-known lemma: "Either the individual, as an individual, has no value, or there is something higher than the universal."[2]

For Hegel, the conjunction of reason and the universal marks the apotheosis of the self-realization of the Absolute: the highest conceivable good. Kant and Hegel did not invent the equation that defines moral goodness in terms of rationality and universality; they articulated a basic moral sentiment that is older than history and even more powerful than ever today. The problem with this sentiment—as none have seen more clearly than Kierkegaard and the existentialists, notably Heidegger and Sartre, who followed him—is that it assigns negative moral predicates to particularity: insofar as an individual acts in such a way as to depart from universal precepts, he invokes moral condemnation.

Although the rites of mate selection are highly conventionalized, the act of mating intrinsically defies convention as such. Indeed, the conventions that constrain sexlove across the spectrum of human culture betray its unruly nature: Bataille got that exactly right. The historical displacement of arranged marriages by marriages based on the socially destabilizing structures of romance might well be viewed as a dawning recognition that sexlove always defies the strictures that would normalize and tame it.

Here, then, is the paradox: the phenomenon I have cited as the ground of ethical consciousness, the structure of reversibility known as recognition, is the source of both the ethics of universality and the departures from it that are endemic to sexlove. The pathos that founds human sociality also founds acts of social upheaval. Love and hate, friendship and enmity, grow out of the same ground; they define and sustain each other, and neither exists in isolation from the other. We care about our enemies, else we would be indifferent; and the difference or particularity of one's beloved, the transcendence that attracts us, is also a threat, a potential source of pain. Seen through this paradox, both ethics and sexlove may reveal themselves in a new light.

3.

Kierkegaard posed the problem, but did not solve it. He wrote and lived as though the call of the flesh, the temptation he called *Anfaegtelse*, beckoned us always downward, toward the aesthetic stage whose governing telos is sensuous pleasure, pleasure felt only at first hand in one's own body. Kierkegaard accepted the wisdom of his day that sensuous pleasure is necessarily a solipsistic experience: to seek it, therefore, is necessarily to live in denial or willful refusal of the demands of others, to live in an infantile state driven exclusively by the desires of one's own flesh. One is either innocent, amoral, and incapable, as was Don Giovanni, of feeling the demands, needs, and pathos of others; or one behaves as Johannes Climacus, the seducer, did, deliberately manipulating the pathos of the other, unethically reducing the other to an instrument of one's own pleasure. The aesthete dwells in the lower particular, for Kierkegaard, because he regarded *aisthesis* as a solitary mode of experience. Had Kierkegaard conceived *aisthesis* through the structures of reversibility, had he recognized our ability to experience another's pleasure directly through the intertwining of flesh, he might have had a healthier consciousness with regard to his own desires and a more fulfilling relationship with Regina Olsen.

The higher particular is the religious stage that one reaches only after having transcended the ethical-universal-rational dimension of sociality and morality. This stage is also solipsistic—the Knight of Faith cannot communicate his vision or defend his actions in ways that others could understand—Kierkegaard defines it as "passionate inwardness": an ecstatic coincidence of self with finite self, which is, at the same time, an absolute coincidence of finite self with the Absolute. Kierkegaard affirms the conjunction of contradictories, the coincidence of finite and infinite, A and ~A, and says that this logical absurdity is intrinsic to faith: true faith is valid by virtue of the absurd.

His underlying argument is one made famous by Camus. The human condition is despair because finite lives cannot be meaningful without the knowledge of the universe denied to us by our finitude. Camus is Kierkegaard without the leap of faith, a man who seeks to affirm his condemnation to absurdity and vindicate it through a metaphysics of rebellion. And Kierkegaard is a wildly optimistic Husserl: the principle of principles for phenomenology (as Derrida is fond of pointing out) is the coincidence of self with self, which is at the same time a coincidence with its object of knowledge. For Kierkegaard, the ideal of pure reason can be achieved by transcending reason in the ek-stasis of faith, which "knows" what it cannot know by coinciding with it.

Derrida's *différance* and Merleau-Ponty's *écart* place this coincidence in the realm of impossibility and wishful thinking. Coincidence is impossible for Derrida because knowledge is always mediated by signifiers that indefinitely defer coincidence with its object. Coincidence is ruled out by Merleau-Ponty by the fundamental structure of the flesh: I can touch myself only because I do not coincide with myself; I can reflect and in that reflection capture my thought, but only at the distance of thinking it.[3] Reversibility is an intimacy of knowing and being that necessarily falls short of coincidence.

The same reversibility of flesh that challenges Kierkegaard's conception of the lower particular also challenges his conception of the higher particular. What, then, of particularity? How, then, does one affirm the departure of the unique individual from the universal claims of reason and ethics in the disruptive act of sexlove? And—Kierkegaard's favorite question—what would be the nature of this affirmation, this "teleological suspension of the ethical"? Is it really true that sexlove is intrinsically disruptive, that it necessarily ruptures the structures and conventions of sociality? If sexlove must rend the fabric of the ethical-rational-universal, then how could one vindicate it?

4.

To form a new union is to disrupt existing structures. The law of exogamy requires us to leave the bounds of one clan or family in order to start another. In sexlove, one's social priorities change: in the initial phases, which are the crucial ones here, the beloved displaces others in the hierarchy of demands and obligations—just as the fiercest seagull creates a ripple effect in a line of pilings by taking the one it wants. Nor, as Marcuse argued, do sexlove and work resonate in harmony. All cultures send their young changelings away during the period of mate-selection; the initiation into the mysteries takes place somewhere beyond the *polis*: either in the forest or desert, or in boarding schools, boot camps, or summer camps. Adolescence is a period of passionate sexlove and also the time of defiance. Falling in love is messy. Go do it somewhere else. Or in the dark. I don't want to see it. Come back when you are safely married and sane again.

If sex is demonized, as it clearly is in our culture, then sexlove is demonic and needs to be tamed, brought under sanctions designed to preserve order and tranquillity in the state. That statement is couched as a hypothetical: *If* sex is demonized . . . Need it be? Well, it always has been: even cultures inclined to tolerate sexual behavior in a more benign spirit than we do still mystify sex with taboo and prohibition. Why?

Freud was not the first to remark on the fact that sexual reproduction promotes the vigor of heterozygosity at the expense of order and regularity. Clone Haydn and you will get fine musicians, but you won't get Mozart. That model led Freud to challenge the fundamental principle of psychoanalysis. In *Beyond the Pleasure Principle*, Freud argues for a new dualism of Eros and Thanatos. Eros is vitality: the formation of new unions and the attendant building of tension. Thanatos is dissolution, compulsion to repeat, entropy, and return to the inorganic. The revolution in thought here is the affirmation of unpleasure in the building of tension or Q or energy that follows from the formation of new unions, the designation of that unpleasure as vitality and life.

Kierkegaard confused the universal with the conventional. As we know, there are widely accepted conventions that are not truly universal, although they may be compelling in the social contexts where they reign supreme. It takes a maverick to break the conventions of white supremacy or male supremacy or human supremacy or divine supremacy to found a new universality more deserving of the appellation, to form a new union. These mavericks are not readily understood; they find it hard to communicate their visions and their faith in what, for the moment, only they can see. They dwell apart from the *polis* and descend upon it in fear and trembling, knowing that they will be a threat to those they seek to redeem, knowing that the flies in the marketplace, the herd animals collected in a mob, can easily dispatch them to preserve the comfortable familiarity of their conventions.

Is sexlove necessarily disruptive of the universal-ethical-rational, as such? Or is it just intrinsically defiant of the conventions that seek to minimize the discomfort and unpleasure that is a consequence of forming new unions and different social structures?

There is something oppressive about the universal, no matter how well-intentioned and rational it may be, when it is codified into convention and enforced. The connection between socialism—socialism in all its radical forms, not just National Socialism—and totalitarianism is a historical fact that warrants contemplation. It may be that the universal as regulative ideal intrinsically requires an engagement with freedom; it may be, as Kant put it, that "the concept of freedom is . . . the regulative principle of reason";[4] it may be that there is an essential opposition between the universal-rational-ethical and the enforcement of convention.

In short, it may be that the engagement of another's freedom at the level of recognition is the genuine locus of ethical consciousness, that the path toward the universal is guided by the pathos of reversibility . . . and misguided by the pure white light of objective reason. It may be that the reason that deserves the name must be impure and informed by that pathos Kant regarded as pathological.

5.

There is a dark side of these speculations that must be brought to light. It has to do with pathos and perspective, and the judgment required to steer between the oppression of convention and the oppression of unbridled freedom, between the aspects of recognition that lead us to love and those that lead us to acts of violence driven by love gone bad.

The enforcement of conventional norms, as enforcement, is oppressive to those upon which it operates. Another name for systems of enforcement of conventional norms is government, the means by which we protect ourselves from ourselves. Given the force of pathos and the variance among perspectives, government is no doubt necessary, and that attenuates its repugnance, but does not render it benign. From which I conclude that the best governance is the least governance needed to minimize the threat we pose to each other. When we love badly, when the other we see is recognized increasingly as threat, the ideal of the universal, the ideal that draws us toward concordance, is displaced by local convention—what de facto has drawn this group together. And then, through a movement of idolatry or political myopia or religious fervor (the terms are functionally equivalent in this context), we reify-deify the conventions to which we have been trained and submit to their yoke.

Infantility demands constraint from above because it is relatively unaware of its own long-term interest and incapable of self-restraint. Maturity allows autonomy or self-governance. The trend I see growing around me is a trend toward displacement of individual autonomy and responsibility in the direction of infantilization: placing the onus of responsibility for individual welfare on the earthly god-father created by the people to protect them, care for them, and nurture them. The leviathan we have created has become oppressive. This, as I have tried to show, is not an accident of history, but a peril essential to historical unfolding, a compulsion to repeat a cycle grounded in our own pathos that needs to be recognized if it is to be broken.

The ethical is, indeed, the universal, but the universal whose lucidity or rationality invites us to accept its regulation in the act of autonomy that gives the law unto itself. Kant saw this as clearly as his own historical placement allowed. So did Merleau-Ponty. And he expressed it most clearly in the existentialist underpinnings of his critique of the Marxist doctrine of solidarity that takes regulation by de facto convention as a necessary step in historical progression. He broke ranks with Communism when Stalin enforced ideological cohesion with banishment, labor camps, and lethal elimination. Sartre went the other way, as we know, and their friendship went awry. Merleau-Ponty's critique is episodic, rather than sustained, but it is thematic, and relatively easy to identify. The positive doctrine is not thematic and requires interpolation. The thread I follow is Merleau-Ponty's critique of the

Hegelian universal: the negativity of his critique points obliquely to the ideal of the universal that would have constituted the nexus of the ethics he did not write.[5] He says: "My access to a universal mind via reflection, far from finally discovering what I always was, is motivated by the intertwining of my life with the other lives, of my body with the visible things, by the intersection of my perceptual field with that of the others, by the blending in of my duration with other durations. . . . Such is the total situation that a philosophy must account for" (VI, 49).

The crux of the issue is the oppression of the particular that is intrinsic to the identification of the universal and the ethical as traditionally conceived. *Sexlove celebrates the particularity of the other and intrinsically constitutes a threat to the universal insofar as it necessarily sets the beloved above general precepts and defies those precepts in acting out its pathos.*[6] How I behave toward the intimate other is qualitatively different from how I behave toward the other in general. Love is an act definitive of humanity, but it is not a humanism. In loving another, I contravene the will of the others to whom my loving is a threat. In elevating my beloved, be it my lover, my child, my family, my clan-state-nation, to privileged status, I introduce an inequity that contravenes the abstract ideal of universal equality. The intimate recognition that grounds ethical consciousness is intrinsically a threat to ethics as traditionally conceived. *Agape*, universal love, is thus a contradiction in terms. At least for finite embodied human beings. The attempt to stretch one's love toward an ideal of total inclusiveness is misconceived because it is based on that contradiction in terms.

Do we then celebrate emotional chauvinism?

No, we separate the pathos of respect from the pathos of love, draw the gradations from lover to unknown fellow human being, and exercise judgment. It is not a matter of treating all humans equally; it is a matter of treating all beings appropriately, according to the difference they make to me and I to them. This is what we have always done, but we have not done it as well as we might, had we not been confused by the precepts of traditional ethics.

If intimate knowledge is a condition of love and a prime measure of its authenticity, it follows that we cannot love those we do not know. We can extend formal respect based on abstract ideals of equality, but even respect, as is indicated by the Latin root of the term *re-spicere* (to see), presupposes some level of acquaintance and allows for the possibility of seeing the other in negative terms as a threat. It is not at all clear to me that there is a common good for humankind, that world community would benefit all members, especially if community entails suppressing human diversity by enforcing general norms. The particular always reasserts itself in individual preferences: we love different persons and things, and we love them in different ways. Nor is it evident that the only alternative to comprehensive community is a Hobbesian state of nature. Nietzsche argued that life is becoming, that becoming is strife, and that agon generates growth and excellence.

There may be no common good that does not afflict uncommon people, which we all are in our particularity. But there is a common bad—pain, sickness, suffering in general—that can be minimized. What I call sexlove might provisionally be understood as an erotic friendship of the good. Not everyone is capable of entering such a relationship, and no body can love every other body in that way. But what Aristotle called friendship of utility is not bounded that way. It may be that the best idea under our circumstances is to make the best deal you can with everybody you have to deal with. It may be that the best deal you can make with somebody intent upon hurting you is to beat him to the punch (or to run away as fast as you can). It may be that ethical consciousness, the reversible structure of recognition, is the ability to discern the *ethos* of those you are dealing with and treat them appropriately, that is, making the best deal you can given the particularities of the persons and circumstances. It's a good deal when nobody gets hurt. Unfortunately, it is not always possible to make a good deal. So we negotiate when we can, and fight (or run) when we can't. That is what it is to be ethical, I think—it begins with the process Merleau-Ponty called interrogation, doing the best you can to recognize persons and discern the intrinsic ambiguity of circumstance, then trying to make the best deal.

6.

What, then, of sexlove and ethics? Does the lawful rule of the universal apply only in the ethical domain, leaving the particularity of sexlove wild and unruly, intrinsically defiant of all normativity? Are lovers' contracts essentially antisocial?

Not if social contracts and sexual contracts are both grounded in reversibility. Not if there is something beyond the de facto universal of convention that incorporates the freedom of particular individuals. Not if there is a continuum between the friendship of utility and the friendship of the good marked by degrees of knowledge, respect, affection, and intimacy. Not if the exclusivity of sexlove relations flexes over time and circumstance and is, in all cases and for better or worse, intrinsically affected by the social/historical horizons that envelop all human relations.

The case I have made here does stress the differences between the end points of the social continuum, between the reversibility of intimate carnal knowledge and the reversibility of relatively anonymous relations. I also contend that, although all adjacent points along the spectrum exhibit continuity, the end points are discontinuous and qualitatively disjunct, mediation notwithstanding: different precepts apply at different points across the spectrum, although all may be subtended by some sort of recognition or respect. The differences come to an illuminating point of compression, however, with the structures of convention. What allows the wider community to come together, to convene, is the respect for individual differences that allows us to focus on agreement: "We be polite."[7] As long as this social accord is built on the demonization of sex, as long as sex is intrinsically impolite and impolitic, it is the fate of lovers to be outcasts. That fate banishes sexlove to margins of darkness, privacy, and duplicity. Demonization doth make hypocrites of us all.

Insofar as sexlove defies the de facto universal predicated upon demonization, it is a founding emblem of a higher universal: the universal as the ideal of autonomy, of giving the law to oneself; the always still-to-be-realized appeal of freedom to act only on those maxims that oppress no body. Respect for the law is not the end of the story, but the beginning. The end of the story is the ability to discern between good laws and bad—the laws that fulfill the criterion of Hobbes's paradox of increasing freedom by limiting it and those that result in a net loss of freedom—and the freedom to act on the basis of that discernment. Genuine lovers have always done that, have always claimed for themselves the freedom, not merely to tolerate difference, but to glorify it in the highest affirmation of the reversibility of flesh. Genuine love has always been—and, I suspect, always will be—precarious in just this way: there is no freedom without risk . . . because there is an essential ambiguity, an intrinsic tension, between the freedom to love as one will and the sedimented conventions that permit us to come together by holding us apart.

It is the founding mistake of the romantic tradition to predicate love on obstacle and prohibition—I do not love you because you are prohibited, I love you because you, more than any other, embody my vision of to kalon[8]—but beneath the error of romanticism is the truth that love will always have to contend with prohibition because it is essentially a threat to convention. It is essentially a threat to convention because it thrives on inequality and difference: it sets its beloved above and apart.

Sexlove is the culmination of the reversibility of flesh. As such, it is both the ground and the limit of the universal. *Agape* is the absolute universalization of sexlove; it marks the end point of the continuum, the impossibility that defines a limit. The reversibility of flesh manifests itself in the transfer of corporeal schema, a recognition qualified by particularity. When it expands centrifugally into ethical consciousness as such, it dilutes and becomes abstract, its power of appeal and repulsion atrophies into indifference. That is the limit of humanism: the value, positive or negative, an individual has for me is proportional to the psychic and spatiotemporal distance between us. Finitude and particularity both ground and limit love. There is an absolute discontinuity between fleshly love and the oxymoron of divine love, or *agape*. It is essential to love to be circumscribed. If ought implies can, if it is a mistake in reasoning to impose a duty that cannot be fulfilled, then the ethics of the universal needs to be reconceived.

Or else we'll just have to take off our bodies.

. . . .

CHAPTER THREE

CONSCIENCE AND AUTHENTICITY

I. THE QUESTION

Can there be authentic obedience to the call of conscience?

Conscience is a name for a rift within the self. Authenticity is a name for unity within the self. When I hear the call of conscience, the caller and the called are not the same. When I am authentic, I am my ownmost self. Just to stipulate that it is my ownmost being not to be at one with myself is not to resolve the issue: one must ask the question of how this identity in self-difference is to be conceived. The axis of my questioning here is the tension between obedience and freedom: If I obey the call of conscience, am I behaving as a responsible free agent?

2. CONSCIENCE AS *VOX DEI*

> And it came to pass . . . that God tested Abraham and said to him, Abraham. And he said, Behold, here I am. And he said, Take now your only son Isaac, whom you love, and go to the land of the Amorites; and offer him there for a burnt offering upon one of the mountains of which I will tell you. And Abraham rose up early in the morning and . . . went to the place of which God had told him. (Genesis 22)

Abraham obeys God and God rewards him for his obedience. Had Abraham not been free to disobey, to reward him would make no sense. Abraham's obedience is exemplary because it is abject: he obeys without question a command whose rationale transcends his understanding, and does so simply because he believes the command came from God. God's command to sacrifice Isaac contradicts Abraham's finite reason because it violates their original covenant,[1] that requires Isaac to live on and generate progeny.

The Old Testament God was inclined to be preemptory. What of the New Testament God? Here is what Aquinas said:

> Human knowledge is assisted by the revelation of grace. For the intellect's natural light is strengthened by the infusion of gratuitous light, and sometimes also the images in the imagination are divinely formed, so as to express divine things better than those which we receive naturally from sensible things, as appears in prophetic visions; while sometimes sensible things, or even voices, are divinely formed to express some divine meaning. (*Summa Theologica*, Q 12, Art. 13)[2]

The natural light of reason is insufficient to know God and must be assisted by supernatural means, but it does reflect our finite likeness to God and our propensity to seek to know him as the source of our happiness and perfection. Natural reason alone can and does go astray, but this is a mark of human finitude, not a frailty of reason itself. God as *ens perfectissimum* is Being itself, sheer intelligibility. When God speaks to us and reveals himself, he does not contravene Reason itself, but draws us beyond our capacity for understanding toward an intelligibility that necessarily transcends us during our time on earth.

The call of conscience as the voice of God calls from beyond ourselves but calls us toward ourselves: it calls us to a potentiality for being more perfectly ourselves than we have hitherto been. If we choose to heed the call and obey it, we must transcend our finite natural reason in order to be in accordance with a more perfect rationality than we can understand. The question posed by conscience as *vox dei* is whether the choice to obey a command we cannot understand can be described as a free choice if personal responsibility is taken to be a necessary condition for freedom. If abject obedience is irresponsible, can it be free? Can I take full personal responsibility for an action I can justify only by appeal to faith in understanding beyond my own? What meaning can be assigned to the notion of transfinite reason, the understanding beyond that differs qualitatively from my own?

3. NIETZSCHE: *ÜBERMENSCHLICHKEIT* AND AUTHENTICITY

> You do not want to kill, O judges and sacrificers, until the animal has nodded? Behold the pale criminal has nodded: out of his eyes speaks the great contempt.

"My ego is something that shall be overcome: my ego is to me the great contempt of man," that is what his eyes say.

That he judged himself, that was his highest moment; do not let the sublime return to his baseness! There is no redemption for one who suffers so of himself. . . .

An image made this pale man pale. He was equal to his deed when he did it; but he could not bear its image after it was done. Now he always saw himself as the doer of one deed. Madness I call this. . . .

Listen, O judges: there is yet another madness, and that comes *before* the deed. . . .

Verily, I wish their madness were called truth. (Z, 149–51)

Nietzsche expresses contempt for the self-contempt of the pale criminal, yet Nietzsche is, himself, the creator of the *Übermensch*, the self-transcending spirit who would be more than what he is. In the enthusiasm of *amor fati*, the overman affirms himself unto eternal recurrence of the same, yet he would be different, stronger, higher, more. The overman is lonely and apart, beyond the good and evil of the flies in the marketplace; unlike the herd animals, he reveres the I and celebrates his own evil, his own excess. Although he goes down from the mountain, seeks followers, and argues his case, he nonetheless destroys without remorse, for that is intrinsic to the affirmation of creation. He regards Socratic self-reflection, self-scrutiny, doubt, as a potentiality for weakness, sickness, yearning for peace and death.

As Nietzsche's thought developed beyond 1886, the Apollo-Dionysus agon of the *Birth of Tragedy* is sublated into a new figure: the new Dionysus, not one who needs the metaphysical comfort of a rational dream, but a truly tragic figure who exalts the madness of death-bound, chaotic becoming, and the tumultuous proliferation of new forms in the vital time that remains to him in this world, the only world that is.

The idea of a conscience-stricken, conscience-directed overman is a contradiction in terms: Zarathustra is no pale criminal; he takes the law from nobody, gives himself his own evil and his own good, and hangs his own will over himself as a law.[3] Zarathustra is not at one with himself: he is drawn into a madness, an incoherence among the selves within and beyond himself. "Lonely one, you are going the way of the lover: yourself you love, and therefore you despise yourself, as only lovers despise. The lover would create because he despises. What does he know of love who did not have to despise precisely what he loved!" (Z, 177). His madness propels him to destroy old and create new values. How does he choose which values to destroy and which to create? When he is obedient to this madness, is he behaving responsibly? Can he be said to be free and autonomous in the Kantian sense that he himself cites, the sense of giving the law unto himself? Given the lover's rift within himself, how can Zarathustra manifest authentic autonomy? How can he claim personal responsibility for an act performed by a self divided against itself? How can his will be willed as law when it includes dissent? Doesn't authenticity require resolution, as Heidegger said?

4. FREUD: ÜBER-ICH AND CONSCIENCE

> It is easy to show that the ego ideal answers to everything that is expected of the higher nature of man. As a substitute for a longing for the father, it contains the germ from which all religions have evolved. The self-judgment which declares that the ego falls short of its ideal produces the religious sense of humility to which the believer appeals in his longing. As a child grows up, the role of the father is carried on by teachers and others in authority; their injunctions and prohibitions remain powerful in the ego ideal and continue, in the form of conscience, to exercise the moral censorship. The tension between the demands of conscience and the actual performances of the ego is experienced as a sense of guilt. Social feelings rest on identifications with other people, on the basis of having the same ego ideal.[4]

Conscience, for Freud, is original ambivalence. It is introjection and identification, but at the same time, prohibition and reaction-formation: "You *ought to be* like this (like your father), [but] you *may not be* like this (like your father), that is, you may not do all that he does; some things are his prerogative."[5] The father figure is the ideal on which the child's identity is both modeled and measured: this is what I am meant to be, and this is what I will never be. The ambivalence compounds with the Oedipus complex and the bisexuality Freud attributes to the psyche. The mother figure is also introjected: the Oedipal object-cathexis is desexualized, sublimated, changed into narcissistic libido, and incorporated among the "general and lasting first identifications made in earliest childhood." The voices of conscience originate beyond consciousness and command the ego from a multiplicity of value systems, desires, and prohibitions, which intrinsically conflict with each other.

Conscience is the origin of civilization and the source of our "higher nature." Conscience is also the prime source of repression, neurosis, and the self-destructive instinct named as Thanatos in Freud's later writings where it is identified as the death wish that inevitably supervenes over Eros, the will to live. Instincts are phylogenetic and archaic: they emerge from prehuman origins, from the sedimented vicissitudes in the encounter of organism and environment recapitulated over ages, and they are inherited.

There is no civilization without a collective ego ideal, a common value system operating beneath the level of social consciousness and informing it. Persons who lack conscience were born without the heritage that makes us human; they are psychopaths and require external restraint. There is no art, no cultural production, no humanity, hence no dignity without the sublimation that proceeds from self-restraint.

What, then, of freedom and authenticity?

If freedom is conceived as requiring deliberate, that is, conscious, choice and the ability to act upon it, then it is difficult to find robust conceptual room for freedom in the mainstream of Freudian psychoanalytic theory. The ego, the *topos* of consciousness, is constantly portrayed as the battlefield upon which larger forces collide, and the actions that result appear to be determinable in principle by some sort of vector analysis. Freud, the scientist, was committed to causal explanation, and that implies a metaphysics in which the past determines the future.

Conscience calls us into the herd. Conscience calls us to reconcile ourselves to the ego ideal percolating down through the eons and measure up to the law invoked in the name of the father in the latter phases of ontogeny. But Freud, the scientist, was rescued from simple causal determinism by Freud, the scientist, committed to the reality principle. Freud's life and works are, above all else, the quest for lucidity, demystification, and the resolute project to retrieve sanity from the bricolage of historical accident. Like his icon Oedipus, Freud defied prophets, gods, and social institutions in order to take his measure from reality, and base his thought and action on that measure.

Conscience, for Freud, is original ambivalence. His ego ideal called him to civilization, to the conflicted value systems informing herd morality, with the ambivalent intent of reconciliation. Not the reconciliation that produces oneness—Freud was neither at one with himself nor with his theories nor with his closest colleagues and family—but the reconciliation with truth that set him apart from the civilization to which he was bound by conscience. Freud saw that the conscience that binds us together makes us sick.

So far as I know, Freud's conscience bound him to the monogamous sexual morality of Victorian Vienna, a moral system that he evaluated early in his career as pathological.[6] Freud's madness was to participate in the herd madness to which he was called by conscience. Is this voluntary complicity in madness on the part of the psychoanalyst compatible with any viable conception of authenticity? (This is not a rhetorical question; I will attempt to answer it later.)

5. HEIDEGGER'S SILENT CALL

> Conscience discourses solely and constantly in the mode of keeping silent. (Martin Heidegger)[7]

Freud's conscience calls us into the herd; Heidegger's conscience calls us out of the herd and returns us to ourselves. The self to which we are returned is a null basis, the nothingness constitutive of our being and the freedom that is revealed to us in anxiety. It is a silent call because it speaks of nothing. Hearing the call is affirming anxiety in the mode of freeing ourselves from the identities established by and for ourselves in our concernful participation in the they-self of *das Man*. It is an acknowledgment of the groundlessness constitutive of our freedom and our sole responsibility for the actions we take. Hearing the call of conscience is understanding that our freedom renders us guilty for being the null basis for all that we do or fail to do.[8]

Conscience does not direct us toward or away from any given thing present at hand in past or future. It is empty of content and speaks from the nullity of our thrownness to the nullity of our being-unto-death. Its positive force is to awaken us to our ownmost being as the being that remains in question because it has no foundation for being anything in particular. We are originally guilty because to exist is to act, to be something, and whatever we choose to be cannot be justified by appeal to any transcendent ground. To posit a ground as justification is a free, hence ungrounded, act. Nothing has meaning apart from the transcendental constitution of Dasein.

The silent call of conscience (*Gewissensruf, Ruf des Gewissens*) calls us to the solitude of our ownmost being, that is, to *Eigenheit*, or authenticity. As

Heidegger puts it, "Understanding the call discloses one's own Dasein in the uncanniness [*Unheimlichkeit*] of its individualization."[9] Dasein's home is in the social world with the familiar identities and associated obligations that make up our concernful dealings with others in the everyday domain of *das Man*. That domain is replete with meaning and value; good things attract us, bad things repel us, and we experience joy and sorrow in the midst of our fellow human beings. The call of conscience is the anxious self-disclosure that all the structures constitutive of the social domain are grounded upon the null basis of my own solitary act of transcendental constitution whereby I endow my world with meaning. Heidegger says, "This distinctive and authentic disclosedness [*Erschlossenheit*], which is attested in Dasein itself by conscience—this reticent self-projection upon one's ownmost Being-guilty, in which one is ready for anxiety—we call 'resoluteness' [*Entschlossenheit*]."[10]

Resoluteness follows from Dasein's authentic recognition that it is thrown into existence, into a situation. Hamlet's question to be or not to be is transformed into the forced issue of *how* to be: inauthentic and unquestioning complicity in the familiar structures of the world of *das Man*, taken for granted as a transcendent reality existing apart from Dasein and providing grounds for its manner of existence. Or authentic assumption of the guilt for constituting the world on the null basis of individual freedom. Heeding the call of conscience in a resolute way allows Dasein to "let the Others who are with it 'be' in their ownmost potentiality-for-Being, and to co-disclose this potentiality in the solicitude which leaps forth and liberates. When Dasein is resolute, it can become the 'conscience' of Others. Only by authentically Being-their-Selves in resoluteness can people authentically be with one another."[11]

Authentic being with one another takes the character of repetition [*Wiederholung*]. Instead of being swept along by events and passively submitting to the accidents of history, authentic Dasein exercises the "power of its finite freedom" to survey the possibilities opened by history and repeat those handed down to it that can be reconstituted into a destiny of freedom. This freedom-granting authentic historicality is achieved through authentic "Being-toward-death" in the mode of "anticipatory resoluteness," which neither abandons itself to the influence of the past nor aims at progress, but lives steadfast in the freedom of its null basis.[12]

Resolute obedience to the call of conscience leads authentic Dasein out of the herd into the historical destiny of people coming together, each as the conscience of the Others, in resolute Being-unto-Death to realize the fate of the freedom of nullity. It lies beyond the purview of my scholarship and imagination to generate a concrete interpretation of what this might mean. Nonetheless, it is full of portent. It is patently incompatible with the pastoral vision of a Moravian village ordered from matins to vespers by church bells ringing through crisp mountain air. It is historically situated during the rise of the Third Reich and Heidegger's complicity with National Socialism.

So far as I know, Heidegger died without giving a public account of his affiliation with the Nazi party or his shabby treatment of Husserl. How does that reflect upon his understanding of the call of conscience? It is, I think, intrinsically related to the silence of nullity: according to his own doctrine, Heidegger's call of conscience says nothing. It explicitly excludes ontic obligation, generates no *nomos*, enjoins no *pathos*. It purports, however, to bring "the Self right into its current concernful Being-alongside what is ready-to-hand, and pushes it into solicitous Being with Others." Heidegger specifies this solicitude in just one way: resolute Dasein "can become the 'conscience' of Others." Authentic Dasein could not function as the conscience of others in the mundane sense of providing counsel or attempting to guide other persons in some ways rather than others. In principle, it could do only one thing: it could stand as the silent exemplar of a human being who leaped forth out of the herd and resolutely did what he did on the basis of nothing at all.[13] Heidegger's silence truly may be an authentic expression of his ownmost being guilty. What, then, are we to make of Heidegger's conscience? Do we affirm his silence? Do we emulate it? Or do we suspect an underlying psychopathology, that is, a *failure* to hear the call of conscience?

Does the call of conscience call us back to the herd with Freud? Or does it require us to transcend social identity and identification to dwell with Heidegger among silent death-bound exemplars of authentic guilt? Can one imagine community among such sentinel figures?[14]

6. MERLEAU-PONTY: CHIASMATIC COMMUNITY

If we can show that the flesh is an ultimate notion, that it is not the union or compound of two substances, but thinkable by itself, if there is a relation of the visible with itself that traverses me and constitutes me as a seer, this circle which I do not form, which forms me, this coiling over of the visible upon the visible, can traverse, animate other bodies as well as my own. And if I was able to understand how

this wave arises within me, how the visible which is yonder is simultaneously my landscape, I can understand a fortiori that elsewhere
it also closes over upon itself and that there are other landscapes
besides my own. If it lets itself be captivated by one of its fragments,
the principle of captation is established, the field open for other
Narcissus, for an "intercorporeity." (Merleau-Ponty, *VI*, 140–41)

The flesh of the world, through the phenomenon of reversibility, calls for
speech to break silence and inscribe its truth where it belongs.[15] The visible
lets itself be captivated by a situated fragment, a human perspective, but a
perspective lived initially in anonymous generality.[16] One sees: the spectacle
is visible from interchangeable places through the typical dimensions of visibility subtended by typical organs of sight attuned to the evidentiality of the
world. When I say what I have seen, I invoke your openness to a vision of the
world to which both of us belong.[17]

The call of conscience opens the rift of self-transcendence, sets me at odds
with myself, and urges me to free myself from myself to become more myself
than I have been. It challenges my typicality and summons the self that is my
new destiny. I can heed the summons or turn away from it and reaffirm my
familiar persona.

The herd thrives on typicality and conserves it: expectations of reliable
behavior are foundational for sociality. If we are going to live and work together, we need to know what to expect from each other and fulfill those
expectations. There are norms to which we must adhere; departures threaten
cohesion and introduce dysfunction. We have to behave responsibly: we have
to accommodate each other's legitimate demands based on lucid and shared
values of legitimacy. In no small measure, each communal self is obliged to
act out the part he has tacitly agreed to play: herd conscience is the pervasive
enforcer that keeps us in role. Freud got that right: civilization needs the superego and could not function without it. Conscience, as the etymology of
the term reveals, is knowledge of what is right in the places where we gather
together.

The problem of authenticity arises when the emergent self realizes that
the herd's shared knowledge of what is right is wrong, or misguided, or sick.
That was Freud's situation in Victorian Vienna. It forces the issue of authenticity postponed above. Assuming that Freud deliberately attempted to adhere to the prevalent sexual morality of exclusive monogamy—contravening
his ownmost belief that it was contrary to health and productivity—we may

challenge his integrity: Is this a failure to be the autonomous self, a lapse of freedom, a relapse into the soothing bath of social approval?

There is presumption in this assumption. We presume to ask the question and to probe, as well-known contemporary historians have recently done, into the personal relationships between Freud, his patients, his acquaintances, and the members of his family. We arrogate to ourselves the right to invade his privacy. We take it as legitimate to investigate his personal life to see whether he practiced what he preached, whether he was true to himself, whether he was authentic. Given the subject matter of psychoanalysis, its confessional methodology, and Freud's own willingness to disclose sexually significant aspects of his own intimate dreams and Oedipal fantasies, we may say that he invited the scrutiny and legitimized it in that way. The investigation might also be warranted by its relevance to the task of critical evaluation of one of the most influential theories to have emerged in the twentieth century.

These issues of privacy are complex and consequential, but, for the most part, tangential to the main line of inquiry here. Except the assumption or presumption itself. The probe is the superego at work, an enforcement tool of herd conscience. To dwell in the polis is to be subject to the scrutiny and regulation of the herd. Introjection of herd values, formation of the ego ideal, extends the regulation beyond the walls of the polis to include all dwelling places, dreamscapes as well as landscapes: the superego's probe is omniscient; the look of the other takes on cosmic proportions; shame lurks on every horizon as a latency for self-punishment.

The rift within ourselves is also a rift within community. Alienation is structural to social being; it is the dark complement of being-with others: the threat of betrayal, exclusion, and ostracism, when the herd reinforces its value system by turning on one of its own perceived to have violated it. This is the social dimension of Merleau-Ponty's *écart*, the social counterpart of the cogito that emerges during adolescence to distance the individual from syncretism and primordial communality. It is *ontological* alienation: alterity is a necessary structure of being human, a correlate of the freedom that manifests itself as authenticity; being-with cannot dispense with its shadow. The self is called by a dehiscent conscience, essentially bound up with herd conscience, to distance itself from the herd, manifest its ipseity, and enact its own *nomos*. This is Freud's reaction formation, the overman's creation of his own evil, Dasein's choice of itself to *be* guilty. The call of conscience is at once and necessarily a call to alterity as well as a call to be the same.

If the call of conscience is essentially ambivalent and never univocal, then obedience must be reconceived, as must authenticity. One cannot simply obey a call that issues ambivalent commands. The *vox dei* that spoke to Abraham put him in fear and trembling, Zarathustra's path was not clearly laid out before him, and Freud had to struggle with hypocrisy. What, then, of obedience and authenticity and the question guiding the thoughts unfolding here, whether it is possible to heed the call of conscience as a responsible free agent?

7. MADNESS: RIFTS AND BLESSINGS

The rift in the Paris circle in the 1950s that set Merleau-Ponty at odds with Sartre and others of his former colleagues centered on the question of how to respond to the Communist revolution when the atrocities of Stalin came to light. The issue was forced for the French intelligentsia, and all those involved acknowledged their ambivalence. Merleau-Ponty broke with the party, Sartre did not, and the two men broke with each other, remaining unreconciled until Merleau-Ponty's death. There is a comparable rift in the community of Heidegger scholars over the issue of Heidegger's silence about his Nazism. Little has been left unsaid about these rifts and I do not intend to address the specifics here, except to say that I think it is crucial that one philosopher spoke and the other did not.

Merleau-Ponty's chiasmatic community incorporates the rift or *écart* between my social identity and my alterity. Heidegger's call of conscience emanates from that part of Dasein that "remains indefinite and empty in its 'what'":[18] it induces anxiety and "puts Dasein's Being in-the-world face to face with the 'nothing' of the world."[19] In both cases, there is the rift of self-transcendence that calls the familiar patterns of our lives into question and demands some sort of response, from creative acts of self-transformation, at one end of a continuum, to tenacious acts of self-conservation coupled with flight from the discomfort of self-confrontation, at the other. Nonetheless, there are consequential differences between Heidegger and Merleau-Ponty that tend to be obscured by the conspicuous similarities. The difference I regard as crucial on the question of conscience and authenticity has to do with the phenomenological description of the call and its origin.

Husserl's thesis of intentionality asserts that "all consciousness is consciousness of an object." The intentional object of Heideggerian anxiety is a non-object, nothingness, nullity; anxiety is an indefinite, horizonal, mood or state of mind in which all specific objects lose definition and meaning. The call bypasses Dasein's social identity: it situates Dasein, but is itself radically unsituated. It forces Dasein to the recognition that it has its existence as its own to be,[20] but it provides no context, orientation, measure: nothing could serve as a guide.

This is madness: to believe, and resolutely to act on the belief, that the social world has no meaning, that every relation constitutive of the fabric of human society is arbitrary and without any ground whatsoever is psychopathological. It may be essential to good philosophical skepticism to entertain the hypothesis as an ascesis in the subjunctive mode, but as we know from Loeb and Leopold, it is madness to take it to the streets. Nietzsche knew that, even in the pits of his own madness. So did Hölderlin. So did Heidegger. So do you.

Nietzsche wrote of "another madness"—different from the madness of the conscience-stricken pale criminal—and said that he wished it "were called truth."[21] This truth is that it is madness to believe, and resolutely to act on the belief that the relations collectively comprising the fabric of human society are sane. They are not sane—they are insane—because they are absurd in the literal sense of embodying contradiction, and for that reason alone cannot be taken to the streets, either.

Sanity is an ideal that transcends the historical unfolding of human behavior: as a species we are always at war. This is the truth hidden in the appeal to the divine from Abraham to Aquinas to Heidegger. We have to look at the good and evil playing out in the streets and see into and beyond them. This, too, is madness—the madness of authenticity. When the world is sick, its denizens are stuck: to behave in accordance with the prevailing norms is to embrace the sickness and suffer the pain that sickness entails; to defy the prevailing norms is to invoke the wrath of the godlings within and without, to suffer the pain of condemnation. The madness of authenticity is to seek a measure in the world[22] that transcends the madness of the world, and to act on that measure—knowing ahead of time that doing this will draw blood. Where in the world is this sanguine madness to be found?

Merleau-Ponty argues that human flesh is always situated, always on the way from some place and time to another, always in context, even (and sometimes especially) in moments of radical reflection and deep alienation.[23] If this is right, then Heidegger's account of the call of conscience is flawed. It may be—indeed, I think it is—philosophically powerful, rich with insight, and resonant with truth, but it is not phenomenologically accurate because it dispenses with human intercorporeity in its opening gesture. It does so on the premise that intercorporeity is an ontic matter of fact present-at-hand within the world that has no meaning other than that assigned by care at the ontological level. Heidegger starts and ends with no ground of measure for authenticity—other than that groundlessness itself—because he cuts himself off from the only possible ground right from the start.[24]

Heidegger's insight is that no call of conscience can tell us definitively what to do, not even the *vox dei*. In the end, we are always thrown back on ourselves, solely responsible for doing what we do and being who we are. In fact, I think it was his reaction against the *vox dei* model that projected Heidegger from divine plenitude to finite nullity, a kind of binary thinking that he usually eschews. Either absolute ground or no ground. No absolute ground. Therefore, absolutely no ground.[25]

We are creatures of flesh who walk upon the earth in the company of others more or less like ourselves. We participate in the communion of flesh through the phenomenon of reversibility. We cannot not be in touch with each other. We cannot *not* respond to human pathos. We can love and we can hate and we always do both, genuine indifference being genuinely pathological, genuinely subhuman. Loving and hating in and across the interlocking nexus of communal structures, we are called upon to accommodate the interests and values of the groupings within which we dwell. We also have demands of our own that necessarily collide with any grouping: it is a brute fact that self-interest and group welfare cannot always be brought into harmony, even in groups as small as two, especially when self-interest is bound to ipseity, as it is in the case of authenticity.

Furthermore, there is no single superego that can function as the uncontested: there is always an agon. The call of conscience is always and necessarily both ambiguous and ambivalent: it always comes contested; it always pulls both ways. There is no question of obeying it. Or of disobeying it. Obedience is not what is at stake. The call of conscience cannot be obeyed because its commands always contradict themselves. In the name of the covenant, violate the covenant. In the name of robust love and vigor, forsake the vows you made to those you love. In the name of humanity, commit terror.

Conscience is the dehiscence of the self that may be the prelude to self-transcendence. It is a call to assess one's values and measure them against the pathos of the others within and without the periphery of one's own epidermis. It is a call to care, just as Heidegger said, but that call cannot come exclusively from within individualized Dasein with the clamoring voices of its internalized loves and hates neatly bracketed by *Angst*. Nor is the call heard by a Dasein totally unconcerned about the effects of its actions upon those who dwell in the same world. Defiance is a social gesture. As is martyrdom. And they are both mediated by calculation. The Zen of spontaneity is disciplined by training: you dashed into the fire and tried to save the baby because you had prepared yourself to be that person.

So, one last time, what does the authentic self do when its emergent truth conflicts with a conscience that is also its own? Do you unsheathe the sacrificial knife, raise the cup of hemlock to your lips, order the bomb to be dropped—or drop it yourself because the order to do so has been authenticated by higher authority? All of these commands issue from a sick world, a world in which violent contradiction is incarnate: do this in the name of the glorious father or the beatific mother in order to expose, expunge, and reduce to defeated infamy all the purveyors of evil lurking behind masks of benign authority. The problem is differentiating the good from the evil when they always come mixed. When conscience calls, I am torn between conflicting ideals; one pathos, one tug from the bricolage of my heritage, has to be measured against another that conflicts with it. Nor can the ideals themselves guide me: just because it is their soundness that is at stake.

Viable answers to this question cannot be generated in the abstract arena of metaethical disputation. The rule of rules in metaethics is consistency. It is a good rule, because inconsistency undermines resolution and betrays conflicted motivations that need to be addressed—if time and the force of circumstance allow—before triggering the deed. Consistency is a good rule, but it is insufficient to guide us, just because we can be consistently wrong and persistently bound to a flawed paradigm.

Heideggerian authenticity, the version delimited to *Being and Time* and analyzed here, is finally an appeal to consistency: it enjoins Dasein to behave in accordance with its ownmost being, the nullity of a being whose Being is in question. *Eigenheit* is the ideal of being consistently what one is. It has the correlate of taking personal responsibility for being what one is, that is, for existing in this mode rather than that, through these actions rather than others. I endorse this correlate for the reasons given throughout this discourse—and one more with which I will conclude, but want to stress its insufficiency. Being my decision, one for which I take total and exemplary responsibility, does not make it a good decision nor me a good human being. I can want to have a conscience, affirm my being guilty, and be truly guilty, as Heidegger, the Nazi, was.

There is another authenticity, an authenticity culled from the interstices of Merleau-Ponty's writings. This authenticity wants to be responsible and *not* guilty. It wants to have found the best possible thing to do and, then, to have done it. Heidegger just got that wrong: responsibility is not equivalent to guilt. In wanting to have a conscience, I want my decisions and actions to matter; I want to make it right for myself and deserving others. I want the dignity of freedom and personal responsibility, to be sure, but I also want to be proud of what I have done.

The call of conscience is not about nothing. The call is always concrete, situated, and consequential. Given this magnitude, it calls everything into question; that is, it shakes the nexus of relations constituting the meaning of the world and commands revaluation of all values. So conceived, the call of conscience is a blessing, a consecration of blood, both in the sense of wounding and in the sense of potentially conferring grace. It is a wrestling with angels from which one always emerges transformed and scarred, but sometimes also ennobled, closer to *to kalon*, and sometimes marked with an ineradicable stain of shame. The problem, again, is one of discriminating the good from the evil when they do not come packed neatly into binary opposi-tions, but arrive mixed in the confused voices of finite temporal unfolding.

The call of conscience calls upon us to listen to the world, articulate its voices,[26] and assess its claims. One does not obey or disobey the call, one ei-ther accepts the responsibility for making one's own decision or one displaces that responsibility on to an external authority and does what *das Man* is sup-posed to do in that situation. The listening does not guarantee the goodness of the decision, nor does the anxiety of the struggle with the angels vindicate a bad decision. The burden of responsibility is to determine what is good and to do it. How does one go about doing that?

8. LUCID REVERSIBILITY

The concluding thought promised above will not answer this question. The account of authenticity set forth here asserts that authenticity is insufficient as a moral precept: it does not provide moral criteria for distinguishing good and evil, and it cannot vindicate bad decisions. What good is it, then?

One cannot be authentic in the sense of taking personal responsibility for a decision that is not one's own. For a decision to be one's own, it must be lucid. This is a matter of degree. To the extent that the call of conscience calls for abject obedience to a command whose rationale is beyond our ken, to obey is inauthentic. The inverse is also true. And that is my concluding thought. One has to listen to the voices of conscience, attempt to understand their rationale, and assess the soundness of their claims. This is the burden of articulation, the demand on the part of the flesh of the world to bring the silent vision, the mute perception, to speech and let it assume its proper place in the chiasmatic community that is the domain of morality.

Authenticity is thus bound to a precept of lucidity: one is called upon to thematize the prereflective. This can be understood in psychoanalytic terms through Freud's famous dictum—where Id was, there let Ego be—but is more comprehensive when understood ontologically through Merleau-Ponty's "fundamental phenomenon of reversibility" founded on the pathos of the transfer of corporeal schema that allows me to recognize you as a fellow human being and identify with you across the space of alterity: the pathos I have described in the previous chapter as the ground phenomenon of ethics. The competing voices in the silence of Freud's unconscious, the organic phylogenetic bricolage subtending our collective heritage, are the voices of the other bodies and beings that linger and dwell in the world we inhabit, pollute, and despoil. We have to listen to them, hear and feel their claims, evaluate those claims, and respond with the lucidity of understanding.

Lucid or dark, one is responsible for what one does. In the chiasmatic community, others hold me accountable for my deeds and deal with me according to prevailing mores. Objectively speaking, that has been and will be the case as far backward and forward as I can see in historical time. Beyond that is the authenticity of reversibility, the dehiscence of the self, that calls me to conscience, now also in the sense of the French *conscience* or consciousness, and demands personal responsibility. Responding to that demand is what I take moral philosophizing to be: an open-ended endeavor that offers the best promise of bringing the objective fact of social accountability, including mercy and revenge, to nobler levels of human behavior.

Nobler levels of human behavior are nobler levels of intertwined love and hate: incarnate human finitude precludes anything resembling the beatific vision of unalloyed love. Strife is a correlate of becoming, conscience will remain an agon, and violence will remain an essential feature of the human condition. In short, alterity—our vulnerability to each other—is guaranteed by intercorporeity and in turn guarantees that love will remain intertwined with hate. The hope lies in understanding it better and dealing with it better. I argued above that bad philosophy produces bad consequences and unhappiness. Here I am asserting that the inverse of that is true, too: there is such a thing as good philosophy, and it pulls us toward nobility.

Nothing should remain dark, silent, and isolated as an emblem of guilt.

CHAPTER FOUR

. . . .

REVERSIBILITY AND ETHICS: THE QUESTION OF VIOLENCE

SUMMARY

This [chapter][1] argues against two theoretical standpoints. The first contends that all human action entails violence. The second contends that discourse, the traditional alternative to violent confrontation, is itself necessarily violent. I contend that the conjunction of these two theses obscures significant differences between violent and nonviolent human behavior and, thereby, atrophies a legitimate moral animus against violence. The standpoint I defend rests on the assertion that humans are capable of direct perceptual experience of the pain of other humans, that this experience is the ground phenomenon of morality, and that it allows us in principle to adjudicate between violent and nonviolent action, to distinguish among kinds and degrees of violence, and to assess evidence bearing on questions of vindication and culpability.

I.

> We do not have a choice between purity and violence but between different kinds of violence. Inasmuch as we are incarnate beings, violence is our lot. . . . Life, discussion, and political choice occur only against a background of violence. What matters and what we have to discuss is not violence but its sense or its future. (Merleau-Ponty, *HT*, 109)[2]

The question of violence: Is violence intrinsically bad, or is it value-neutral? The question cannot be answered by definitional fiat because any definition put forward would have to be shown to be adequate to the relevant phenomena, and relevance is determined by definition.[3] The etymology of "violence" is nonetheless revealing. The proximal source is the Medieval Latin *vis* ("force";[4] "strength, especially as exercised against someone"[5]), which can be traced to the Indo-European *wi-*, *weiá-* ("vital force"[6]), the root of the Latin *violare* ("to force, to do violence to, hence especially to rape"[7]). The roots are value-neutral, but the derivatives are laden with negative value. The ambiguity here, I will argue, is essential: force has the essential propensity for destruction; the question remains whether that propensity ineluctably manifests itself in some way, as Lord Acton implied in his well-known assertion to the effect that power inevitably leads to some degree of corruption.[8] The question is illuminated by etymology, but cannot be answered by appeal to etymology.

I should also acknowledge that the question as posed presupposes a narrowing of the domain of violence to the human sphere. I am writing here of violence as forceful imposition of human will. This excludes the notion of violence as rapid change. Thus, hurricanes are not violent unless they are conceived as means used to impose the will of some anthropomorphic being, and even then the violence would properly reside in the domain where agency intersects with the means employed to carry out its intention.

Merleau-Ponty, writing in 1947 before his momentous break with Sartre over the issue of Communism,[9] outlines the argument that contends the question is not one of violence, which, being the human lot, is inevitable, but of the deployment of violence. The context of the quotation cited above is an exposition of Marxist doctrine set forth as a prelude to a critique of Communist ideology and praxis. The critique was precipitated by the unearthing of the atrocities of Stalinism, the party purging, the labor camps, the eradication of human life in the name of humanism, and in response to Arthur Koestler's depiction of the Bukharin trial in his novel *Darkness at Noon*. Given Merleau-Ponty's evolving attitudes toward Marxism, one cannot definitively say that in the passages cited here Merleau-Ponty was speaking only for Marx and not for himself as well (although I am quite sure that he did not subscribe to the position stated in the quotation).[10] Whether in 1947 Merleau-Ponty endorsed the position stated in the quotation is only marginally relevant to the question of the soundness of the supporting arguments. What is relevant is that the political standpoint he attributes to Marxism is challenged by the ethical implications of the thesis of reversibility he developed in his later writings.

"What matters is not violence but its sense (*sens*) or its future." The issue raised in this assertion is not reducible to the tired old ends-means dispute.[11] That debate presupposes that we have a choice whether or not to deploy violent means. This presupposition is ruled out by the claim that "we do not have a choice between purity and violence but between different kinds of violence." Merleau-Ponty states the case for this claim later in the same paragraph:

> He who condemns all violence puts himself outside the domain to which justice and injustice belong. He puts a curse upon the world and humanity—a hypocritical curse, since he who utters it has already accepted the rules of the game from the moment that he has begun to live. Between men considered as pure consciousnesses there would indeed be no reason to choose. But between men considered as the incumbents of situations which together compose a single *common situation* it is inevitable that one has to choose. (*HT*, 110)[12]

We have no choice but to be violent. That is, our only choice is how to behave in a common situation, and that action or inaction will necessarily produce violence. Only if we were disembodied consciousnesses could we have the choice to be pure, that is, the choice not to violate others by imposing our will upon theirs in a manner contrary to their interests and wishes. The only choices, forced upon us by our situation, are whom to violate, and how; and those choices are driven by the crucial question of why. To oversimplify, humanism amounts to a choice to promote universal ends rather than particular ones, but either choice—to serve human interests at large or those of a narrow elite—involves some form of terror. One cannot cite terror and violence as grounds for condemning action for they are the consequences of all action, including inaction: "to abstain from violence toward the violent is to become their accomplice" (*HT*, 109).

This is a radical position. Like all radical positions, it simplifies complex judgments. For example, it rules out pacifism as a political ideology; it obliterates the distinction between those committed to nonviolent means and those who deliberately use terror; de jure it conflates all moral differences between warfare conducted between combatants in accordance with the Geneva conventions and warfare conducted in the streets against noncombatants. We are all complicit; we are all combatants. The operative moral disjunction is between the hypocrite who thinks it is possible to remain pure or aloof and the authentic person who resolutely acts with the awareness that purity of any kind is an impossible ideal, one that is finally guilty of obscuring moral responsibility.

2.

The opposite position is equally radical (as is generically the case with binary oppositions). This position holds that violence is essentially related to some form of moral negativity, although that premise does not serve to distinguish this position from its Marxist opposite. The differentiating postulate is that there is always an alternative to violence, always a viable choice between violent and nonviolent action. Given this postulate, complex judgments are once again simplified: all other factors being equal, the morally justifiable choice is always to seek out nonviolent means.[13]

The always available alternative to violent action is discourse, in particular or, more generally, an appeal to ideality, symbolism, moral exemplarity. Discourse, communication based on principles of rationality, is ceteris paribus always preferable to violence. The deployment of violence is war; the peace process is essentially linked to rational discourse.

Here we arrive at the crux of the matter at hand. Only if there is a genuine distinction between the sword and the pen, between warfare and discourse, can there be an alternative to violent action, given the inevitability of conflict among divergent perspectives. If one holds that discourse is itself a form of violence, that discourse is inseparable from violence, then the first form of radicality, the Marxist thesis of the inevitability of violence, wins by default, and violence becomes once again a morally neutral category. Mooting the question of which has the stronger force, if the pen is intrinsically mighty, if it has force (*vis*), and if force rigorously entails violence (*violare*), one can no longer cite discourse as an always available alternative to violence.

The argument in support of one currently popular version of the thesis of the violence of discourse draws its force from semiological reductionism.[14] The violence of signifiers is inescapable because all experience is mediated by signifiers and is meaningless without them. Signifiers assign events to places within a symbolic matrix, and this assignment, given human finitude, is always to some degree arbitrary. The violence is the arbitrariness. Merely to perceive another is to assign that person a place within my matrix of concepts and symbolic sensitivities, within the worldview that has evolved from my cultural heritage. Thus, to perceive a thing is exactly *not* to perceive that thing as it is in itself; it is to violate the ipseity of the thing, to force it into a place that cannot be its own. This is inevitable because we are always on the near side of the bar that bars us from the signified.

Regarded through the semiological reduction, language is the primal mother of all acts of violence. Even the deliberate attempt to deal with others in an appropriate way, in a way that is proper to given persons or groups, depends upon a transcendental projection of appropriateness that has its source in the system of signifiers that, being superscribed upon me, governs my saying, thinking, feeling, and doing. To do what is right is always and only to do what one thinks is right from one's own point of view. Human action is, thus, violent in its appropriation of others: it necessarily violates the other's propriety. The meaning others have for me, including the meaning I have to the other that is my unknowable self, derives from the ideality of the system of signifiers within which I dwell, not from any reality that anyone could know or experience directly.

Is there, then, no significant difference between the violence of perception or experience and the violence of rape[15] or other forms of physical abuse? At the level of the first intention, clearly there is: even within the semiological reduction, one distinguishes between raping and looking, touching and talking, between physical and nonphysical forms of abuse. At the metalevel of reflective analysis, however, ambiguity and obscurity intrude. *Whatever distinction might be drawn, it cannot be a distinction between violence and nonviolence.* Can it then be a matter of kinds or degrees of violence? Perhaps an example would be helpful.

In the brochures that define sexual harassment at my institution, no juridical distinction is made between forms of behavior that involve touching, speaking, and looking (they are all and equally forms of harassment); nor do these brochures assign different degrees of culpability, different levels of punishment (although I trust that these differences are taken up when specific cases are tried). The difference between the violence of a sexually harassing look and that of a non–sexually harassing look would reside in the *presence* or *absence* of sexual content. And that would depend upon the mental state or intentions—conscious or unconscious—of the looker. But within the context of the semiological reduction, that would be beyond the ken of all parties. It would depend upon the system of signifiers operative within the person passing judgment: in no case would it be possible to *present* evidence relevant to the judgment. The evidence would have to be as intrinsically ambiguous and multideterminable as the offending look itself. Even if, contrary to the deconstruction of the notion of presence, one were to grant that person X looked at person Y, that such an event occurred—was *present*—at a given time and place, it would be impossible for both jurors and participants

to determine whether or not the look itself had sexual content or sexual significance.[16] The look itself falls on the side of the signified.

Is there a fallacy[17] embedded in this example? The question about discriminating among kinds and degrees of violence is answered by an example illus-
trating the indeterminability of one species, sexual harassment, of one kind
of violence, the look. Surely there is a difference between this kind of violence (looking) and others that belong in the domain of touching, the generic
category of rape. The difference would have to do with some distinction such
as that between physical and psychological damage. Here is one person who
has been sodomized with the wooden handle of a toilet plunger.[18] And there
is another who has been offended by a prurient look or genital exhibition or
perhaps even a verbal proposition requesting fellatio.[19] The first has internal
injuries requiring hospitalization and surgery, the second has suffered an in-
dignity but no physical abuse.

If violence is defined as a collision between semiological systems, the
prima facie distinction between the presence and absence of physical damage
to body or property atrophies. It atrophies because the damage referred to,
that which is signified, can never be *present*, even to witnesses or the victims
themselves.

What can be inferred from this example? Within the context of semiological reductionism—in which all meaning derives from transcendental
violence—violence atrophies as a measure of moral judgment. *In fact, transcendental violence itself, conceived as a violation of ipseity, is parasitic upon
a latent appeal to some form of presence just because ipseity presupposes the
presence of a being whose meaning is irreducible to any string of signifiers,
but which can be the subject of experience and cognition.*

The philosophical mistake of semiological reductionism illustrated by the
examples offered lies in a basic error in reasoning, a non sequitur. From the
true premise that language, as the vehicle of culture, pervades the entirety of
human experience, one infers that the significance of all persons, places, and
events is *exclusively* determined by the cultural forms or signifiers that inform
our experience of them. The non sequitur resides in the claim that meaning
derives exclusively from signifiers. To arrive at this conclusion, one needs the
additional premise, supplied by radical forms of transcendental epistemology, that meaning (or significance or the relations among persons, places,
and events) is ideal, always and only the projection of immanent forms such
as the concepts and categories constituted by signifiers. This premise has
the effect of ruling out the possibility that the persons, places, and events

themselves play a crucial role in the formation and application of immanent forms or signifiers. It forecloses the thesis, defended here, that to call a given creature a cat is determined in some measure by the nature of the beast itself, and that the same is true of all objects of experience, even though they may be as ambiguous as human sexual behavior and the motives or intentions influencing its various forms.

Ambiguity resides in the multideterminability of things, in the fact that things can be interpreted in the context of a host of competing systems of signifiers. Judgment, the ineluctable element in all moral assessment, is the process of determining which of the competing systems of signifiers, or schemas of interpretation, best fits the case at hand. And that requires empirical research, the attempt to assemble evidence that favors one interpretation above its competitors. The fact that evidence is also ambiguous and multideterminable complicates the process of judgment. It is also true that evidence can be compelling: eyewitness testimony, fingerprints on the murder weapon, presidential DNA in the traces of semen that might have been found on Monica Lewinsky's clothing.[20]

In assessing the many sources of evidence in cases of violence, there are two that are both highly relevant and highly ambiguous: one concerns the suffering of the victim, the other concerns the intentions of the agent. I have argued that the fundamental tenets of semiological reductionism exclude both sources. Now I must try to show that we do, in fact, have access to them.

Within the context of the ethics of reversibility,[21] where I am capable of direct experience of another—where I can directly perceive the intentions of others in their bodily comportment, where it is possible for me to sense the sense of another's sensing of me—that perceptual experience provides an evidential basis for judgments I may make about it. And, given the phenomenon of context, the evidence can be supported by other evidence relevant to the first, other evidence that is in principle communal and accessible to third parties.[22] Within the context of the ethics of reversibility, it would be possible, at least in principle, for jurors to decide whether an act of sexual harassment involving looking had taken place. This is not to deny the ambiguity that pervades experience, not to assert that clarity is anything more than a goal to be approximated; it is, however, to claim that there are grounds for judgment and that these grounds, being commonly accessible, are capable of eliciting agreement from others. It would be possible to make a fallible but still nonarbitrary judgment as to whether the plaintiff's claim was true. In the other case, the fact of sodomy could be much more easily established because the evidence is far more tangible and concrete, that is, perceptible. And, in both cases, the degree of severity of punishment in the case of guilt could also be assigned in a nonarbitrary way: jurors could assess the degree of damage, not only through evidence, but also through reversibility, the human capacity to feel the pain of those who suffer.

3.

Back to the question of violence, the question of whether violence is intrinsically bad or value-neutral.

We have before us two theoretical edifices that support the thesis of the inevitability of violence in human action. One, the Marxist position, is a materialism: all action in a common situation violates others by its material impact upon their bodies and lives. The other, the deconstructionist position, is a transcendental idealism: signification itself violates ipseity. Taken together, they erode the distinction between violent and nonviolent human action, and thus obscure the issue of whether violence is itself morally objectionable. The classical alternative to violence is discourse, but if discourse itself is conceived as intrinsically violent, the recourse to discourse is, at best, but a shift from one modality of violence to another. If all action is violent, violence atrophies as a useful category in the moral evaluation of human behavior.

The failure of both positions lies in their radicality, their global pronouncements in a domain where discernment and judgment are essential. This failure is not without merit. Marx reminds us that every action has a political dimension: the baker is not as close to armed conflict as the general or the covert insurgent, but no war or guerrilla insurgency was ever waged without tacit consent and logistical support from the noncombatant infrastructure. And deconstruction has succeeded in demonstrating the pervasive and insidious effects of systems of signifiers operating beneath the level of deliberation and awareness: no war or insurgency was ever waged that did not draw its fervor from inchoate systems of symbols. As George Bernard Shaw once said, a good cry is worth half the battle.

Granting that, there are still consequential differences between generals and bakers, ideologues and poets; history judges them differently. International war crimes tribunals punish combatants and, for the most part, leave the civilian infrastructure alone. The distinctions operating here can find no ground in global pronouncements and radical theses. How do we assign moral responsibility when it is a matter of the violence of the pen and the sword? How should we?

The primordial ground of moral assessment is the transfer of corporeal schema, the recognition of another human body as like unto oneself, coupled with the transitivity of pathos.[23] This recognition or identification of living bodies across the difference of spatial separation is founded upon the phenomenon of the reversibility of flesh. Violence, as the forceful imposition of one will upon another, is a refusal to respect and honor difference or ipseity, that is, a refusal of the mutuality revealed through the perceptual intertwining of flesh.

The transitivity of pathos is not exclusively positive, but rather runs the gamut from love through hatred to indifference. Indeed, the very recognition that grounds love also grounds hatred, intimacy being a condition for intensity of both positive and negative pathos. The hypothesis that informs my present thinking is that neither can appear in pure form: no love without its shadow, no hatred without affinity.[24] I cannot develop this thought here, and can only set it forth as a postulate: intensity of pathos is inversely proportional to distance in psychic and physical space.[25] Nor can I explore the psychosocial motivations of vengeance and threat; I can only stipulate as fact that we do inflict damage on one another, that the threat posed by others who differ significantly from oneself can be real as well as imaginary. The affinities that promote friendship are mirrored by differences that generate enmity; both are grounded in recognition and reversibility: I can sense your hostility as directly as I can sense your amity. (Of course, these perceptions are far from apodictic and discernment is crucial; as Freud pointed out, the reality principle is essential to survival among all higher primates, ourselves included.)

Given the reality of hostile others, given a threat that is genuine, consequential, imminent, and beyond mediation, violence will occur. Terror abounds—we have no dearth of instances—and when terror touches us, it co-opts, engages us one way or another; terror also preempts, can narrow our real alternatives down to the primordial choice between fight and flight. Whether or not it is always preferable to negotiate, it is not always possible. To attempt to negotiate in the teeth of an implacable foe may sometimes be heroic; at other times it may be fatally stupid.

On these grounds, I am prepared to argue in favor of justifiable fights, justifiable recourses to violent means.[26] But that is tangential to the question of violence as I have posed it here, that is, the question of whether violence is intrinsically bad. My conclusion is that violence is, indeed, intrinsically bad, even when it is warranted and can be justified. In a fierce fight, the victors do not walk away unscathed; those who are not killed are marked or maimed.

There can be "good fights" and "just wars." But the injunction against moral binaries is well taken: good people die in wars and everybody gets injured in a fight. There is no purity, but there is moral vindication. Some acts of violence are justifiable, and some are irredeemable. And there is a third class rife with imponderables. As Merleau-Ponty puts it: "All action and all love are haunted by the expectation of an account which will transform them into their truth. In short, they are haunted by the expectation of the moment at which it will finally be known just what the situation was."[27] This means, among other things, that it may take a long time for the vindicating or condemning judgment to consolidate historically. And every case is always open for review: those who are celebrated at one time may be ridiculed or condemned at another.[28]

If violence can, in some instances, be vindicated, then the violence of an action is, *eo ipso*, insufficient grounds for its moral condemnation. But its intrinsic badness also means that violence is, *eo ipso*, the court of last resort, the least favorable alternative, something to be avoided, a moral negative. Violence is harmful, but there are other things that are worse. To master the means of violence is to confront the invitation to abuse it; not to master the means is to deliver that invitation to others. As I read history, there seems always to be some who have been willing to accept the invitation, to exploit weakness.

Given the negativity intrinsic to violence, mediation is always preferable if not always possible. The ultimate ground of mediation is truth. Truth commands assent, and hence can provide a common measure across differences in perspective. Discourse can conceal truth as well as reveal it. Discourse as falsification and dissimulation is, no doubt, a form of violence. But discourse of itself is not originary violence; fallible as it is, it is our prime recourse against violence. As disclosure of truth, as expression of a perspective,[29] discourse allows us to measure conflicting perspectives against a nondiscursive and obtruding perceptual reality that provides a measure among them. We are all openings upon the world, openings separated by differences in perspective. Through the reversibility of transfer of corporeal schema, we are capable of seeing through eyes other than our own. Through the reversibility of discourse, through the listening that opens us to otherness, we have the option of transcending the biases that separate us and discovering a common ground.[30] Discourse can create meaning and establish relations, to be sure, but that creation is mimetic: the viability across perspectives of discursive meaning has its measure in the world. Meaning derives from the world: From what other source could it come?

CONCLUSION

Let me begin with two disclaimers: I do not deny that discourse can be violent, or that some instances of discourse are more violent than some instances of physical injury. Spanking a child to enforce a precept that will guide the child toward his or her own higher interests is far different, far less violent, than to teach the child through shame that he or she is worthless. My thesis depends rather on the assertion that not all acts of discourse are necessarily violent. Think of a weather report: it does not do justice to either sunshine or rain, certainly not to a hurricane or a moonrise, but in violating the ipseity of these events, it benignly helps us to dress appropriately and provides work for poets. Still, pressing questions remain.

Is it always preferable to choose the least violent option? Is discourse always preferable to physical means? Can this distinction between pen and sword, diplomatic and military means, rational discourse and brute force, ultimately be sustained?

I have characterized violence as the imposition of one will upon another contrary to the volition of the latter. Given the ethics of reversibility, the recognition of the will of another embodied intelligence reinforced with the resonance of pathos, the suffering of the patient is shared and constitutes a negativity that dissuades. Good parents avoid violence and maximize co-option whenever that is possible, and do so for the sake of their own sensibilities as well as those of their child. Given that children require discipline to develop their capacities for reasoning, a program of rearing that completely eschews violence may serve as an ideal, albeit one that cannot be fully realized: babies do not willingly forsake the breast, do not seek to control their processes of evacuation voluntarily, have to be taught to respect and honor the legitimate needs and wishes of others.

The threat of a rogue, be it state or individual, might be attributed to infantility equipped with machinery of destruction. One seeks—if one can—to discipline rogues. In the best case, one educates the headstrong infant to recognize that the locus of its genuine long-term interest lies in the universal, that is, in the ideal state of affairs that minimizes the suffering of all (as opposed to a de facto universal that may not be genuinely universal at all but merely serves the interests of a currently prevailing power). It is well if the benign parental figure[31] in this scenario is equipped with the means of reinforcement but is appropriately reluctant to deploy them. Failing that, there is only moral suasion and the long-term power of truth. Only history can determine whether that power is sufficient; and history, one hopes, is without end. My optimism here is tempered by the awareness that individuals have always suffered in the process of historical change.

My answer to the first question is, thus, affirmative: the optimal course is always the one that genuinely seeks to enlist the freedom and reason of all parties.

My answers to the second two questions are far more ambiguous—and necessarily so, given the nature of the answer I have given to the first. The optimal course is not always open, and the crucial tests come when it is not. The difference between violent and nonviolent means is not abrupt, but a matter of degree and circumstance. A big stick is a strong argument, even when it remains resting on the shoulder of might. There is merit to the argument that contends that discursive (or psychological) suasion is parasitic upon the peripheral presence of real (or physical) power, that brute force is finally decisive. For the individual, at least, death is an absolute to which there is no riposte, and brute force is vectored toward death.

Notwithstanding the power of this argument, however, I contend that the distinction between physical and psychological force is nonultimate. If time allowed, I would defend my belief that beneath this distinction there are others at work such as those between immediate and long-term consequences, and between individual and global effects. Martyrdom is a case in which the violent death of an individual (for example, Socrates, Jesus, Martin Luther King Jr.) is decisive, to be sure, but decisive in exactly the opposite way from that intended by the perpetrators of the violent acts.

In the first section of this essay, I quoted Merleau-Ponty's assertion that "between men considered as pure consciousnesses there would . . . be no reason to choose [between violent and non-violent action]." This is admittedly a contra-factual hypothetical statement and subject to criticism on those grounds, but the point it makes is crucial. The patient of violence is a sentient body, a corporeal intentionality for whom the line between intelligence and embodiment is always only provisional and discernible only under specific circumstances. We do not go to a psychiatrist with an aching tooth, but the dentist has to contend with our pain and our fear. My thesis is that there is a spectrum of psychophysical force bounded by the impossibility of purity on either end: no purely physical force, no purely psychological force, but always an intertwining in which one aspect or the other may weigh more heavily.

This continuum of psychophysical force does not coincide with the continuum from greater to lesser violence in action. As noted in the case of spanking or shaming a child, there can be an action that is more psychological than physical on one continuum, but still belongs toward the violent end of the other. This exception to what may otherwise be a reliable rule has important consequences for the thesis being set forth here.

Although the threat of brute force subtends most cases of psychological violence, it is minimal in cases falling in the domain of pride and shame. Although it is a human weakness to behave shamefully when fearful of physical harm, it is a prime source of human nobility to go in harm's way for the sake of pride and the need to act in conformance with one's highest ideals. Our heroes large and small are ones who have chosen to suffer physical harm rather than shame, to bear the ennobling scar on their flesh. Conversely, we may be driven by ill-founded pride and psychological-historical commitment to inadequately considered ideals to use force in shameful ways.[32]

Here we arrive at the thought that has guided the broad strokes of this chapter from the start, the thought that the question of violence is finally a question of love-hate-indifference. Nobility, acting in accordance with one's highest ideals, ideals founded ultimately on the pathos of reversibility, is the locus of the criteria by which to judge violence. The Greek word inadequately translated into English as "nobility" is "*to kalon.*" The Greek idea expresses an ideal of comportment, prior to any distinction between inner and outer or spirit and body, designated by the famous triad that names the object of desire: the good, the true, the beautiful. *To kalon*, as it informs the flesh of the world, is what we love, what we need, lack, want, and desire in others as well as ourselves. It is the basis on which we judge all things, including violence.[33]

· ·

CHAPTER FIVE

DOES MERLEAU-PONTY'S ONTOLOGY PREDELINEATE A POLITICS?

I. PHILOSOPHICAL CONTEXT

Merleau-Ponty's philosophy is situated in the context of the transcendental-ism of contemporary continental thought. The main thesis of transcendental philosophy is that human experience is mediated by formal structures vari-ously conceived as categories of understanding or essences or *Existenzialen* or linguistic signs, etcetera. When questions arise concerning the origin or ground or warrant of these formal structures, transcendental philosophy di-vides along the axes of a binary opposition: absolute ground or absence of ground, *Grund* or *Abgrund*, onto-theology or nihilism. Neither axis is ca-pable of providing foundations for human knowledge or action: human fini-tude precludes access to absolute grounds, but the total absence of grounds precludes foundations of any description. Current attempts to generate non-foundational guidelines for thought and action merely put the problem at one remove: guidelines based on unrelieved negativity must ultimately be ar-bitrary, derived from some variant of the *argumentum ad ignorantiam*, and fail for that reason, since ignorance cannot provide viable guidance.

Politics presupposes ethics. I take this to be self-evident but, to temper the dogmatic tone of the pronouncement, will say that any attempt to order the polis betrays a desire for order of some sort (the limiting case being abject anarchism), and that desire, like all others, projects values. The limiting case establishes the point: to make a case for the absence of any arch is to engage in ethical argumentation.

However one defines ethics or moral philosophy, if one demands of it, as I do, that it be relevant to the assessment of human behavior, either one's own or that of others, then it must provide foundations for that assessment. It must provide means of inquiring about available options for future actions and choosing among them, and also provide means of evaluating decisions made and actions performed. Absent such foundations, the notion of responsibility loses all content.

The conclusion I draw from these general reflections is that, if contemporary Continental philosophy is to be capable of generating an ethics worthy of the name, it must find and articulate a tertium quid, a way around or beneath the mutually exclusive alternatives of crypto-onto-theology or self-dissembling nihilism. I will argue here that Merleau-Ponty does point the way toward this third alternative by demonstrating that the exclusive disjunction of *Grund* and *Abgrund* does not exhaust the realm of philosophical possibility, and that finite grounds can be found. Finally, I will argue that the very attempt to found values on finite grounds does, indeed, predelineate a politics, albeit a politics that may not be immediately recognizable as such.

2. HISTORICAL CONTEXT

Why try to generate grounds for political theory by extrapolating from the values implicit in Merleau-Ponty's ontology when he wrote two books and a series of essays devoted to politics? My answer to this question is that Merleau-Ponty's explicitly political writing is situated within a discourse and historical setting framed by Hegel, Marx, Stalin, and the crisis of the Communist Party in post–World War II France. The problems Merleau-Ponty addressed demanded treatment in the lexicon that generated them, a lexicon structured by Marx's appropriation of Hegel's understanding of historical process and how it addresses the polarization of universality and particularity. My contention here is that Merleau-Ponty's explicitly political treatises suffer from being framed within this polarity, this understanding of historical process, instead of attempting to undercut the binary opposition that subtends it. The central thesis of this paper is that Merleau-Ponty nonetheless does manage to undercut the dualistic universality-particularity opposition, but does so in writings less constrained by the lexicon of the political debate dominating his situation, writings that explicitly take up broader issues of intersubjectivity, alterity, expression, and communication. It is in these works that one can find conceptions of history and being-with that generate values capable of supporting a politics freed from some of the constraints of the Hegelian-Marxian lexicon.

With the defeat of Nazism, postwar European intellectuals on the left wing of the political spectrum were committed to Marxist principles and the Communist revolution. The revelation of atrocities committed by Stalin in the name of Communism produced an ideological crisis. Dialectical materialism, as a historical force, necessitated a movement toward the universal concretized in the proletariat and pointed toward the inherent telos of humanism: the *Aufhebung* of terror, the end of humanity's violation of itself. Violence had long been an issue for Marxist thought, which both affirmed it as a necessary means for historical change and negated it as a source of injustice and human suffering. The problem here was to discriminate between good and bad violence, between means that were vindicated by their ends and those that could not be justified [as elaborated in the previous chapter].[1] Stalin's use of violence produced a division within the Communist Party intellectuals who believed it to be justifiable and those who did not. This schism then articulated itself around the issue of the historical roles of the party elite and the proletariat: Which one is to drive historical progress? As Merleau-Ponty puts it in *Humanism and Terror*: "We [are faced here] with abstract alternatives: either history is made spontaneously or else it is the leaders who make it through cunning and strategy—either one respects the freedom of the proletarians and the revolution is a chimera or else one judges for them what they want and the Revolution becomes Terror" (117).

As is well known, the differences between Merleau-Ponty and Sartre on this issue were critical factors in their bitter split. Sartre, in his typical style of polarized thinking, accepted the dilemma and chose between the opposed options: he chose allegiance to the party. Merleau-Ponty, in his typical rejection of binary opposition, sought to undercut the dilemma by finding the ambiguous ground beneath the polarized abstractions. The operative idea here is that of situated freedom, heralded in the chapter on "Freedom" in *Phenomenology of Perception* and brought to bear on the issues raised by Stalinism in *Humanism and Terror*.

In his exquisitely lucid "Translator's Introduction" to *Adventures of the Dialectic*, Joseph Bien articulates Merleau-Ponty's response to the party-versus-proletariat debate and, in a deft two-paragraph sketch, points in the direction of the broader thinking to which I just alluded. Revolutions go astray when they generate bureaucracies that separate strategic and ideological leadership (the party) from the engine of historical process (the proletariat). Bien says that Merleau-Ponty realizes that the mistake lies in continuing to adhere to the ideal of a homogeneous society, a society in which conflicts at the level of particularity have been resolved in a dialectical elimination of alterity achieved in the universality of a single non-class, the proletariat.

The solution lies in "the possibility of changing the social relations within one's own lived situation" (*AD*, xxvii) and pointing toward another ideal. Not an ideal configured around mediations between the axes of history, party, and proletariat, but, as Bien puts it, "a mediation among men for a totality which is man. . . . We must renounce the proletariat as the necessary vehicle by which man will overcome the barriers that exist between himself and his fellow men, [and] instead of looking at man's relationship to the production process, . . . look at his social relations" more globally (xxvii–xxviii). Bien then concludes: "Merleau-Ponty points us this way when he speaks of situated consciousnesses. The 'human condition' is to be a historical being in situation and to find that one's situation is not unique but opens onto and demands others for its own definition" (xxviii).

Although I find difficulties in his lexicon of "mediation" and "totality" (about which more later), I think Bien is exactly on target when he recognizes that alterity is not simply the source of conflict that has to be overcome, but is also intrinsic to the solution to the problem of conflict among humans. He is also on target when he expands the domain of being-with one another beyond economics to include "language, work, law, and art . . . [in an] appeal to culture as the *expression* of man's historical situation with respect to all mankind" (*AD*, xxix; emphasis added).

3. UNIVERSALITY AND PARTICULARITY

Simply put, the problem for Merleau-Ponty is Hegel: Hegel mediated through Marx, but primarily Hegel. For Hegel, particularity is negativity, a negative to be negated. Kierkegaard's proto-existentialist critique of Hegel consists largely in the attempt to restore to particularity the positivity of individual differentiation. Merleau-Ponty, the existentialist, stands in tension with Merleau-Ponty, the Marxist. This tension is exacerbated by Merleau-Ponty's commitment to embodiment in general and the particularity of the lived body in particular: in the passage to the return of the Absolute *Geist*, Hegel must find a way to transcend embodiment, the body classically defined as differentiating materiality. Marx's dialectical materialism does not provide an adequate means to reconcile Hegel's idealistic conception of the universal with Merleau-Ponty's commitment to embodiment: it translates the dialectic into an economic framework, to be sure, but its commitment to the proletariat, as the historical concretion of the universal, is finally a commitment to the obliteration of difference, specifically the economic difference of class, and does not satisfy the Kierkegaardian requirement for assigning positive value to the individual, as such.

In a piece titled "East-West Encounter," the transcript of a conference held in Venice in 1956,[2] Merleau-Ponty spoke of "a new kind of universalism." As opposed to the universalism of "bourgeois philosophy"—"an abstract reason that imagined one could, on the basis of principles truly common to all human beings and independent of all situations, pronounce truths and discover values"—this new universalism would encompass "the idea that if we place ourselves on the level of what men *live*, it is possible . . . that living men will freely express what they live, and that they will find themselves going beyond the boundaries of their class or society" (*TD*, 29). Merleau-Ponty associates this free expression with "the notion of engagement."

Not the Marxist notion of engagement, which "would oblige us to consider the act of writing as an action like any other [and therefore] enacted according to rules . . . of action in the political sense of the word," not an engagement encumbered by the responsibility assigned to the writer by Lenin to "keep silent, or even lie, rather than be disloyal to the institution" (*TD*, 30). Such engagement would leave "no reasonable choice for writers," they would "simply have nothing more to write" (31). The engagement Merleau-Ponty affirms is quite the opposite. "Nothing would justify a choice that would oblige the writer to lie. There is, in an immanent manner, a convergence [rather than a divergence] between the values of culture and those of action. The writer does not have to choose between them, to put the one set of values before the other, to subordinate one set to the other" (31). Nonetheless, although the writer is not constrained by antecedent ideological commitments, what he or she writes does have "a political bearing; . . . [it] has the potential to teach those who read a certain way of situating themselves within the world, and consequently a certain political way of being" (31).

The key ideas here are situation, individual freedom, expression, and political consequence. Somehow, under the "new universalism," individuals would be free to write (and, one assumes, express themselves in other cultural or artistic forms) about the situations in which they find themselves in such a way as to affect how other individuals perceive their situations and act upon them. How is this freedom of individual expression related to the issue of universality and particularity?

A partial answer may be found in Merleau-Ponty's 1952 essay, "Indirect Language and the Voices of Silence":

> The Hegelian dialectic is what we call by another name the phe-
> nomenon of expression, which gathers itself up and launches itself
> again through the mystery of rationality. And we would undoubt-
> edly recover the concept of history in the true sense of the term if we
> were to get used to modeling it after the example of the arts and lan-
> guage. For the fact that each expression is closely connected within
> one single order to every other expression brings about the junc-
> tion of the individual and the universal. The central fact to which
> the Hegelian dialectic returns in a hundred ways is that we do not
> have to choose between the *pour soi* and the *pour autrui*, between
> thought according to us and according to others, but that at the mo-
> ment of expression the other to whom I address myself and I who
> express myself are incontestably linked together. (S, 73)

This is a straightforward statement of a common theme in Merleau-Ponty:
language and expression have the power to overcome individual differences
and generate unity. Language reveals the world and the world has the unity
of style, hence in speaking I can beckon you to take up my vantage, look at
the world from here, and leave it to the world to convince you. Expression
can generate accord: it can "bring about the junction of the individual and
the universal."

Merleau-Ponty's reference to Hegelian dialectic here is not accidental and,
I will claim, manifests a tension in Merleau-Ponty's thought. Hegelian dialectic sublates or negates the negative of difference. Accord is conceived as
the overcoming of alterity. This stands in tension with the thought developed
above that alterity has positive value, that it is part of the solution to the
problem of conflict that is its negative dimension. If we talk long enough—or
signify in other ways—we will come to agreement and share a common or
unitary perspective on the world.

Such optimism is dampened by the realization that dialogue generates as
well as mediates conflict. Dialogical intimacy can intensify violence as well as
mitigate it. The ethnic groups in the Balkans, in Ireland, in the Middle East,
etcetera, have been in dialogue for centuries. It is my view that the hatred
that has festered over these years is fostered by dialogical intimacy and tribal
memory. My country recently fought in some of the fiercest wars in human
history, World War II, Korea, and Vietnam. We are now closely allied with
Germany and Japan, and relatively cordial ties with Vietnam, and even North
Korea, are being established. The difference is distance and the possibility

of forgetfulness it affords as generations embittered by war are displaced by generations in search of peace. The Serbs and Croats that clashed in World War II came into violent confrontation again just ten years ago: that fight has been simmering and erupting throughout modern history, nurtured by geographical proximity, cultural intimacy, and a common language. My point is that dialogue, of itself, is insufficient to move us toward the "new universality" and mediate the differences that produce conflict.

The problem here is that the "new universality" is still a Hegelian universality aimed at unity and totality, hence intolerant of alterity. The problem here is that some kind of cultural homogeneity remains presupposed as a condition for coexistence. This presupposition must be challenged, and can be challenged on the basis of fundamental doctrines in Merleau-Ponty's teaching: most relevant here are the doctrines of situated freedom and alterity (or *écart*). Freedom, the correlate of Merleau-Ponty's widely misunderstood conception of rationality, is always situated in space, time, and culture. That follows as a corollary to the thesis of human finitude. Culture is the glue of community, and community presupposes limit, hence alterity; that is, community is exclusive of and defined by its other, its outside. Conceived in this way, the very idea of community renders the notion of global community oxymoronic. Alterity is a condition for existence: our bodies are separated in space and time by the peripheries of our skins and lifetimes. Dialogue cannot overcome that separation, indeed, alterity is what necessitates and sustains dialogue. Angels neither talk nor sing: they don't have to and couldn't if they wanted to. Which, being in perfect accord, they wouldn't.

Alterity generates conflict. How can it provide any positive value enabling us to contend with the conflict it generates?

The contemporary answer to this question is well known. We are told that we must learn, not only to tolerate difference, but to celebrate it. Totalizing universality is always oppressive because it always takes the form of domination of all perspectives by one whose privilege rests simply on de facto power. Humans, unlike angels, can sing. But always in different registers; it is just a matter of learning to harmonize: let the diversity of notes be cause for celebration. A pretty thought. How is this to be brought about? How do we foster harmony and minimize cacophony? Well, there has to be a common score. Once again, we are right back to totalizing universality. If all voices are to be heard, the predictable result is a shouting match, and verbal warfare has always been the prelude to violence. No matter which side you are on, Durban was scary.[3]

History gives us only one model of relatively long-lasting peace. Serbs and Croats didn't fight when Tito was running the show. Under Alexander, the caesars, Genghis Khan, and their ilk, there were extended periods of peace. Oppressive to many, no doubt, but relatively tranquil for a while. The more absolute the governing power, the fewer the fights. One doesn't mediate irreconcilable conflicts; one simply stifles them. At this point in world history, conditions are ripe for peace: there is but one superpower, and it just happens to have the best form of government ever to exist on earth. Pax Americana. We are the Leviathan.

But of course we cannot deduce from Merleau-Ponty's teachings a justification for taking charge and bringing peace through a new world order. Such a notion is antithetical to all of his writings and his deepest sensibilities. So where is the positive value in alterity capable of counterbalancing the inevitability of conflict brought about by alterity?

4. EXPRESSION AND TRUTH

The answer I favor lies hidden in Merleau-Ponty's discourse on expression and the responsibility of the writer to defy all political coercion that would force him or her to lie, the responsibility to address the limits of his or her situation and transgress them, the responsibility to take the circumscription that always attends freedom as something to be contested. It is this thought that takes Merleau-Ponty beyond Hegel, beyond the Hegelian dialectic of mediation, beyond Hegelian *Sittlichkeit*, and beyond the oppression of Hegelian universalism. Hegel did not adequately understand the problem. The problem is not only the conflict produced by alterity; the problem is also the use of violence to resolve the conflict. Conflict conceived, as Nietzsche did, in terms of agon, or, as Plato did, in terms of his kind of dialectic (the contest of ideas), is the engine of progress, change for the better. It fosters the agon in which a better set of ideas defeats a lesser set of ideas, even if that lesser set of ideas happens to be the conventional wisdom, the de facto universal, of a given time and place.

There is a pessimistic, misconceived notion of hermeneutics beneath much of the discourse in Continental philosophy today that assumes that it is impossible to see through and beyond the limits of one's language and culture, that we are inevitably trapped within the transcendental horizons that establish the de facto universals around which our communities are constructed.

When separate communities differ with regard to custom, ritual, cuisine, dress, and other such relatively benign modes of comportment, the politically correct attitude to take is one of tolerance or even affirmation: *de gustibus non disputandum est*, and furthermore, the dispute would be fruitless, each side being committed to its tastes and incapable of seeing beyond its ideological framework. When, however, alterity obtrudes in dramatic ways and communities collide over such forced issues as abortion, gay and lesbian rights, territorial boundaries, class privilege, distribution of wealth, social justice, and so forth, the politics of tolerance break down, leaving but one recourse: the deployment of power and violence. The sanctimonious appeal to dialogue, although omnipresent, is thoroughly hypocritical because the ground or measure needed to adjudicate between conflicting perspectives has been ruled out in advance by the pessimistic premise of hermeneutic blindness. In this framework, dialogical encounter can only be semiological violence, the attempt to impose a value-laden system of signifiers by nondialogical strategies of enforcement and coercion. Two examples in our profession are the guidelines for nonsexist language published by the American Philosophical Association and the Society for Phenomenology and Existential Philosophy, which are enforced by rejection of papers that fail to comply: Nietzsche and Freud, among hosts of others, would be silenced today.

The point here is that the de facto universal operating within a community is intrinsically oppressive to minority voices, and that this oppression is exacerbated by the pessimistic understanding of hermeneutic circularity. This is the Hegelian universal at work: the attempt to achieve unity by negating alterity, and carrying out that project through a transcendental formalism aimed at its own arrogant onto-theological ideality posited as the end of philosophy.

There is another universal, another understanding of hermeneutics and transcendental constitution that has antecedents in Kant and Hegel but has been confused with the mistaken project of imposing de facto unity by formal enforcement. Kant called this alternative "the ideal of pure reason." It is the universal as regulative ideal. Under my interpretation, the universal can function as a regulative ideal, not by appealing as Kant did to divine omniscience, but by appealing to the power of finite truth to command assent. There is much still to be learned in the sphere of virus research, but the power of its current findings is sufficient to command more assent than the original explication for influenza as occasioned by the influence of heavenly bodies. You pray; I'll get a flu shot.

Merleau-Ponty addressed the issue of the universal and its relation to finite truth throughout his writings. Attune yourself to it, and you will find it
everywhere. The text I will take up here is from the chapter on "Interrogation
and Dialectic" in *The Visible and the Invisible*. Interrogation, as I understand
it, is the process of questioning the world in the process of seeking solutions
to our problems. It involves openness and wonder; it is Merleau-Ponty's alternative to Husserl's *epoché*: the resolve to look to the world and listen, to
prepare ourselves to hear something different from what we have seen before
and taken for granted. It requires the courage to identify our presuppositions
and expose them to the challenge of worldly transcendence. It is experimen-
tal philosophy; it involves expression, testing, critique, and judgment as the
project of subsuming one's findings under the most appropriate conceptual
schema one can find or create, even if and especially when that collides with
what is most familiar and comfortable. It is the affirmation of alterity.

In the text I just mentioned, Merleau-Ponty appeals to interrogation to
discriminate between good and bad dialectic. Bad dialectic is Hegelian formalism, the imposition of a transcendental schema on historical unfolding,
the commitment to an a priori structure come what may. "The bad dialectic
[is] that which imposes an external law and framework upon the content and
restores for its own uses the pre-dialectical thought. Dialectical thought by
principle excludes all *extrapolation*, since it teaches that there can always be
a supplement of being in being. . . . [Bad dialectic] is what happens as soon
as the *meaning* of the dialectical movement is defined apart from the concrete
constellation" (VI, 94).

What is good dialectic? It is self-critical interrogation that opens itself to
changing its presuppositions:

> There is no good dialectic but that which criticizes itself and sur-
> passes itself as a separate statement; the only good dialectic is the
> hyperdialectic . . . a thought that . . . is capable of reaching truth
> because it envisages without restriction the plurality of the rela-
> tionships and what has been called ambiguity. . . . The good dia-
> lectic is that which is conscious of the fact that every *thesis* is an
> idealization, that Being is not made up of idealizations or of things
> said, . . . but of bound wholes where signification never is except in
> tendency. . . . What we seek is a dialectical definition . . . that must
> rediscover the being that lies before the cleavage operated by reflec-
> tion, about it, on its horizon, not outside of us and not in us, but

there where the two movements cross, there where "there is" something. (*VI*, 94–95)

Here, in the chiasm of inside and outside, is Merleau-Ponty's tertium quid,
the finite ground beneath the abstractions of absolute ground and abyss. It
is the "there is" that is not foreign to us because it obtrudes and encroaches
upon us, but, for the same reason, is not entirely constituted by us, either.
Recall what Merleau-Ponty said at the 1956 East-West conference: "Our
concern [is] the definition of truth, the definition of culture, the practice of
truth and culture" (*TD*, 31). I take "the practice of truth and culture" to refer
to art, conceived broadly as creative expression, as the process of generating
new ways of perceiving, feeling, and understanding the emergent situations
in which we find ourselves. Staying with Merleau-Ponty's example of writing, what the writer expresses is a particular way of seeing, feeling, and assessing his or her situation. It has a political bearing because the descriptive
"is" frequently implies a prescriptive "ought." Some forms of description are
intrinsically value-laden: "Cigarette smoke contains carbon monoxide," for
example. Or "More than three thousand people were killed in the terrorist
attacks on September 11."

The prescriptive force in both examples is a demand that something be
done. What is to be done, however, remains to be specified. That depends
upon further investigations that generate more precise descriptions, which, in
turn, suggest a range of possible responses. Given that situations are always
ambiguous, there are always competitive descriptions, conflicting narratives
that portend differing responses. This creates an agon. Merleau-Ponty's venture beyond Hegel consists in asserting that the grounds for adjudicating
among the alternatives for action are to be found, not in a supervenient formalism based on the metarule always to negate difference or suppress alterity,
but on the unpredictable nature of the concrete situation itself.

In the relatively easy task of deciding what to do about the fact that cigarette smoke contains carbon monoxide, medical research is needed. In the
second case, a much wider range of research is mandated to answer such
questions as who is responsible for the attack, and what form of response
is appropriate. Noam Chomsky's descriptions and prescriptions differ radically from those being proposed by President Bush and his advisers. These
are but two contestants in the huge agon now being aired before the jury of
the world at large. Is the real culprit, the real enemy, to be found within or
without the community who suffered the loss of life on September 11? Or is

the true source of misery both within and without? Differing descriptions of the reality will suggest differing prescriptions for responsive action. The coalitions that form on the various sides of the debate will be determined by the relative power of the competitive descriptions to command assent. Ultimately, in the court of history, that is, the world court deliberating over time, it will be the power of truth that gains the greatest support. The problem for us, now, is to perceive that truth as clearly as we can in the short span of time available before we need to act, as we remind ourselves that inaction is action in the privative mode and generates its own consequences. The decisions and actions we confront are forced.

Merleau-Ponty can't tell us what to do now any more than he could tell France what to do in the late fifties. Or any less. Which is just to restate his thesis that the emergent situation demands an appropriate response that cannot be predelineated by some historical a priori, by some Hegelian formalism. Indeed, the novelty of contemporary terrorism demands a vision beyond any de facto universal now sedimented in the heteronomous collection of communities involved.

Merleau-Ponty can, however, set the parameters of debate and offer guidelines. The governing parameter is that of history conceived in terms of becoming as unending conflict, on one hand, and, on the other, the emergence of a better apprehension of truth, one whose power to command assent surpasses its competitors . . . until yet a stronger claim is heard and tried. The guidelines he offers, the value system presupposed in finding an appropriate response, are founded on transfer of corporeal schema and reversibility as the ground phenomenon of ethical behavior. This encompasses but is not reducible to traditional humanism because it extends the range of recognition beyond the human sphere to the flesh of the world.

This ground phenomenon of ethics and politics must be translinguistic just because it is the ground and measure of expression, of how we talk and what we say. If prescription is predelineated in description, if how we describe or narrate the emergent situation prefigures how we respond to it, then the agon between competitive narratives cannot be decided within a given narrative, but requires opening ourselves to some ambiguous thing beyond narration, beneath interpretation. Our organs of sense are configured in such a way that we tend to see the same things—we can actually agree that we are witness to the same event, and we can actually move our bodies to see what the other sees. We can interrogate the situation. That interrogation allows us, not so much to mediate between conflicting perspectives, but rather to move to new and better perspectives capable of transcending the limits of the narratives with which we began. The ambiguity with which we began will give rise to new ambiguities, of course, but interrogation will have made some things clearer. Like who did what and why.

Is this a politics? Not in the traditional sense, because it is predicated on the idea of modulating conflict and violence rather than seeking to eliminate them. [In the previous chapter],[4] I argued the case for differentiating within the sphere of violent confrontation between linguistic and nonlinguistic violence and between combatant and noncombatant participation in the violence. Such distinctions allow one to modulate violence, to attempt to contain and delimit it. I think, following Merleau-Ponty, that is the best we can hope to do. It is always better to debate with words than with more lethal weapons, but sometimes your opponents don't afford you that luxury. It is, I think, the measure of civilization, hence the measure of a politics, to maximize the appeal to truth in the adjudication of conflict. But the appeal to force is primitive, primordial, and always on the horizon as a last resort. Because an enemy can always preempt debate by violent intervention, I do not advocate reducing one's arsenal. But while we develop our weaponry, I think it would also be well to develop our rhetoric, our ability to co-opt our competitors into forms of engagement that produce less misery than war produces.

CHAPTER SIX

MERLEAU-PONTY AND THE ONTOLOGY OF ECOLOGY, OR

APOCALYPSE LATER

What can a philosopher contribute to the contemporary debate about ecology? As philosophers, we have no claim to technical knowledge about how to stop global warming, protect endangered species, or reduce the pollution of our planet's earth, air, and water.

Philosophers provide ways of thinking about things. We are also trained to identify errors in the words, concepts, images, symbols, and the like that guide the ways in which we already think about things. Although some positive theses will emerge toward the end, the main thrust of this paper is critical: I will argue that there are fundamental flaws in the conceptual structures that inconspicuously inform contemporary discourse about our environment.

The very word "ecology" is misleading and should be abandoned. The planet we inhabit is, indeed, our dwelling place, but it is not at all like a house. We build houses to protect ourselves from our surroundings. Most of the people who concern themselves about the environment spend most of their lives in structures designed to provide shelter from wind, rain, fire, and moving earth. Our primary habitat is that part of the world that has been tamed to be fit for human dwelling. David Abram,[1] who knows about such things, tells me that people we regard as more primitive than ourselves and closer to nature also sometimes think of the world at large as a house or congenial dwelling place. Perhaps that is because they, too, have been reared to believe that a superior power created the earth to provide a place for us to live.

That belief reflects the familiar desire to influence (by worship, supplication, and arcane rites) the powers whose sendings take our destinies out of our hands. There are, indeed, awesome powers at work in the universe, but they did not contrive Being for human dwelling and do not operate by transforming the *logos* into reality—although it is well to employ *logoi* in the attempt to understand them. Anthropomorphic design, intention, and intelligence belong in the sphere of *anthropos*, which is but one part intertwined with others in the flesh of the world.[2] So, it would be wise and prudent to think and speak differently about the uncanny place mutating around us. "Ecology" is an inept neologism: what we need to develop has an older name. "Phronesis" resonates with the archaic motives of fear and arrogance, but in a more mature way, governed by a reality principle that seeks understanding. It is not latently informed by a metaphor based on primitive superstition.[3] *Phronesis*, or practical wisdom, is the endeavor to find out how the world works, and to incorporate that understanding into our actions with the hope that it will produce consequences more to our liking than those that follow from acting in ignorance. Or on the basis of superstition.

Merleau-Ponty writes about brute being, and uses terms like "wild" and "savage" to characterize the natural world into which we have been thrust. Unlike his sometime friend and colleague Sartre, who argued that being could have only the significance we impart to it, Merleau-Ponty had a robust sense of the transcendence of the world. For him, being does not lack meaning and oppress us by being sheerly contingent and de trop; rather, it overflows with *sens*, not all of which is congenial to human needs. The world limits our freedom and has its own transcendent fate, which we have no choice but to accommodate, even though we are largely ignorant of it and bereft of reliable information about any origin or destiny it might or might not have.

The French word "*sens*" can be translated into English as "sense" or "meaning" or "direction." "Direction" is a spatial term, but, as such, refers also to time. A one-way street, in French, is *une rue sens unique*, a street with a specific direction of movement through time. My point here is that meaning, as Merleau-Ponty conceives it, is bound up with time, time that is inseparable from space, culture, and nature. Merleau-Ponty's ontology is an ontology of becoming; it asserts the reality of time, and in doing so denies the a-temporality definitive of all ontologies of Being. His is a pivotal point in what I have to say, so I will take a moment to explain it.

Kant and his successors in the tradition of transcendental philosophy espouse various forms of the thesis of the ideality of time, that is, the thesis that time is a formal structure projected onto experience—in Kant's case, by the understanding informed by the pure forms of intuition and governed by the transcendental unity of apperception. Temporal categories should not be applied to the thing in itself because the thing in itself is defined by appeal to the *Ens Realissimus* or *Ens Perfectissimus*, which is a-temporal. Derrida also asserts the ideality of time, but bases his grammatological account on *différance* and the play of signifiers: for him, it is by virtue of the *gramme* (rather than Kant's transcendental unity of apperception) that time is synthesized in human experience.

Merleau-Ponty is initially enticed by this transcendentalism with regard to time, but quickly moves away from it. He does assert the thesis of the primacy of lived time, that is, that all our objectifications of time are grounded in time as perceived, but goes on to acknowledge the reality of natural time. We conceive time as transcending our temporal experience. We think of a time that preceded us and will continue beyond us. And we are correct to do so: archaeology and carbon-14 dating substantiate the transcendence of time, and evolution teaches us that a temporal process led us to perceive time and other things as we do; hence our experience of time presupposes a passage of time that transcends us. This is not to say that the human apprehension of natural time is everlastingly true; quite the contrary, as it is with other things that transcend us, our understanding of time is finite, corrigible, and is being modified right now in physics labs. Nonetheless, our apprehension of natural time is, albeit finite and partial, an apprehension of time itself as it unfolds in the natural world. There is but one time as there is but one space, but there are many aspects of both, and many perspectives upon them, all of which both reveal and obscure the transcendent reality that grounds them.

At first, Merleau-Ponty designates the relationship between lived time and natural time with Husserl's term *Fundierung*, but then subsumes it under his own notion of reversibility. We come to be in natural time and in that coming-to-be develop a capacity to experience it. Lived time, the time of perceptual unfolding, allows us to form an understanding of the time that transcends us, but is itself grounded in that time. Ultimately the two are intertwined in a process of genesis that does not permit the isolation of either in what Husserl called a fulfillable intention.

Given his understanding of time as both transcendental and real, as both immanent and transcendent, Merleau-Ponty is committed to an ontology of becoming: he rejects the belief subtending all ontologies of Being that time is but a human projection and ultimately an illusion.[4]

How does this ontology of becoming based on the thesis of the transcendence of time affect our understanding of ecology? "Profoundly" is the one-word answer, meaning all the way down. But I will start at the surface with the notion of protecting endangered species. Physicists tell us that the sun will burn out in ten to the "whatever" years. Some geologists tell us that another ice age is coming fairly soon. And other sciences of a softer nature predict an even sooner end: if thermonuclear warfare doesn't wipe us out, then biological or chemical warfare will. The best we can hope for is rearguard action that will save the whales and spotted owls for a little while longer. Now, why would we want to do that? Evolution tells us that species mutate, and that some mutations displace their ancestors: no more dinosaurs or three-toed horses. Does it make sense to try to interfere with this process, especially when we have a pretty good idea of our planet's destiny? Why not embrace the new species that emerge as life adapts to changes in global habitats?

Consider one endangered species, *Homo sapiens*. We have come a long way from the Pleistocene. We are now civilized, in some measure at least, and in some sense of the term. That is, we have adapted to living in cities, in the *cives*. Some of us tolerate smog, traffic, crime, police, noise, gang warfare, graffiti, ubiquitous filth, and so forth, and, in short, inure ourselves to close proximity to the other noxious creatures we call fellow human beings. Some of us not only tolerate it, but actually prefer it. Is this a new species? Will it (or has it already) developed discernibly different DNA from persons who are descendants from an unbroken heritage of farmers? Which DNA will the longest survivors bear? Which species or subspecies would we prefer to survive? Note that the judgment to be made here is driven by preference, by the need to be lucid about what one wants.

"Conservation," as the term is used in discourse about ecology, is a curious notion. The Greens are typically regarded as left wing, not conservatives in the political sense who usually prefer capital profit to preserving the habitat of endangered species. People committed to preserving the environment typically repudiate all forms of power generation except some that are derived from sun, wind, and renewable resources. Why not develop supersafe nuclear generators? Because it cannot be done? Because the cost and the risk are too high? How would an environmentally friendly aircraft be powered? How would an environmentally friendly military go about its business? What is to be conserved? What is to be forsaken in the process of conserving what we choose to conserve? Do we deprive lumberjacks of jobs and Weyerhaeuser of profits for the sake of spotted owls? How does one make such decisions and defend them in rational ways? To conserve is to protect something from change: What can be protected from change? Why would one want to do that? And how would we go about grounding our judgments about what to conserve and what to relinquish?

Note that the technical questions of how to deal with the ecosphere have given way to prior questions of a discernibly philosophical nature. What is worth saving? What is worth saving when every attempt at conservation is likely to involve forsaking something else some human beings value?

Surrounding the question of conservation is the question of restoration: patching the ozone layer, cleaning the land and water and air, replanting the forests, cleaning up the mess we have made. Well, then, what do we restore? The way things were back then. But when? Before there was nuclear waste? Before the industrial revolution? Before men and women devised means of exerting control over their surroundings, a process that always involves artifice, hence transformation of nature?

The ancient Greek poets were not the first to characterize their species as the intruder, the corrupter, the species that, by its very nature, upsets *moira*, the cosmic balance, but they provide a familiar exemplar. Is there a cosmogony that does not portray our species as the one that trashed paradise? As Anaximander said, we are the ones who change things; we upset the balance, and we pay penalties for doing so, according to the assessment of time.[5] Time. What goes down, comes round. Like it or not, the karmic debt will be paid. By our very nature, we provoke the nemesis. If you are a Green and want to identify the enemy, look in the mirror.

This is a big idea. Our species is a curse on the environment. We are the species that fouls its own nest, its own *oikos*. We are the ones who, by nature, break natural law.

Three philosophers I know contest this view. The other two are de Sade and Derrida. Derrida does not think there is such a thing as natural law, hence it follows that it cannot be broken. I could refute Derrida by strapping a scuba on him, taking him down sixty feet or so, and inviting him to defy Boyle's law by holding his breath and swimming to the surface. De Sade argued that everything we do occurs in nature, that, for example, the primordial prohibition of incest is regularly violated by us and other species, hence that nature permits libertinage—and anything else we natural beings are capable of doing. Merleau-Ponty argues along similar lines that we are worldly creatures, as natural as any others, not above or beyond nature. There is dehiscence of nature, differentiation within nature, of course, and we can distinguish ourselves as that part of nature that reflects upon the natural order. What does this have to do with ecology? In a word, everything.

"Conservation" and "restoration," key terms in ecological discourse, both appeal implicitly to a natural ordering informed by design, by some sort of teleology, some sort of purposiveness. Ordering is for the sake of something.

What is the teleology operative in ecological valuation? The de facto answer is a confused teleology. Confused because distinctions are typically not drawn between the different entelechies manifested by different species,[6] nor is the crucial distinction between divine and finite teleology given its due.

I believe, but do not have the space here to demonstrate, that much if not most of ecological discourse covertly presupposes some sort of appeal to a natural teleology that is onto-theological at its core. For example, the notion of a cosmic balance upset by self-seeking human projects that subtends the idea of karma as well as the fear of tampering with natural species through artificial manipulation of DNA is largely crypto-onto-theology. Balance is stasis, rest, and perfection, none of which are apparent in the turmoil of continental drift, global warming on the earth's surface, cooling at its core, and the chaos of weather. Suffice it to say that I believe that the teleologies implicit in projects of conservation and restoration should be made explicit. Let me, then, be explicit about my own standpoint on this matter.

First off, I believe in Boyle's law and other natural laws that articulate causal relations in the physical and organic world, but I do not believe that these laws serve a cosmic design or divine purpose that is discernible and serves to provide a measure for our values and decisions. Nonetheless, I do believe that *our* purposes are served by discerning natural laws like the one discovered by Boyle and that they do provide a measure for our behavior (as I tried to illustrate with the example of scuba diving). The more you know about how the world operates, the better able you are to deal with it: ignorance is costly.[7]

I also believe that teleology presupposes ends, ends presuppose needs and desires, and perfect beings have no needs or desires. Therefore, the very notion of cosmic teleology grounded in divine perfection is internally incoherent. Finite beings, organisms, are all driven by goals, all behave purposively. We attribute to our own species some ability to set goals for ourselves in a deliberate way, but tend to think of other organisms as driven by instinct. A rough distinction can be made between those who incorporate the needs of species other than their own in their thinking about conservation and restoration, those who implicitly appeal to divine authority, and those who limit their concerns to their own kind (which may not and typically does not include all members of their species). Savers of whales and spotted owls belong in the first category, many of those who fear genetic engineering fall into the second, and some recent presidents of the United States belong in the third. Where do I belong? Definitely not in the second group.

The question underlying debates about conservation and restoration is always a question about competing goals, competing needs, desires, and values. That competition includes decisions as to the extent of one's concern for beings other than oneself. Do we do what we think is best for ourselves in the singular or in the plural? Do we prioritize the family, clan, state, species, vertebrates at large, or every living being except mosquitoes and slimy things that live under rocks? My answer to that is Dillon's law of proximity: the value, positive or negative, of other beings is a function of psychic and physical distance; we love and hate up close, and indifference sets in with remove. I was more touched by the death of my cat last summer than I was by the famine in Somalia. How one limits the scope of one's concerns is no easy question to answer—think of Agamemnon and Iphigenia—and I will make no further attempt to do so here . . . except to say that I have argued [in the previous chapter] that conflicts of interest are best addressed through the agon of expression and debate, and should whenever possible be adjudicated by appeal to the co-opting power of truth rather than by taking the always available last resort first. Violence will remain forevermore on the horizon, but the ability to contain it is the prime measure of civilization.

Let me now go directly to the overriding issue: How do we stand—how should we stand—with respect to the world in which we dwell?

In his influential essay "The Question Concerning Technology," Heidegger has both illumined and obscured this issue. The fulcrum of the essay is the distinction Heidegger draws between *techne* and *poiesis*. On the one hand, there is the self-dissembling horizon presupposed by our technological era in which we tacitly take the world for granted as *Bestand*, as standing reserve, as a resource to exploit in various modes of mastery and control. On the other, there is the listening or attunement to Being that he describes in terms of *poiesis*, *aletheia*, and *Gelassenheit*. Heidegger acknowledges that the two orientations, *techne* and *poiesis*, are related—*techne* is but one of the orientations revealed through the wonder of *poiesis*—but the thrust of his essay is that the hegemony of *techne* in our era poses a serious danger. The danger is that of our being closed off from the wonderful and awesome aspects of Being that might be revealed if we approach the world with wonder and awe. In sum, Heidegger argues that there is an intimate agon between *techne* and *poiesis*, that *techne* has supervened in our era, and that this supervenience constitutes a bad or dangerous state of affairs.

Contemporary readings of Heidegger frequently miss the point that he, like his prime mentor, Nietzsche, is a philosopher of transcendence, and hence they miss the main point of the essay, the call to awaken to what lies beyond our daily concerns. That, in my view, is the message that resounds throughout Heidegger's *corpus*, a constant theme perduring through the many twists and *Kehren* of his writing. It is a message that needs to be heard. It is a message obscured by the onto-theological attempt to deliver it in bite-size pieces designed for comfortable consumption. It is the one thing that was right about old-time religion.

But Heidegger also erred in separating our daily concerns from our awe of transcendence. Erred in seeing the agon between *techne* and *poiesis* as abyssal. *Techne* is essentially a response to *poiesis* as houses are a response to brute being. Our houses have stout walls and roofs, but they also have windows, and we place them carefully in order to view what lies beyond. Anyone who has made it a project to find an appropriate *templum* for her dwelling place, anyone who has lived on the land before building her dwelling in order to sense the spirit of the place . . . any such person knows that *poiesis* informs *techne*, knows that the quality of what he makes depends as much on the quality of his listening as the respect he has for his materials and the mastery he has over his tools. You don't build an igloo in equatorial Africa. You do learn from the wisdom of generations of successful builders how it is done here, and why. And the why tells you how to do it better in the place you have chosen. Which is equally a place that has chosen you.

In his essay, Heidegger momentarily forgot that the flight of *das Man* from transcendence is itself an awareness of transcendence in the privative mode. In issuing the wake-up call, Heidegger momentarily forgot that sleep, as opposed to death, always includes a tacit monitoring of the world from which it is seeking temporary surcease. If it weren't, no call could interrupt the slumber, and Heidegger's writing would be sheer vanity.

There is an element of mastery implicit in *techne*, but that mastery is a bit more subtle than contemporary critics of mastery and power seem to realize. From farmers to heavy-equipment operators to civil engineers, the ones who work the land know the land better than most of us who walk on it, even if we carry cameras. I have seen a dozer driver scoot out of a pond site he was excavating because he felt what was indiscernible to me, a little ripple in the hardpan that said he would bury his machine if he didn't get the hell out right now.

Men and women who go to sea in technical contrivances know the sea and the sky, are attuned to their moods, sensitive to the inflections that betoken change, and hence appreciative of the beauty that portends a fate. They are truly masters and wonderful to behold in action, but their mastery is full of respect: for the most part, they attempt to control themselves and their vessels, not the sea. Read Melville and Conrad, and you will get a remote sense of this. Go to sea in rough weather with such a master and you will see it at second hand. Try to do it yourself, and you will learn that *poiesis* drives *techne*, all the way from the design of the craft to the craft of handling it.

The sea can teach us much if we will listen. The first lesson is ceaseless motion and change. The earth is also restless, but, for the most part, moves more slowly and less dramatically than the sea; nonetheless, it, too, is constantly becoming. In neither case is there any question of restoring the status quo ante or reaching equilibrium; that is a lesson the sea can teach us about the earth. Another is that neither earth nor sea provides a comfortable and secure habitat for our species, although the earth is somewhat more accommodating. Both earth and sea command respect and vigilance.

The sea feeds us, waters our crops, replenishes our lakes and streams; it also changes its boundaries, amps up our hurricanes, and regularly wrecks mariners who lack respect and prudence. When it seems calm, it is brewing its next storm. It is a mistake to regard the sea as anything other than implacable. The sea is not a woman. It has no human characteristics at all, although it is a fecund source of anthropomorphic metaphors.

The sea can be defiled and polluted. I have been sailing and diving the waters of the northern part of the Western Hemisphere for half a century, and I have seen it happen. Waterfowl and fish, coral reefs and shorelines, sheltered bays and ocean reaches—all bear traces of human waste. The sea transforms itself to accommodate our garbage. Some species of fish can eat the filters of our cigarettes and survive; others cannot. The sea will endure. Not forever. Only change is forever. But it will last longer than we will. It may have a different aroma; it may swell or shrink; it inevitably will breed different inhabitants in its depths and well beyond its shores.

What can we learn from this? We are the species that has evolved in such a way as to surpass all others in the capacities to calculate and to produce garbage. We are now wondering how to combine those skills. The answer to the how lies in reversibility.

To touch is to be touched. To pollute is to be polluted. We need to learn to calculate the positives and the negatives about wrapping things in plastic, driving cars and flying planes, generating energy this way and that, and, in general, using the world for our purposes. That learning is best conceived as developing our capacity for *phronesis*. Phronesis is best conceived as the cure for dogmatic ideology. I doubt that we will ever stop generating garbage, but the answer to that problem does not lie in turning off our powers of calculation; it lies in tuning them up according to the revelations that come from *poiesis* or wonder, on one hand, and our penchant for comfort, on the other.

As it is with seagoers, so it is with earthmovers, hunters, gatherers, and, ironically, Heidegger's silversmith in "The Question Concerning Technology." The smith that crafts the chalice that beckons toward the unknown beyond must sense the beyond he is invoking, must listen to the silver and respect its limits as well as its beauty, and only then can he exert his power and ply his trade. If he can't wonder, he can't make; he can only duplicate.

How, then, do we stand—how should we stand—with regard to the world in which we dwell?

I have addressed two issues, both having to do with care. Who or what do we—should we—care about? And how do we exercise that care?

My answers lie in the questions themselves, as I posed them here: that is, both in the questioning of what to do or not to do, and in the questioning of the grounds that might serve to justify the judgments we make. My belief is that the warrant for judgment is ultimately local. Judgment is bound to specific circumstances; it may be informed by one or more of the mixed bag of principles we confusedly call universal, but it cannot be derived from principles, simply because one needs some warrant for appealing to this principle rather than that. Judgment, in classical terms, is the process of deciding what general category a particular thing properly belongs in. One has to attune oneself to the thing and then ask which among the competing categories it calls for. That query needs to be situated within the context to which the thing properly belongs, and, ultimately within the context of one's sense of the global horizon. How would changing this thing resonate with its environs?

Interrogation, as Merleau-Ponty conceived it, is exactly the undertaking that does *not* blindly adhere to ideology and predetermine itself by an overriding dogma. Interrogation is oriented toward uncovering the truth of the matter at hand, and doing that with the hope and belief that the expression of truth will command assent among the parties in dispute. The choice here is between phronesis and violence as engine of change. And the problem is that wisdom and power do not always reside in the same place. Think of Lord Acton's famous dictum.[8]

Finally, I believe that the relevant categories are ultimately aesthetic, that is, based on desire. One has to determine what one wants. There are desires and needs that all human bodies have in common. There are others that are more particular. Identifying the basic needs for clean earth, air, energy, and water is the sometimes obscured *telos* of the ecological movement. The question of distribution of resources, however, will always involve conflicting local interests, and those issues point to the intersection of ecology and politics. Where incompatible aesthetics collide is the familiar battlefield of conflicting interests.

How will the eco-battles be resolved in the long run? Here are my speculations.

The losers will be members of that subspecies of the human order who, like myself, value privacy, personal autonomy, and individual responsibility. We are the endangered species that wants distance from the burgeoning mass of humanity, remove from neighbors, and freedom to live as we choose. I currently live in the sequestered protection of a hundred or so acres of privately owned woodland. It is true that I have to get the permission of bureaucrats to build a house or a septic system, or to dam a stream to create a lake, or to kill a marauding bear or a succulent doe, to open a road or manage timber or . . . the list goes on. It is also true that the bureaucrats are free to condemn my property and appropriate it at their price to build roads they think are necessary for people I don't know or want to know, to cut down my trees or spray them with something that behaves like Agent Orange to protect their power lines and phone lines, and to tax me for funds to use as they see fit (including paying their own salaries and hiring more people like themselves).

Still, I am remote enough for the time being that nobody pays much attention, and I can do pretty much what I please as long as I don't annoy other people who will invoke bureaucratic retribution.

Nevertheless, it is inevitable that *das Man* will drive people like me into proximity with itself, just as my desire for telephone service and electricity entails submitting my trees to its defoliants and chain saws. The needs of the many will continue to supervene over the desires of the few. Taxes alone will ensure the disappearance of my subspecies from its chosen habitat. My kind will be eased out of existence by legislation enacted for the sake of *das Man*. That is inevitable. It may even satisfy some variation on the theme of what is now being called "social justice." I am reconciled to it because I think I will beat *das Man* to the punch by dying before it encroaches too much more than it already has. That is one consolation. Another is that becoming is as implacable as the sea: species change behavior or die out. I have that in common with the spotted owl. But the human species at large is resilient: *das Man* is, as Heidegger suggested, fairly close to being immortal, and will die out or mutate beyond recognition only when its own self-proliferation finally makes the planet unfit for habitation by anything resembling what I respect as human. *Das Man*'s contribution to the gene pool will engulf the DNA of the likes of me.

Subsequent generations will have intermittent access to places like the one in which I live if they are willing to pay an entrance fee to the public park, obey the signs that will be nailed to the trees, and pack out their own excrement. A half century ago I actually ate the fish I caught in the Potomac River a mile or so upstream from Watergate. A half century from now, my descendants may be able to eat the salmon they take from the sea, but they will have been bred in fish farms. A few generations further on, people will read in history books that humans used to feed themselves from the wild, and they will not know whereof they read, just as I can't quite imagine what it might have been like to live as Native Americans did when the woods and streams were rich with game. I can still hunt wild grouse and woodcock, but I stock my land with pheasants and chukars bred in incubators, and fill my ponds with farm-raised trout.

I think that *das Man* will have crowded my subspecies into extinction long before the sun burns out. And that might actually be a happier end to the brief chapter of human existence in the endless book of becoming than the far more likely scenario suggested by Freud in *Beyond the Pleasure Principle*. In that scenario, it is not the slow degradation of habitat that will kill humanity as we know it or morph it into some alien being that thrives on its own waste, but rather the bellicose nature of our own kind. In individual cases, Thanatos always prevails over Eros, and the same might well be true for the species. The greatest threats to the lives and welfare of people like ourselves do not come from recurrent catastrophes in the natural world, but rather from that part of the natural world we call human, that is, from the hostility and contagion of members of our own species.

We are now learning what we should have known from the start, that nonproliferation treaties drafted by the possessors of nuclear, biological, and chemical warfare capabilities will be contested by peoples who do not belong to the club. The force and direction of the vector from battle-axes to stealth bombers to MRVd missiles is clear enough to see: the force is increasing and the direction is unwavering. Weaponry has always been at the cutting edge of technological development. There is no slogan for forging plowshares into swords, because the swords were always there first.

My guess is that, one way or another, and sooner rather than later, we will kill ourselves, and the world will have to chug along without us and the gods we invoke when, once again, we prepare to cut loose the dogs of war.

Or maybe phronesis will prevail. I'd like to think so.

· ·

CHAPTER SEVEN

LIFE-DEATH

I.

The philosophers I admire are those who are humble enough to place themselves in service to their thoughts and arrogant enough to push those thoughts
toward their limits. The philosopher has the thought and the thought has the
philosopher. If the philosopher is true to the thought, it will lead him beyond
himself to the thinker he wants to be. If the philosopher shrinks before the
demands of the thought, he slips back into the paradigms and prejudices that
confine him to what he has been and delimit his thinking to the unthought
hidden beneath it. Such admirable philosophers are torn between these two
faces of the unthought: the unthought that calls for recognition and expression, and the unthought whose power is its elusiveness, its propensity to evade
the recognition that will expose its vulnerability to scrutiny.

   To study such a philosopher is to seek his unthought in both its guises. To
be true to such a philosopher is not always to be stalwart in defense of what
he said, although that must be given its due; it is rather more to be true to
what he did not say, but which sought expression through him as a congenial
vehicle for its self-manifestation. Thoughts that are uniquely one's own are
necessarily without value to others, but to have developed a unique perspective may provide an opening through which others can see things that eluded
one's own grasp.

2.

So far as I know, Merleau-Ponty did not leave us with a sustained thematic
on life-death, yet it would not be mistaken to take that theme as encompassing all he wrote. It would not be a mistake to classify him as an existential
thinker.

Concluding his short essay "Man, the Hero," Merleau-Ponty wrote: "It is not fascination with death, as in Nietzsche, which allows the hero to sacrifice himself, nor is it the certainty, as in Hegel, that he is carrying out the wishes of history; rather, it is loyalty to the natural movement [that] flings us toward things and toward others. It is not death that I love, said Saint-Exupéry, but life."[1] There are two mistakes in this passage that are both trivial and consequential. The first is a misinterpretation of Nietzsche, who was in service to the same thought that called Merleau-Ponty, and the second is in endorsing Saint-Exupéry's opposition of life and death—as though one could affirm life without thereby affirming death.

The "natural movement [that] flings us toward things and toward others" is becoming. As with Nietzsche before him, Merleau-Ponty was a philosopher of becoming. To be a philosopher of becoming is to espouse the metaphysical principle that identifies the real with change.[2] The philosophy of becoming is committed to the thesis of the transcendence of time. Time is not primarily an immanent form projected on things that are otherwise timeless (although immanent projections derived from natural time are possible variants, as, for example, in music and cinema); time is the transcendent modality of the being of everything. Heraclitus said it: Everything changes. To that must be added: including the *logos* (and his instantiation of it). Time is inseparable from things; it is the *manner* in which things are, not something separable from things. Parmenides and the Eleatic school got it exactly backward: coming into being and passing away are what is real; stasis, rest, permanence, atemporality, and the like all belong in the realm of wistful ideality, and that, too, ceaselessly changes.

Merleau-Ponty earned a place in the history of philosophy by demonstrating the falsity of the ancient and abiding dogma that our bodies are impediments to thought and reason. He showed that intellection is not hampered by the body's motility and desire, but rather dependent upon them. Socrates's death had been the emblem of a mind that needed to free itself of its own body in order to become truly itself and fulfill its own highest destiny. After Merleau-Ponty, that emblem—and the Eleaticism it portended—had to be reconceived. Socrates was wrong: there can be no minds without bodies. How could such a palpably false idea have gained so much popularity in the face of overwhelming empirical evidence to the contrary?

Nietzsche gave us the answer, Freud articulated its psychopathology, and Merleau-Ponty developed its philosophical consequences. Nietzsche's answer is that our desire for metaphysical comfort, our need to believe that my death is not the end of me as an individual person, is the source of our wistful longing for afterworlds. Freud showed that our belief in the possibility of personal immortality is the product of self-deceptive wish fulfillment. And then the existentialists, Merleau-Ponty among them, explored the portents of authentic finitude and mortality for human life.

Philosophers from Socrates forward wrote in willful denial of the biological fact that living beings always die. Kant, for example, contended that there could be no morality without the promise of immortality and reward for good behavior in the life hereafter. The hidden truth behind this manifest untruth is that the fact that individual lives culminate finally in death is a fact laden with value. To live a life predicated on a metaphysics of Being that posits an invisible realm of eternal peace, rest, stasis, and beatitude is necessarily to endorse a set of values that has enormous qualitative portent for the manner in which one lives. Likewise, there are values, different values, latent in the metaphysics of becoming. The values of Eleaticism have been the subject of philosophical inquiry for at least three millennia; the values of the metaphysics of becoming have surfaced hither and yon throughout this time, but in a minor key, and have yet to be articulated adequately.

3.

Pascal made a bad bet. If reality is becoming, then gods are illusory, and afterworlds are dreams that take place in this one. To live as though these dreams were real is infantile, self-deceptive, and ultimately psychopathological. (And it would not fool an omniscient god, anyway.) It is, as Nietzsche wrote, to "lie" reward and punishment into the structure of things.

In his *Critique of Judgment*, Kant wrote cryptically about art as being driven by "purposiveness without a purpose." Can there be goal-oriented behavior that is rational when there is no ultimate finality, no ultimate goal, no ultimate reward? We do *alpha* for the sake of *beta*, *beta* for the sake of *gamma*, and so on: What if there is no *omega*? Does the whole of human endeavor amount to zero, nullity, *Nichtigheit*? That is what Heidegger wrote in *Being and Time*. He was wrong, as we shall soon see, and he may or may not have realized that later on. The sound and the fury do signify something. What they signify is life, in this case human existence, terminally finite, to be sure, but real and meaningful. Indeed, that terminal finitude is one of the horizons that impart significance to the course of human existence.

Merleau-Ponty knew this to be the case. In the chapter on "Temporal-ity" in *Phenomenology of Perception*, he wrote that "the subject . . . cannot be eternal," that "existence . . . cannot be temporal without being so in its entirety" (410). He concludes the previous chapter on "The Cogito" with this thought: "Insofar as, when I reflect on the essence of subjectivity, I find it bound up with that of the body and that of the world, this is because my existence as subjectivity is merely one with my existence as a body and with the existence of the world, and because the subject that I am, when taken concretely, is inseparable from this body and this world" (408). Descartes was simply mistaken: the inner truth of the cogito reveals the self to be finite, embodied, and worldly—not an invisible and immortal soul substance des-tined to dwell forever in eternal beatitude or eternal perdition.

Can there be goal-oriented behavior that is rational when there is no ul-timate finality, no ultimate goal, no ultimate reward? There can be because in fact there is. Unless, of course, you define rationality in Eleatic terms as grounded in an omniscient and atemporal mind, which is strictly inconceiv-able for mortal beings (as all theisms acknowledge). In that case, all finite distinctions between irrational and rational behavior are ultimately ground-less. And *that* is truly irrational.

"Meaning" and "significance" are terms designating relations. The mean-ing of a thing has to do with how it is related to other things and things in general. Causality is one such relation. Love is another. Relations are real, else there is no science, else qualitative distinctions between types of human interaction designated by such terms as noble and base, good and bad, are illusory.

This is where Heidegger went astray. He superimposed a variant of El-eatic teleology (genuine purposiveness presupposes ultimate finality) on an otherwise lucid phenomenology of death. Here is how he defines "the full existential-ontological conception of death": "Death, as the end of Dasein, is Dasein's ownmost possibility—non-relational, certain . . . not to be out-stripped [*unüberholbare*]. Death is, as Dasein's end, in the Being of this en-tity towards its end."[3] Because life is the advent of death, because death is the end in which all my goals terminate, and because death is nonrelational and thereby without meaning, all purposiveness is grounded in nullity, a mean-ingless finality. Life goes precisely nowhere. This is straightforward Kantian dogma: for life to have any meaning whatsoever, one must presuppose god, freedom, and immortality as "the ideal of pure reason." Absent god and im-mortality, we are left with groundless freedom, that is, nullity.

4.

I have chastised Merleau-Ponty for endorsing Saint-Exupéry's opposition of life and death, for loving one and not the other. But what is death if not the negation of life? And if one affirms death, as Socrates did, does this not imply a negation of life, as I think it did in the case of Socrates? Can one authentically espouse Nietzsche's doctrine of *amor fati* and affirm human existence as "truly tragic"?

Merleau-Ponty ties the existence of the self to the existence of its body, yet the body remains after the death of the self. There must be something that transcends the body, something that vanishes at death. As every hunter knows, there is a huge difference between a living body and a dead one. A radical change has taken place, as when a caterpillar turns into a moth, as when a responsive human being turns into a decaying corpse. Where did the caterpillar go? Where did the person go? The body of the caterpillar sprouted wings in the chrysalis, the body of the person sprouted maggots in the earth. In both cases, there is a routine, ordinary, and predictable biological change of state. In both cases, the change of state portends further changes of state. That is the nature of becoming: everything changes; nothing stays the same.

At death, the process of decay that began shortly after sexual maturity accelerates: the process of decomposition breaks down the organization of the body in such a way that it is no longer capable of functioning as a whole, but life goes on at lower levels of organization. Death, like adolescence, brings about drastic change within the human body. If you affirm life, you are committed to affirming the whole enchilada. To love life is to love death just because you can't have one without the other.

Selfhood can and, I think, should be conceived as a product of that kind of reversibility we call reflection. Reflection is a capacity developed in varying degrees by living bodies that terminates at death. Reflection is properly construed as bodily self-transcendence. Growth is a taken-for-granted aspect of bodily self-transcendence, as are the projects of losing weight, developing skills, changing habitualities, controlling anger and fear, and so forth—all of which presuppose some degree of self-alienation, some degree of the organism not wanting to be what it now is. That not wanting to be what it is now goes on at both conscious-reflective levels and subconscious-prereflective levels. Freud realized in mid-career that the life-instinct he correlated with growth and higher levels of organization had to be complemented with a death-instinct involving decay and reduction to lower levels of organization.

His mistake lay in conceiving that complementarity dualistically as a binary opposition.

Life-instincts and death-instincts: our bodies want to live, to preserve themselves against threats to existence, and our bodies also want to die, to bring conscious existence to an end. Both of these statements are true; truer still is the statement that our bodies, like the bodies of salmon swimming to their spawning grounds, want to live until it is time to die. That is what our bodies want. Why don't we?

I think that we can want to die and sometimes do want to die. Fatigue, surcease from pain and disability, choosing death as the most preferable of the options open under the circumstances: there is a plethora of nonmorbid motivations to die at a certain time and under certain circumstances.[4]

5.

If life is not vindicated by finality on the far side of death, if the individual self is grounded in bodily organization that enables it to be reflective or self-conscious and that self ceases to be at death, then what does vindicate life with all the suffering it always entails? Or, to ask this question in another way: Is it truly the case that the vindication of every human action lies exclusively in the consequences to which it leads—and that for the individual who disappears at death in the witnessing of those consequences? Martin Luther King Jr. martyred himself in the cause of civil rights, but what does that matter to him now? And, on another side, would we be contending with suicide bombers if they did not believe in the promise of fifty black-eyed virgins in the hereafter?

Anyone as fond of Scotch whiskey as I am knows that the vindication of drinking it does not lie in the consequences it frequently produces the following morning. *Au contraire*, it is a "now" kind of thing: consequences be damned; it feels good right now, and that is vindication aplenty. Is life like that? Shall we live, love, laugh, and be merry—exactly because tomorrow we will surely die? Is hedonism the meaning of life? Or was Nietzsche right when he said that only the Englishman lives for pleasure?

Speaking as the Irishman I am, I can say that pleasure is surely part of the meaning life has for me. Without my alcohol, tobacco, and firearms, life would be a lesser thing. I can also say that if that were the whole story, life would also be a lesser thing, not worth the effort when assessed according to a hedonistic calculus.

What beyond pleasure would suffice to vindicate life? If we adhere to the premise that there is nothing beyond life, then we have to say that only life could provide its own vindication. In the sense of vindication as justification by results, self-vindication is an oxymoron. That same would be true of such cognates as self-redeeming, self-warranting, and the like.

Nietzsche once wrote that "it is only as an *aesthetic phenomenon* that existence and the world are eternally *justified*" (*BT*, 52), but then retracted that thought in his frequently repeated assertion that the attempt to justify life from within the standpoint of life is a vicious form of circular reasoning. I am convinced that he is dead-right: the question of vindicating life is one of those philosophical traps generated by self-reference so acutely identified by Wittgenstein.

Heidegger responded to Nietzsche in a different way by appealing to hermeneutics: it is not a matter of getting out of circularity, but rather getting into it in the right way. What is the right way? As I interpret interpretation— which may not be what Heidegger had in mind and certainly is not the way that some contemporary Heideggerians view the matter—one explores a perspective from within by teasing out its presuppositions, abandoning those that fail tests of coherence and factuality, and accepting, if only provisionally, those that pass both those tests and the admittedly dicey test of inconceivability of the contrary. This is, indeed, a dicey test: for Anselm, the nonexistence of God is inconceivable; for Kant, the nonexistence of the transcendental unity of apperception is inconceivable; for Merleau-Ponty, Husserl's transcendental reduction is inconceivable because it is inconceivable to suspend our primordial faith in perception. I think Merleau-Ponty was right and the other two wrong, but my present purpose prevents me from elaborating.[5]

In Heidegger's hermeneutics of death in *Being and Time*, he argues that death individualizes: only I can die my death, nobody else can do it for me. In dying, I am absolutely alone. But life is the advent of death; hence I am absolutely alone throughout my life. To recognize this aloneness is authentic. Thus, I attribute to Heidegger the fundamental impossibility of authentic being-with.

Only I can void my bladder; nobody else can do it for me. In urinating, I am absolutely alone, even though others may witness the event. The same is true for all bodily functions: nobody else can eat my food for me, go to the dentist for me, sleep for me, or suffer through my hangovers for me. Death is a bodily function. How does it differ from the rest? There are qualitative differences between sleeping and urination, for example, such that it is well not to perform the two acts simultaneously, as there are between death and the other bodily functions. But why does dying cut me off from others when, as much as I might want it to be the case, urination does not?

There are dentists, probably most of them, who do not experience my pain when their drills hit my nerves. But they have to be trained to this insensitivity. When my eldest daughter had her first cavity drilled out and filled, I was there and had no choice but to feel her pain. I did not feel it in the same manner as she did, but it was the same pain that we both felt. Reversibility is a real structure of intercorporeity.

There are differences between pain and death, to be sure, but they share with all bodily events the structure of reversibility. If you have witnessed the death of a human being, you know this. You are touched by the dying person, and the dying person feels your being touched. This may go on in the context of denial on both sides, but, as is the case in every form of denial, there is awareness of that which is being denied conscious acknowledgment. Freud was right in regarding death and its advent as involving separation anxiety: an irrevocable distance is about to separate the living person from the dead; that is part of the shared pain. And to that extent, Heidegger was half right: the living persons are separated irrevocably at death. There is no reversibility between living bodies and dead ones.

But there is reversibility in the intercorporeity of the dying during the advent of death we call life. And it pervades the entirety of life. This pervasiveness is the basis of the peculiar qualitative aspect of life we place under such headings as intersubjectivity, morality, and love. To the extent we care about others—that is, that we care about the ways in which they care about us, care being a preeminently reversible relation—we care about things that will take place in the world from which we have departed. The quality of life for those alive now is necessarily bound up with anticipations about the hereafter because it matters to us now what will happen to others later when we are dead and gone. It is well to die well, not to die poorly, because we care now what people will think of us then. That, or something like that, underlies the psychology of martyrdom.

The reversibility of intercorporeity also takes the value of living beyond hedonism. It feels good to forsake one kind of pleasure, leisure perhaps, for the kind that comes from having improved the life of another.

Whether intended by the author or not, I read the conclusion to Alphonso Lingis's *Deathbound Subjectivity* as contending that mortality is the emblem of human vulnerability that makes us care for and about each other, that, in that sense, death confers value on life. I agree and would go on to say that becoming, the transience of life, is a source of its value. The irreversibility of time and its consequence, the irretrievability of events, make the moment meaningful. As Nietzsche should have known—I contend he actually did know—eternal recurrence or samsara (the cycle of rebirth) is a Buddhist nightmare, not a truth about Being.

6.

Life entails life-death. We are caught up in a process of becoming. Whether Silenus was right in saying that it is better never to be born, that point is mooted by the fact that not having been born is no longer—actually never was—an option for any of us. Nor, if I am right, do we have the option of living in a certain way that will earn us eternal gratitude in some hereafter.

We can, however, live in such a way that will earn us respect, bring us closer to nobility, and even generate love. Personal growth and self-transcendence breed intercorporeal gratitude in *this* world. Contingent as that gratitude has to be, it is nonetheless—maybe even all the more—a *good* thing to strive for.

In order, however, not to end on an upbeat, I must add that the transience and vulnerability of human life also engender other aspects of Thanatos recognized by Freud, such as the aggression and violence we routinely and voluntarily bring into our lives when, for example, we go to war. Just as life is always life-death, so is love always love-hate. Humanity is occasionally noble; it is regularly contemptible. I will end by reflecting briefly on this troubling thought.

I have tried here to trace the outlines of a thought implicit in Merleau-Ponty's thought, but left by and large unthought when he abruptly died un-be-times. That thought is the metaphysics of becoming, which he did explicitly espouse, but did not develop its implications for this-worldly human values. I have tried to articulate some of these values by contrasting them with the values associated with Eleatic ontology, the metaphysics of Being, what Heidegger called onto-theology, and I have attempted to show that the values of becoming have a stronger claim to validity.

The salient thought here is that the metaphysics of Being is a demonstrably false metaphysics, not least of all because it rests on a category mistake: the mistake of attributing reality to ideality, turning an ill-conceived wish into a self-deceptive and wistful belief. Truth is the column in the temple of god that grows to destroy the rest of the edifice.

Or so Nietzsche argued, but was he right? Martin Luther King Jr. made the world a nobler place riding the horse of divinity. Just as the suicide bombers, not despite their fervor, but because of it, perform contemptible acts in the name of their divinities. What do we learn from this?

I believe that gods of all sorts have generated more misery than they have relieved. Can this be shown by listing the Martin Luther Kings with the Mother Teresas and the Gandhis on one side of a ledger, with the bombers, the crusaders, and the Grand Inquisitors on the other? That would be an interesting bit of research, but not what I propose to do by way of conclusion.

Truth, finite truth and the persistent quest for it, is the foundation for what I have to say. Philosophy offers us many competing and incompatible ways of thinking about the world and the things in it. How one thinks about the world determines how one acts in it, and the consequences of those acts produce or relieve misery. Philosophy, as I conceive it, is the endeavor to think about the world as truthfully as one can with the hope that truth, even unpleasant truth, provides our best course for mitigating misery.

The kind of truth that is germane here is lucidity, being as aware as one is capable of being about the motivations of one's actions and their intended consequences. As I have argued elsewhere,[6] lucidity is a prime condition for personal responsibility, and personal responsibility is the ultimate basis for decision and action. Freedom is the condition for moral responsibility, and lucidity enables freedom. From this, I infer that we are responsible for failure to seek lucidity, the truth that confers freedom.

Theism, blind faith, is, in my view, self-mystification and self-deceit. Belief in a god whom one must obey—regardless of whether the command is comprehensible and warranted according to one's own lights—can be explained psychologically, sociologically, and historically. Such accounts have merit. They say, in effect, that some people at some times and under some circumstances have no choice but to believe, and that may be true. And, freedom being the measure of responsibility, such determination mitigates culpability, although it does not mitigate the misery generated.

But these considerations are not relevant here, because they do not apply to the people reading these words. We are privileged to choose our gods, hence responsible for choosing to obey this commandment or that. If that is true, then all gods are irrelevant—at best poetic, at worst demonic, but finally irrelevant—because lucidity gives us the freedom and the responsibility to determine how we will act. All the rest is mystification and evasion.

· ·

CHAPTER EIGHT

EXPRESSION AND THE ETHICS OF PARTICULARITY

I.

[Throughout this book],[1] I have argued for an ethics of expression in which the recurrent problem of reconciling the particular individual with the universal is achievable through the agon of discourse. Discourse, I have claimed, is different from, and generally preferable to, violent confrontation because it minimizes the amount of human misery generated through the process of adjudicating differences in the values embedded in the competing perspectives across the spectrum of diverse individuals. What Merleau-Ponty called "the new universalism" in his later political writings is a regulative ideal that, although never realizable in fact (because human finitude and embodiment ensure constant emergence of difference), nonetheless allows value differences to be expressed, articulated, critiqued, and measured against the transcendent reality of the perceived world. There is no final and stable accord, but a process of reconciliation by means that maximize freedom and reason and minimize the misery of violent confrontation.

Recently, I have begun to think that this modified Hegelianism needs to be counterbalanced with renewed respect for the recalcitrance of difference because, like all Hegelianisms, it regards difference as a negativity to be negated and leaves no room to affirm particularity as such.

2.

The irreconcilable tension between private right and public welfare, between the individual and the collective, is a ground phenomenon of law and morality. A single person living in solitude is bound by no law or obligation, and need be ruled by no other precept than self-interest. As soon as another person enters the environment, accommodations become an issue. When the population density reaches that of the borough of Manhattan, the list of statutes becomes incomprehensible by virtue of length alone (never mind inconsistency), and ignorance of the law becomes inevitable (but not exculpatory). That is a problem unto itself, but not one I intend to take up here.

That there is an irreconcilable tension between the individual and the collective presupposes values on both sides of the equation that necessarily come into conflict. And that presupposes there are grounded values on the side of the particular individual; otherwise, all disputes would have to be resolved in favor of the collective. What might these values be and how might they be warranted?

Our culture is not unique in granting individuals rights to private property, self-defense, and privacy as such. The extent to which personal survival, dignity, and freedom are respected may vary from culture to culture, but I doubt that there ever has been a culture in which these rights are disregarded altogether. Why not?

Following the general trend of Merleau-Ponty's thinking, I have argued that the ground phenomenon of ethics is recognition at the prereflective level at which transfer of corporeal schema takes place. Pathos is not a new idea. The idea that it is grounded in corporeality rather than spirituality, the idea that spirituality is a refinement of corporeality and founded upon it, is a new idea, a better idea, and one capable of redirecting our traditional ideas about ethics and morality. We are all separated from each other by our skins, but capable of recognizing each other as like unto ourselves: that is the ground of both the pathos of compassion and love, and the pathos of enmity and hatred. Discrete embodiment is the source of the value accorded to particularity.

3.

The perceived world is the always presupposed foundation of all rationality, all value, and all existence. This thesis does not destroy either rationality or the absolute. It only tries to bring them down to earth.[2]

If one brings the absolute down to earth, one destroys the absolute. Merleau-Ponty waffles on this point. In the concluding paragraph of this essay he writes: "Nietzsche's idea that God is dead is already contained in the Christian idea of the death of God.[3] God ceases to be an external object in order to mingle in human life, and this life is not simply a return to a non-temporal conclusion. God needs human history."[4] This statement betrays the lingering presence of Hegelianism in Merleau-Ponty's early thinking, a presence that he had purged from his thought when he wrote the chapter on "Interrogation and Dialectic" in *The Visible and the Invisible*. There he writes: "In Hegel, God, defined as abyss or absolute subjectivity, negates himself in order that the world be, that is, in order that there be a view upon himself that would not be his own and to which he would appear as posterior to being; in other words, God makes himself man—so that the philosophy of Hegel is an ambivalence of the theological and the anthropological" (*VI*, 93).[5] The Hegelian a-temporal absolute is a presupposition of what Merleau-Ponty designates as "bad dialectic" (*VI*, 94). "The good dialectic is that which is conscious of the fact that every *thesis* is an idealization, that Being is not made up of idealizations . . . , but of bound wholes where signification never is except in tendency" (*VI*, 94). Good dialectic or "hyperdialectic" replaces the atemporal idealizations constitutive of Being with the temporal ambiguities of becoming. When the Absolute or Being is brought down to earth, all signification, all meaning, exists only in tendency, in a "plurality of relationships" in continuous emergence. When God, Being, and the Absolute are brought down to earth, they cease to be themselves.

One immediate consequence of forsaking the immutable Absolute for earthly becoming is the recognition that there is no absolute ground for morality. Earthly morality can be nothing other than earthly mores. There can be no categorical imperative grounded in pure Reason because there is no pure Reason on earth: there is only embodied reason intrinsically intertwined with pathological interest, that is, intertwined with the pathos of love and hate, compassion and enmity. No pure reason, only phronesis: only hypothetical imperatives more or less accurately associated with a plurality of antecedents—antecedent desires more or less lucidly identified in the ambiguity of plural relationships. Morality, such as it is on earth, is founded upon the pathos of compassion, not upon pure reason that seeks to exclude all pathological interest. Kant was simply mistaken.

No Morality with a capital "M," only mores embrangled in the turmoil of existence and inseparable from the vagaries of space, time, and circumstance; mores that are inevitably tied to cultural affinities and the unfolding of history. To say that mores are generally relative to cultural variables is, however, *not* to recoil from absolutism only to plunge into the abyss of relativism and nihilism.

Like many binary oppositions, the dilemma of absolutism versus relativism results from the mistake of imposing polarized abstractions upon the rich field of experience and reducing complex phenomena into mutually exclusive categories of purely good or purely bad. Gutenberg's press gave us widespread literacy, but also precipitated centuries of religious war. In the phenomenal world of becoming, things are mixed and values are ambiguous. But ambiguity does not undermine rational moral debate; rather, it fosters and grounds it. Some mores are worse than others; hence some are better, although becoming precludes any of them from being designated as finally the best.

Some of the authors of the U.S. Constitution and Bill of Rights were slave owners, and none advocated universal suffrage. Were they then hypocrites? I think not. I think that what they lacked was lucidity. They were working in the realm of hypothetical imperatives, but they were not fully lucid about the antecedent desires that drove their precepts. They presupposed a flawed anthropology that circumscribed and undermined their understanding of equality. They were not lucid enough to identify and examine their presuppositions, not lucid enough to do better than they did. Advances have been made. In this sphere, contemporary mores are demonstrably better than those that obtained in eighteenth-century America. Denial of moral absolutes does not entail moral relativism, although it may induce the humility of critical reflection and the attendant quest for lucidity.

What follows from this attempt to bring rationality and the absolute down to earth and earthly bodies? Specifically, how does it shed light on expression and the ethics of particularity? I will approach these questions indirectly: a detour through Heidegger may illumine the path opened by Merleau-Ponty.

4.

My generation of Heideggerians has been on a quest to found an ethics of communality on the scanty grounds provided by Heidegger's purportedly value-neutral phenomenology of authenticity. I will leave it to others to evaluate the success of this venture. Instead, I will assert that in *Being and Time* Heidegger gave us a profound, but flawed, phenomenology of the ethics of communality in his portrait of *das Man*.

Nietzsche's contempt for the human herd animal is legendary, but it is a problematic contempt. "The long and serious study of the *average* man . . . constitutes a necessary part of the life-history of every philosopher"

(*BGE*, 38). One must be able to recognize the herd animal in oneself in order to free oneself from the herd. Heidegger accepted the assignment from his primary mentor, and delivered just such a long and serious study of the average man. In doing so, he identified the adherents to an ethics of communality and described the psychopathology underlying this kind of ethical comportment.

Das Man internalizes the norms guiding the mores of the herd in which he finds himself, but does so without lucidity or critical reflection; indeed, he protects himself from lucidity by numbing himself against the anxiety or call to conscience to which authentic Dasein responds. *Das Man* takes his measure from herd values and nurtures his self-esteem on the approval that is the reward of conformity to shared values. *Das Man* lives unquestioningly within what I call the de facto universal, the mores that happen to apply in the space and time into which he has been thrown. Anyone who listens to a fund drive on National Public Radio knows the appeal: come join the community of members who are people just like you. This warm bath of the pathos of approval costs just a few cents a day, but the price of admission to such a magic theater is your mind: in order to dwell among those who are just like you, you have to be just like them.

This pathos of approval is at the same time the pathos of recognition that I have designated as the ground phenomenon of ethics. Shared values are the basis of community, the *ethos* or character fostered by the community, and departures from these values are sanctioned by exclusion and punishment. The herd tramples upon any maverick who runs contrary to its stampede. The de facto universal does not tolerate recalcitrant particularity, even when tolerance is an explicit value within the community.

We are all born into community, failing which we would not survive. *Mit-Sein* is a fundamental existential structure of *Dasein*. The advent of death, the individualizing anxiety that is the call to conscience, requires a departure from community into the solitude of authenticity. Authentic Dasein cannot dwell in community; authentic Dasein cannot participate in the shared values constitutive of community: to the extent that communal values, the de facto universal, constitute the mores of community as such, and to the extent that there can be no earthly morality apart from situated mores, authentic Dasein cannot be ethical; hence there can be no ethics of authenticity. Authentic Dasein must perforce be sociopathological.

Before leaving this detour through Heideggerian authenticity, let it be noted that we are, once again, back in the binary opposition of particularity and universality. The isolated individual cannot survive as such in the herd.

5.

Merleau-Ponty solved the problem of intersubjectivity by turning it upside down. The traditional problem of intersubjectivity is the problem of explaining how an isolated, solipsistic consciousness can ever recognize another human being as like unto himself. Merleau-Ponty solved the problem by arguing that we are born into prepersonal communality, a domain of indistinction of perspectives, and only later in life, through achievement of the cogito, experience the alienation that is constitutive of personal identity. *Mit-Sein* is primordial. Once the recognition of separation is achieved, once we become aware of the divergence of our own perspective from others', we learn to mediate across these differences by expression and discourse.

The apparent *telos* here is the universal, the shared perspective. The problem with this standpoint, as noted at the beginning of this paper, is that particularity is indexed as a negativity that is to be sublated or sublimated or *aufgehoben*. There is then a tension between this Hegelian understanding of the universal and the existentialist affirmation of particularity or authenticity. Heidegger and, following him, Sartre both responded to this tension between universality and particularity by reversing the values assigned to the opposed poles, that is, by assigning positive value to particularity and negative to universality. I have contended that Merleau-Ponty provides the basis for a different response, one that undercuts the polemics of binary opposition and mutual exclusion. The crucial idea Merleau-Ponty provides is that of conditioned or circumscribed freedom.

Merleau-Ponty argued, against Sartre's doctrine of radical freedom (that is, freedom unconstrained by situation and circumstance), that human freedom manifests itself in contesting constraint. His model, taken from Marx, was that of workers uniting in rebellion against the oppression of economic coercion. For Merleau-Ponty, again, Kant was wrong: we must not presuppose noumenal freedom as a condition for human dignity; human dignity is something to be won through acts of freedom in the phenomenal world of everyday life. Freedom thus stands in a necessary relation with coercion and constraint; neither is conceivable apart from the other. The middle term and the underlying analogue is the motility of the lived body in its particularity: insofar as it can move at will, its freedom is not constrained.

No freedom without antecedent constraint; there is a paradox here, actually a plethora of paradoxes. Freedom is situated; its situation in geography and history always constitutes bounds, limits, and constraints. Thus, freedom is tied to finitude and hence cannot be conceived on absolute terms. Freedom and its negative must be thought together: first paradox.

The goal of freedom is freedom. This is one way of understanding Nietzsche's will to power: the *Übermensch* symbolizes the unending task of freeing oneself from the fetters of circumstance in order to will one's own creative will. To do so, one must slay the dragons without and within. Freedom is a correlate of self-transcendence, an agon of self with itself, a non-coincidence of self with self: no selfhood without self-estrangement. Second paradox.

The goal of freedom is to secure its freedom. But, as we are now learning as we stand in line to pass through airport security, the price of security is surrender of freedom. Third paradox. This paradox calls for delicate judgment, genuine prudence—phronesis beyond the apparent capacity of Mr. John Ashcroft.[6] How does one make such a judgment? What criteria could be properly invoked?

Hobbes provides a crucial guideline. In surrendering the freedom we have in the state of nature to kill others and take their property, we gain a greater freedom: security from threat. Fourth paradox: in some negotiations, we surrender freedom for greater freedom. This provides a criterion for surrendering freedom: only do it when there is a net gain of freedom.

There are more paradoxes, but I will stop here to investigate this one. There is more to Hobbes's social contract than immediately meets the eye. The prime threat to freedom is freedom, specifically the freedom of others to do us harm. The threat to us is ourselves, bellicose and nasty beings that we naturally are. Of all the natural catastrophes, including the hurricanes to which we assign human names, we are the worst. Suffering from our self-inflicted wounds, we gather together and voluntarily submit to the rule of laws designed to protect ourselves from ourselves. But we know ourselves well enough to know that laws are only as effective as the means we devise to enforce them. So, we create the leviathan. As a human contrivance, the leviathan is driven by the will to power and responds as Lord Acton decreed: it runs amok and defeats its own purpose by seeking its own autonomy. It rules us against our own individual will; it deprives us of the very freedom it was designed to protect. We have created a servant who now masters us.

As Freud said, civilization has produced discontent. To be civilized is to comport oneself as one must if one is to live in the *cives*. Remember the book of statutes for the borough of Manhattan: to live in the *cives*, one must submit to the rule of law. Laws constrain individuals for the sake of the collective.

Law and its enforcement necessarily favor the herd over the individual. As Kant said over and over, the rule of law is the universal, and the substance of ethics is lawfulness as such. The generalizability criterion, expressed in the various formulations of the categorical imperative, assigns negative value to any behavior that deviates from universal norms. For Kant, we must, contrary to the evidence found in the phenomenal world, presuppose that we are noumenally free in order to reach our highest level of dignity and reason, the level at which we give the law to ourselves and submit to it voluntarily. Autonomy—freedom—is the capacity to make and submit to our own law. Lawfulness as such, couched in terms of the universal, is our highest calling.[7]

Kant could be right only if we were disembodied intellects operating on the basis of reason purified of all pathological interest. What happens if we acknowledge that there is and can be no absolute Morality, only finite and situated mores subject to vicissitudes of geography and history? Do we continue to respect lawfulness as such when there is no Morality as such? How can one respect lawfulness as such when there are always bad laws among the good? In the absence of any absolute universal, do we continue to default to the de facto universal?

We do if we want to live in the *cives*. If we want civilization, we must obey the statutes governing the real estate we happen to occupy. In Manhattan, it is illegal to spit on the sidewalk. In the woods of northern Pennsylvania, you are free to void your body of any substance it contains anywhere you want. And so is your dog.

Let me be clear: I am not advocating a return to the state of nature. I do not want everybody in Manhattan to move to the woods of northern Pennsylvania. Then I would have to go find somewhere else to live. What, then, am I advocating?

6.

Freedom. I am advocating freedom. Or a particular understanding of freedom that conceives it as rooted in particularity, at root the freedom of an individual body to move as it will, subject only to the constraints of the laws of physics, biology, and human contrivance. The problems I have addressed have to do with various collisions between the particularity of freedom and the de facto universality of human laws. In sum, I have argued that the balance between the universal and the particular has, for essential reasons, gone awry, and that the result of this imbalance is an increase of human misery that takes the form of an unwarranted oppression of the one by the many. In simple terms, I have argued that our mores constitute a threat to the freedom, dignity, and creativity of the individual in his or her particularity: the herd is trampling the maverick whose only threat to the herd is exemplarity or refusal to conform. Examples of this oppression abound, but two stand out in my mind.

Well-intentioned as it may have been in conception, political correctness has become an insidious force that undermines the very idea of difference it sought to reinforce. It has degenerated into a power struggle on the part of the militant to impose an ideology on the reluctantly compliant (or indifferent) herd. As I have observed [in chapter 5 above],[8] both the American Philosophical Association and the Society for Phenomenology and Existential Philosophy have sought to regulate the use of language in such a way that the works of Nietzsche, for example, would be largely unacceptable. Shakespeare, at his bawdy best, would have to find alternate means of expression. If what one writes offends nobody, rattles nobody's cage—if one joins ranks with the prevailing ideologues and speaks just like them—then one's own voice is lost in a choral response to the person with the bullhorn.

Regulation of sexual expression among consenting adults is not a newcomer to the domain of ethics and politics. Love and sexuality belong in the domain of the particular insofar as sex involves intimate contact between individual bodies and genuine love is always directed toward the unique one rather than a replaceable token. The state or collective may (or may not) have an interest in regulating marriage as a contractual arrangement, but it has no business in regulating the partners involved and stipulating racial homogeneity (as it once did) or sexual heterogeneity (as it now does). What individual bodies do in private to express and fulfill their sexual desires and fantasies need be constrained only by consent among the persons involved.

What these two isolated examples seek to show is that Nietzsche and Heidegger were correct in regarding the hegemony of the herd as stifling to individual expression, hence as conservative of the status quo, when what is needed is the agon of competing ideas that generates lucidity and the possibility of the self-transcendence that augments individual freedom and responsibility.

Absent an absolute, situated morality is always a matter of local mores. Local mores are contingent upon time and circumstance, but that does not preclude evaluating their comparative merits. The mores underlying Jim

Crow laws were bad in comparison to the mores underlying the decision made by the Supreme Court in Brown v. Board of Education. Is there a criterion that could be used in adjudicating among competing mores?

I have argued that there is such a criterion and that it is to be found in the notion of circumscribed freedom delineated here. The herd has to protect itself from the threat to the many posed by the violence of sociopaths. Laws and ethical sanctions contrived to curb the more brutish among us satisfy the criterion latent in Hobbes: there is a net gain in freedom. But laws and ethical sanctions contrived to produce cultural homogeneity, that is, to constrain the benign behavior of the atypical few to conform to the patterns of the "just-like-us," do not satisfy that criterion. Not only is there a net loss of freedom for individuals, but there is also a net loss of freedom for the herd itself. It is from the expressive exemplarity of such mavericks as Martin Luther King Jr., D. H. Lawrence, Carrie Nation, Copernicus, Simone de Beauvoir, Nietzsche, and others of their ilk that new ideas and greater lucidity bubble up to the surface of general cultural awareness and bring humankind closer to the ideal of individual freedom and personal responsibility.

No criterion, this one included, can guarantee good judgment. Decisions are always responsive to situations and situations are always unique, always emergent. In order to judge, to subsume this complex event under that general rubric or principle, one must strive to be lucid about the presuppositions and the consequences of one's judgment. And lucidity, like freedom, is an open-ended, never to be fully realized, ideal. Some failures in judgment—and some successes—can be identified as such, but others remain opaque and require further elucidation.

Individual judgment is a flawed ground for ethical behavior, but there is no other. Absent individual judgment and responsibility, there is only conformity to inculcated herd morality . . . and that provides no basis for condemning those who lived according to the popular precepts of apartheid, Nazism, and Texan liberationism that have governed in some places and some times.

The point of the universal, of lawfulness as such, is to protect the freedom of the individual as such.

NOTES

....

EDITOR'S INTRODUCTION

1. Dillon, *Semiological Reductionism*, 2.

2. Ibid., 3, 4.

3. Derrida, *Of Grammatology*, 158.

4. For a more complete presentation of my views about the distinct, yet essentially complementary relationship between phenomenology and deconstruction, between Merleau-Ponty and Derrida, see chapter 5 of my *Merleau-Ponty's Philosophy*.

5. Dillon, *Semiological Reductionism*, ix.

6. "To sustain my claim to relevance, I want this book to reach beyond the academic sphere to the larger world of critical minds who bring other sorts of criteria and other funds of experience to bear, people who live their lives thoughtfully and want to dig a bit deeper than popular media sometimes allow. . . . And, for those readers, the technical terminology required for condensation and precision, and the references to the relevant works . . . is a kind of academic shorthand that allows scholars to allude to complex thoughts without taking up limited time. . . . This is a hybrid work in the sense just explained" (Dillon, *Beyond Romance*, xiv).

7. Dillon, *Beyond Romance*, 1–2.

8. Nietzsche articulates his Dionysian pessimism as an alternative to all versions of romanticism and aestheticism throughout book 5 of *The Gay Science*, but especially in §370; pp. 327–31.

9. I did this kind of close editorial review for the fourth time during April 2011 in preparation for submitting the final manuscript to Ohio University Press.

Art, Truth, and Illusion: Nietzsche's Ontology

CHAPTER 1: ART, TRUTH, AND ILLUSION: NIETZSCHE'S METAPHYSICAL SKEPTICISM

Editor's note: A version of this chapter was published as "Art, Truth, and Illusion: Nietzsche's Metaphysical Skepticism," *Symposium* 8, no. 2 (2004): 299–312.

1. I have adopted here the convention of capitalizing such terms as "Real" and "True" when the reality and truth they designate is conceived in absolute, infinite, or non-perspectival ways.

2. "Judgments, judgments of value, concerning life, for it or against it, can, in the end, never be true: they have value only as symptoms, they are worthy of consideration only as symptoms; in themselves such judgments are stupidities. . . . *The value of life cannot be estimated*. Not by the living, for they are an interested party" (*TI*, 474).

3. "*Would it not be necessary* for the tragic man . . . to desire a new art, the *art of metaphysical comfort* [*die Kunst des metaphysischen Trostes*] . . . ? —No, thrice no! O you young romantics: it would *not* be necessary! But it is highly probable that it will *end* that way, that *you* end that way—namely, 'comforted,' as it is written, in spite of all self-education for seriousness and terror, 'comforted metaphysically'—in sum, as romantics end, as *Christians*" (*BT*, 26; *W1*, 18).

4. *Editor's note*: Dillon will refer to the "wisdom" or "saying" of Silenus many times in the course of this book; it is a frequent touchstone for Dillon's own views about what makes life worth living. Dillon's use of the saying is drawn from *BT*, §3, where Nietzsche is quoting what seems to be an unnamed text: "There is an ancient story that King Midas hunted in the forest a long time for the wise Silenus, the companion of Dionysus, without capturing him. When Silenus at last fell into his hands, the king asked what was the best and most desirable of all things for man. . . . At last, urged by the king, [Silenus] gave a shrill laugh and broke out into these words: '. . . What is best of all is utterly beyond your reach: not to be born, not to *be*, to be *nothing*. But the second best for you is—to die soon'" (*BT*, 42).

Nietzsche uses quotes around this entire paragraph, but it is not clear what text— if one at all—he is quoting. At the end of the paragraph, he does offer the following citation: "Cf. Sophocles, *Oedipus at Colonus*, lines 1224ff." However, those lines of the play—chanted by the chorus—are not the above passage: they refer to the basic sentiment, but with no attribution to Silenus. The sentiment can also be found expressed in Cicero's *Dialogues*, again without reference to Silenus.

Thus we have here an ancient saying—a piece of Greek folklore—with no clear attribution. Nietzsche is the earliest person I have found who attributes the saying to the satyr Silenus, and all later such attributions I have found do so because of Nietzsche.

5. We fear what threatens to disrupt our tranquillity. This grounds a utilitarian morality that Nietzsche traces to Platonic eudaimonism, the position that only ignorance leads to bad acts, that good acts flow from those who know what is in their own self-interest.

Nietzsche says: "This type of inference smells of the *rabble* that sees nothing in bad actions but the unpleasant consequences and really judges, 'it is *stupid* to do what is bad,' while 'good' is taken without further ado to be identical with 'useful and agreeable.' In the case of every moral utilitarianism one may immediately infer the same origin and follow one's nose: one will rarely go astray" (*BG*, 103).

Nietzsche yearns for something higher than the useful, and is willing to suffer pain to get there. Utilitarianism is associated with leveling out in his mind, a necessary by-product of the social contract to achieve comfort by refraining from threatening one another.

6. "The problem of *culture* is seldom grasped correctly. The goal of a culture is not the greatest possible *happiness* of a people, nor is it the unhindered development of *all* their talents; instead, culture shows itself in the correct *proportion* of these developments. Its aim points beyond earthly happiness: the production of great works is the aim of culture" (Nietzsche, "The Philosopher," in *PT*, 16).

7. "When one considers . . . the *value* of knowledge, and, on the other hand, a beautiful illusion which has exactly the same value as an item of knowledge—provided only that it is an illusion in which one believes—, then one realizes that life requires illusions, i.e., untruths which are taken to be truths. What life does require is belief in truth, but illusion is sufficient for this. That is to say, 'truths' do not establish themselves by means of logical proofs, but by means of their effects; proofs of strength. The true and the effective are taken to be identical; here too one submits to force" (Nietzsche, "The Philosopher," in *PT*, 16–17).

8. Support for regarding the early Nietzsche as espousing a form of totalitarian thought may be found in the following passages from "The Philosopher" in *PT*:

> The entire life of a people reflects in an unclear and confused manner the image [*Bild*] offered by their highest geniuses. The geniuses are not the product of the masses, but the masses show their effects. . . . There is an invisible bridge from genius to genius which constitutes the genuinely real "history" of a people. (§17; p. 3)

> The philosopher is a self-revelation of nature's workshop; the philosopher and the artist tell the trade secrets of nature. . . . Together with art, [philosophers] step into the place vacated by myth. (§24; p. 6)

> Science is totally dependent upon philosophical opinions for all of its goals. . . . That philosophy which gains control also has to consider the problem of the level to which science should be permitted to develop; it has to determine value. . . . Philosophy reveals its highest worth when it concentrates the unlimited knowledge drive and subdues it to unity. (§§28, 30; pp. 8–9)

> *The last philosopher* . . . demonstrates the necessity of illusions, of art, and of that art which rules over life. The only criterion which counts for us is the aesthetic criterion. (§§38, 41; pp. 12–13)

9. Nietzsche, "The Philosopher," §59 in *PT*, p. 22, emphasis added.

10. *Editor's note*: The two figures in this chapter are reproductions of Dillon's actual pencil drawings. The executive editor of the university press and I entirely agreed we should publish Dillon's own drawings, rough as they are, because of their historical value, personal quality, and charm.

11. *Editor's note*: Aristotle, "On Interpretation," in *The Basic Works of Aristotle*, 40.

12. The "creator of language" described here corresponds closely to the "genius in the act of artistic creation" (*BT*, 52) described as the source of the unifying vision in *The Birth of Tragedy* and *The Philosopher*.

13. Note that Nietzsche is here violating his own injunction against causal explanation. Just as Kant does.

14. This point has yet to be demonstrated, but will be defended shortly. Support for it now, however, can be found in the following passages: "The illusion which is involved in the artistic transference of a nerve stimulus into images is, if not the mother, then the grandmother of every single concept" (*TL*, 85); and "It is not true that the essence of things 'appears' in the empirical world" (*TL*, 86).

15. "Every word instantly becomes a concept precisely insofar as it is not supposed to serve as a reminder of the unique and entirely individual original experience to

which it owes its origin; but rather, a word becomes a concept insofar as it simultaneously has to fit countless more or less similar cases—which means, purely and simply, cases which are never equal and thus altogether unequal. Every concept arises from the equation of unequal things" (*TL*, 83).

Nietzsche distinguishes the rational person who operates through categorial reason (Apollo) from the intuitive person who sees things as unique and individual (Dionysus), and describes the latter as happy and redeemed by illusion and beauty (*TL*, 90).

16. See *TL*, 81, where Nietzsche argues that "a uniformly valid and binding designation is invented for things, and this legislation of language likewise establishes the first laws of truth. For the contrast between truth and lie arises here for the first time." He illustrates this claim with the example of the liar as one who sees something as it is ("I am poor") but misrepresents it in language ("I am rich"). If we cannot see things except through universally binding concepts, there can be no lie. Liars must be able to work within language and also to work upon it from without.

17. "Each perceptual metaphor is individual and without equals and is therefore able to elude all classification" (*TL*, 84–85).

18. "The genesis of language does not proceed logically in any case, and all the material within and with which the man of truth, the scientist, and the philosopher later work and build, if not derived from never-never land, is at least not derived from the essence of things" (*TL*, 83).

19. "This is how matters stand regarding seeking and finding 'truth' within the realm of reason. If I make up the definition of a mammal, and then, after inspecting a camel, declare 'look, a mammal,' I have indeed brought a truth to light in this way, but it is a truth of limited value. That is to say, it is a thoroughly anthropomorphic truth which contains not a single point which would be 'true in itself' or really and universally valid apart from man. At bottom, what the investigator of such truths is seeking is only the metamorphosis of the world into man" (*TL*, 85–86).

20. "To be truthful means to employ the usual metaphors. Thus, to express it morally, this is the duty to lie according to a fixed convention, to lie with the herd and in a manner binding upon everyone. Now man of course forgets that this is the way things stand for him. Thus he lies in the manner indicated, unconsciously and in accordance with habits which are centuries old; and *precisely by means of this unconsciousness* and forgetfulness he arrives at this sense of truth" (*TL*, 84).

21. "Truth cannot be recognized. Everything which is knowable is illusion. The significance of art as truthful illusion" (*TL*, 97).

22. As Nietzsche puts it:

How is it that art is only possible as a lie? . . .

Art includes the delight of awakening belief by means of surfaces. But one is not really deceived! [If one were] then art would cease to be.

Art works through deception—yet one which does not deceive us?

What is the source of the pleasure we take in deception which we have already tried, in an illusion which is always recognized as illusion?

Thus art treats *illusion as illusion*; therefore it does not wish to deceive; it *is true*. (*TL*, §184; p. 96)

This conception of the truth of art, its lucidity with regard to its means and claims, is incompatible with the beautiful lie that is politically effective. The contradiction tacitly acknowledged here is explicitly confronted in the "Attempt" and other works of the 1880s.

CHAPTER 2: NIETZSCHE'S METAMORPHOSIS

1. *GS*, 328. This passage is repeated in *Nietzsche Contra Wagner*, almost verbatim. I take it to be significant that the word "madness" is deleted. Also, the phrase "revenge against life itself," which does not appear in the *GS* text, is added.

2. This date is not quite arbitrary. It is the date of publication of Nietzsche's fourth *Untimely Meditation*, *Richard Wagner in Bayreuth*. As will become evident, this public announcement of Nietzsche's break with his erstwhile patron marks a dramatic change in Nietzsche's life, one which ramifies across the entire spectrum of his philosophy and existence.

3. Kaufmann cites *Human, All-Too-Human*, vol. 2, preface, §3, as the source of this quotation. I cannot find these words in *Werke*, although the farewell expressed is clear. Section 3 of the preface to volume 2 of *Menschliches, Allzumenschliches* begins as follows:

> —Es war in der Tat damals die höchste Zeit, *Abschied zu nehmen*: alsbald schon bekam ich den Beweis dafür. Richard Wagner, scheinbar der Siegreichste, in Wahrheit ein morsch gewordener, verzweifelnder Romantiker, sank plötzlich, hilflos und zerbrochen, vor dem christlichen Kreuze nieder. (*W1*, 739)

> —At that time it was indeed high time *to say farewell*: and I immediately received a confirmation of the fact. Richard Wagner, seemingly the all-conquering, actually a decaying, despairing romantic, suddenly sank down helpless and shattered before the Christian cross. (*HH*, 210–11)

4. Here Kaufmann notes that when Nietzsche puts this passage into *Nietzsche Contra Wagner* he adds: "Confronted with the theater, this mass art par excellence, I feel that profound scorn at the bottom of my soul which every artist today feels. *Success* in the theater—with that one drops in my respect forever" (*GS*, 325n111).

5. *Editor's note*: At this point, Dillon refers the reader to his essay "Conscience and Authenticity" in *Chiasmi International*, vol. 5, 2003. The unabridged version of that essay appears in this book as chapter 3 of *The Ethics of Particularity*.

6. *Editor's note*: Dillon's original clause was "that defines the essence at stake." I have rephrased the clause so it is grammatical.

7. *Editor's note*: The manuscript had the word "Nietzschean," but that doesn't cohere with the subsequent pronoun and the surrounding text, in which "Nietzsche's style" is used.

8. "Thus Spoke Zarathustra," in *PN*, 145.

CHAPTER 3: ILLUSION, APPEARANCE, AND PERSPECTIVE: NIETZSCHE'S HONEST TRUTH

1. This interpretation is subject to challenge. There are Nietzsche scholars I respect who contend that his philosophical orientation was closer to Hegel than to

Kant. I acknowledge that there are instances when this is the case. As particular issues emerge, it will become evident whether or not it is appropriate to frame them in one philosophical context or another. Here the touchstone is patently Kant.

2. I reproduce here in full section 3 of the *Transcendental Aesthetic*, "General Observations on the Transcendental Aesthetic," in which Kant defines "appearance," "illusion," and "thing in itself." This is drawn from *Critique of Pure Reason*, 88–89:

> When I say that the intuition of outer objects and the self-intuition of the mind alike represent the objects and the mind, in space and in time, as they affect our senses, that is, as they appear, I do not mean to say that these objects are a mere illusion [*Schein*]. For in an appearance the objects, nay even the properties that we ascribe to them, are always regarded as something actually given. Since, however, in the relation of the given object to the subject, such properties depend upon the mode of intuition of the subject, this object as appearance [*Erscheinung*] is to be distinguished from itself as object in itself. Thus when I maintain the quality of space and of time, in conformity with which, as a condition of their existence, I posit both bodies and my own soul, lies in my mode of intuition and not in those objects in themselves, I am not saying that bodies merely seem [*scheinen*] to be outside me, or that my soul only seems to be given in my self-consciousness. It would be my own fault, if out of that which I ought to reckon as appearance, I made mere illusion.(a) That does not follow as a consequence of our principle of the ideality of all our sensible intuitions—quite the contrary. It is only if we ascribe *objective reality* to these forms of representation, that it becomes impossible for us to prevent everything being thereby transformed into mere *illusion*. For if we regard space and time as properties which, if they are to be possible at all, must be found in things in themselves, and if we reflect on the absurdities in which we are then involved, in that two infinite things, which are not substances, nor anything actually inhering in substances, must yet have existence, nay, must be the necessary condition of the existence of all things, and moreover must continue to exist, even although all existing things be removed—we cannot blame the good Berkeley for degrading bodies to mere illusion. Nay, even our own existence, in being made thus dependent upon the self-subsistent reality of a non-entity, such as time, would necessarily be changed with it into sheer illusion—an absurdity of which no one has yet been guilty.

At the point marked (a) in the text above, Kant inserts the following footnote:

(a) The predicates of the appearance can be ascribed to the object itself, in relation to our sense, for instance, the red color or the scent to the rose. That which, while inseparable from the representation of the object, is not to be met with in the object in itself, but always in its relation to the subject, is appearance. Accordingly the predicates of space and time are rightly ascribed to the objects of the senses, as such; and in this there is no illusion. On the other hand, if I ascribe redness to the rose *in itself*, or extension to all outer objects *in themselves*, without paying regard to the determinate relation of these objects to the subject, and without limiting my judgment to that relation, illusion then first arises.

3. *Editor's note*: For no reason I can discern from any of the manuscript versions, Dillon placed this entire paragraph in brackets. I have removed them as unnecessary.

4. "Buddha . . . found a human type, in his case scattered through all classes and social strata of his people, that was good and good-natured from inertia (and above all inoffensive); also from inertia, this type lived abstinently, almost without needs. He understood how such a human type must inevitably roll, with its whole *vis inertiae* [force of inertia], into a faith that promises to *prevent* the recurrence of terrestrial troubles (meaning work and action in general)" (*GS*, 296–97).

5. "A couple more signposts from my morality. A big meal is easier to digest than one too small. That the stomach comes into action as a whole, first precondition of a good digestion. One has to *know* the size of one's stomach. For the same reason those tedious meals should be avoided which I call sacrificial feasts, those at the *table d'hôte*. No eating between meals, no coffee: coffee makes gloomy. Tea beneficial only in the morning. Little, but strong: tea very detrimental and sicklying o'er the whole day if it is the slightest bit too weak. Each has here his own degree, often between the narrowest and most delicate limits. In very agaçant climate it is inadvisable to start with a cup of thick oil-free cocoa. —Sit as little as possible; credit no thought not born in the open air and while moving freely about—in which the muscles too do not hold a festival. All prejudices come from the intestines. — Assiduity—I have said it once before—the actual sin against the holy spirit" (*EH*, 53–54). See also *TI*, 47.

6. "Inwieweit verträgt die Wahrheit die Einverleibung?" The word "incorporation" should be understood literally as embodiment.

CHAPTER 4: ZARATHUSTRA: TRANSCENDENCE HERE AND HEREAFTER

Editor's note: A shortened version of this chapter was presented in 2002 to the Nietzsche Society at the Society for Phenomenology and Existential Philosophy, Loyola University, Chicago, Illinois. A version was also presented at the University of North Carolina at Asheville, Asheville, North Carolina, during the 2002–2003 academic year.

1. This is clearly oriented around the Christian tradition, and important distinctions would have to be made to justify calling it the essence of religion. I leave it unqualified here for two, perhaps insufficient, reasons. First, Nietzsche's attack on religion is primarily motivated by and centered on his reaction to his own Christian tradition. Second, the resentment, self-deception and quiescent longing for peace he finds underlying the Christian tradition he also finds in Judaism, Buddhism, and just about every other religion he addresses. The Buddhist and Taoist traditions, for example, conceive God, freedom, and immortality through figures that differ from the Christian figures, but a plausible argument can be made that nirvana and reunion with the One in the Tao are functionally equivalent to the Christian beatific vision, hence are variations on the immortality function. One can stress similarities or differences; the matter is of little consequence in the interpretation of Nietzsche being set forth.

2. It is not insignificant that Nietzsche addresses himself primarily to Kant in the opening phases of *Beyond Good and Evil*, the book immediately following *Zarathustra* and described by him as a more prosaic attempt to explicate the thinking in the poetic work.

3. Kant, *Critique of Pure Reason*, 29.

4. Ibid., 640–41.

5. The ouroboros is the "emblematic serpent of ancient Egypt and Greece represented with its tail in its mouth continually devouring itself and being reborn from itself. A Gnostic and alchemical symbol, Ouroboros expresses the unity of all things, material and spiritual, which never disappear but perpetually change form in an eternal cycle of destruction and re-creation." *Editor's note*: Dillon names *Encyclopedia Britannica* for this quote; the passage can be found *verbatim* in the online *Encyclopedia Britannica* at http://www.britannica.com/EBchecked/topic/435492/Ouroboros.

6. Nietzsche devotes only one short paragraph on the child in the speech "On the Three Metamorphoses." The paragraph describes the child as "a new beginning, . . . a self-propelled wheel, a first movement, a sacred 'Yes.' For the game of creation . . . a sacred 'Yes' is needed" (Z, 139). The child is to be understood as a figure for the link between affirmation and creation. This link is developed in the section "On the Way of the Creator." Here the image of "a self-propelled wheel" (Z, 174–75) is again invoked, which provides additional warrant for interpreting the child through the section on the creator.

7. Although all such thinking is necessarily idolatrous.

8. *Autonomia* means "freedom to use one's own laws, independence," per Henry Liddell and Robert Scott, *Liddell and Scott's Greek-English Lexicon* (London: Oxford University Press, 1964).

9. Kant, *Critique of Practical Reason*, II, 2, i, 117f.

10. Kant, *Groundwork of the Metaphysic of Morals*, 123.

11. Ibid., 89.

CHAPTER 5: BODY AND SOUL: NIETZSCHE'S SELF

1. "Where there is affinity of languages, it cannot fail, owing to the common philosophy of grammar—I mean, owing to the unconscious domination and guidance by similar grammatical functions—that everything is prepared at the outset for a similar development and sequence of philosophical systems; just as the way seems barred against certain other possibilities of world-interpretation" (*BGE*, 27).

2. *Convenire*: to come together in social formation.

3. See chapter 4, section 1, above. Also, see my essay "Am I a Grammatical Fiction?—The Debate Over Ego Psychology" in *Merleau-Ponty's Later Works and Their Practical Implications*.

4. "Nämlich das Gefühl des Zustandes, von dem <u>weg</u>, das Gefühl des Zustandes, zu dem <u>hin</u>, das Gefühl von diesem >>weg<< und >>hin<< selbst" (W2, 581).

5. In this context, the German "*Affekt*" and the English "affect" are cognates insofar as both betoken an emotional state.

6. *Editor's note*: This insertion clarifies the sense.

7. [(mineness Þ oneness) & (oneness Þ mineness)] Þ (mineness Û oneness).

8. Kaufmann translates the German "*Lust*" as delight. That is not incorrect, but it overlooks the fact that "*Lust*" also betokens pleasures and satisfactions that are not particularly joyful or merry, but are rather satisfying in contemplative ways that have to do with feeling good about ourselves.

CHAPTER 6: MORALITY IN A GOD-FORSAKEN WORLD

1. See chapter 3 above.

2. *Editor's note*: Dillon has an incomplete endnote here that reads "See _____ above."

3. *Editor's note*: Again, Dillon has an incomplete endnote here that reads "See _____ above."

4. "[We] laugh at the way in which . . . science at its best seeks most to keep us in this *simplified*, thoroughly artificial, suitably constructed and suitably falsified world—at the way in which . . . it loves error, because, being alive, it loves life" (*BGE*, 35).

5. "Every concept arises from the equation of unequal things" (*TL*, 83). See chapter 1, section 3 above.

6. *Editor's note*: Dillon has an incomplete endnote here that reads "Refer to 'Truth in Art.'"

7. *Editor's note*: The sentence is incomplete. I have inserted "beings" here as the most logical choice of words.

8. This "typology" is loosely isomorphic with the "genealogy" undertaken in the next work to be considered here; indeed, anticipates it in seminal ways.

9. I take this to be a variation of the sentiment articulated a few paragraphs earlier that universal accord is generally, but mistakenly, assumed to be the supreme goal or regulative ideal that drives political and moral theorizing.

10. *Editor's note*: Dillon has an endnote here that reads "Refer to SemRed." No doubt, he intends to make some kind of reference to his book *Semiological Reductionism: A Critique of the Deconstructionist Movement in Postmodern Thought*.

11. See chapter 1, section 3.

12. "The *over-all degeneration of man* down to what today appears to the socialist dolts and flatheads as their 'man of the future'—as their ideal—this degeneration and diminution of man into the perfect herd animal (or, as they say, to the man of the 'free society'), this animalization of man into the dwarf animal of equal rights and claims, is *possible*, there is no doubt of it. Anyone who has once thought through this possibility to the end, knows one kind of nausea that other men don't know—but perhaps also a new task!" (*BGE*, 118).

APPENDIX: TEMPLATE FOR CHAPTER 7

1. Doctrine of "original repetition": Signifiers signify by virtue of iteration. A signifier used only once cannot signify. Signifiers are ideal, they bring about the linkage or unification of time by bridging moments. They do this by repetition.

"For X to be meaningful, X must be re-cognized as having the meaning X. That recognition requires subsumption under the signifier X. The signifier must be a double for the return or subsumption to take place: that is, the signifier is both a prior condition of re-cognition and the means of the return or subsumption that grants the re-cognition. And this must have been the case from the first" (Dillon, *Semiological Reductionism*, 73).

2. *Editor's note*: Dillon's citations in this template refer to *On the Genealogy of*

Morals in *Basic Writings of Nietzsche*, ed. and trans. by Walter Kaufmann. "S" refers to "Section"—so "S4" refers to "Section 4"—and the number in the bracket refers to the page number in that text.

3. Passage to be considered in the sequel. The lamb v. bird of prey passage in section 13. It is because of the seduction of language, the grammatical fiction of the I, that we are able to enjoin people to behave as lambs. But N seems to argue against this that "the belief that the strong man is free to be weak and the bird of prey to be a lamb" is *false*. What then becomes of the overriding theme of self-transcendence—which seems to depend heavily on freedom? *Editor's note:* I have no idea what the reference to "sequel" in the first sentence of this note means.

The Ethics of Particularity

CHAPTER 1: SEXUAL ETHICS AND SHAME

Editor's note: A shorter version of this chapter was presented at Rutgers University during the 1999-2000 academic year.

1. The term "sexlove" is a coinage I have adopted to refer to the forms of loving that involve sexuality in an explicit way. Hitherto I have used "erotic love," but now have come to think that that term is permeated with associations drawn from the romantic tradition. As should become evident in the course of the [book], the boundaries between the traditional conceptions of love (and between them and my notion of sexlove) are ambiguous and shifting. In my view, all forms of sociality are based on the structure Merleau-Ponty names reversibility, hence there is affinity and overlapping among them. Nonetheless, the structures of reversibility in the sexual domain are discernibly different from those in the domain of economics: a sexual liaison may be contractual at some level, but differs from a business deal in important ways. One of my goals is to show how the ethical consciousness that informs sexlove (which depends upon the unique particularity of the individuals) stands in dynamic tension with the ethical consciousness that generates a morality of equality or universality.

2. *Editor's note:* Dillon is referring here to the eighteenth-century Scottish poet Robert Burns, but it is not clear which of Burns's poems he has in mind.

3. Defiance is a form of pride, hence essentially related to shame. Like all binary oppositions, they are interdependent; neither can be thought apart from the other. Oedipus's shame is a measure of his pride.

4. The word "menarche" means "beginning" and is derivative from the root for "measure." In the measure of human life, menarche is the time to begin.

CHAPTER 2: SEXLOVE AND ETHICS

Editor's note: A shorter version of this chapter was presented at the Twenty-third Annual Conference of the International Merleau-Ponty Circle at Salisbury State University, Salisbury, Maryland, in 1998.

1. The Oedipal structure is, of course, held by Freud to be both sexual and competitive and, thus, the source of rivalry between siblings and same-gender parents and children. I maintain that infantile sexuality differs from the character of sexuality after puberty, and that the threats one encounters within the family differ significantly from the threats one encounters when seeking a mate outside the family. One does not choose one's parents and siblings as one chooses a mate; one cannot divorce and remarry. Familiarity is not a potential negative within the family, nor is boredom a threat: taking a parent's affection for granted is a positive unless it verges on disregard. In short, the dialectics of wonder and intensity within the family romance differ from those in sexlove: Oedipal longing is something to be resolved and overcome; erotic desire is something in which to rejoice. See M. C. Dillon, *Beyond Romance*, chapter 7, "Motherlove and Sexlove."

2. Kierkegaard, *Fear and Trembling*, 113.

3. See Dillon, introduction to *Écart & Différance*.

4. Kant, *Critique of Practical Reason*, 50.

5. "The only good dialectic is the hyperdialectic. The bad dialectic is that which . . . becomes autonomous, and ends up at cynicism, at formalism. . . . What we call hyperdialectic is a thought that . . . is capable of reaching truth because it envisages without restriction the plurality of the relationships and what has been called ambiguity" (*VI*, 94).

6. As noted earlier, the threat to the de facto universal posed by sexlove is exacerbated by the fact that the taboos and prohibitions surrounding sexlove are primordial (for example, the claim that the rule of exogamy is the first law whose institution marks the birth of the rule of law or civilization as such) and engraved upon the collective conscience with an intensity and persistence nowhere else to be found. We are disturbed far less by Orestes's act of matricide than we are by Oedipus's violation of the *Ur-taboo*.

7. *Editor's note*: This clause is ungrammatical, but it is unclear how it should be resolved. We might think of it as a "Dillonism," that is, an ungrammatical, humorous turn of phrase of the sort Dillon liked to use in conversation.

8. The Greek word "*to kalon*" is usually translated as "nobility." The Greek term is rich and overdetermined; it means aesthetically attractive or beautiful, it also means morally good or virtuous; indeed, it means both of these things at once, the intersection of goodness and beauty, as though one could not be either good or beautiful without being both. *To kalon* is that which one seeks in one's beloved; to see someone as an instance of *to kalon* is already to feel the tug of eros. See Dillon, *Beyond Romance*, chapter 9, part 3, "Mimesis and To Kalon."

CHAPTER 3: CONSCIENCE AND AUTHENTICITY

Editor's note: A substantially shorter version of this chapter was presented at the Twenty-fifth Annual Conference of the International Merleau-Ponty Circle, George Washington University, Washington, D.C., in 2000; and at the Twelfth Annual Conference on "Time, Memory, Text," organized by the Department of Romance Languages and Literature at Binghamton University in 2001. A longer version than that, but considerably shorter than this chapter, was published as "Conscience and Authenticity," *Chiasmi International*, vol. 5 (2003): 15–28.

1. "And God said to Abraham, Truly, Sarah your wife shall bear you a son; and you shall call his name Isaac; and I will establish my covenant with him for an everlasting covenant, and with his descendants after him" (Genesis 17).

2. Thomas Aquinas, *Basic Writings of Saint Thomas Aquinas*, 110–11.

3. "'He who seeks, easily gets lost. All loneliness is guilt'—thus speaks the herd. And you have long belonged to the herd. The voice of the herd will still be audible in you. And when you will say, 'I no longer have a common conscience with you,' it will be a lament and an agony. Behold, this agony itself was born of the common conscience, and the last glimmer of that conscience still glows on your affliction" (Z, 174).

4. Freud, *The Ego and the Id*, 27. First published in 1923 by Internationaler Psychoanalytische Verlag, Leipzig, Vienna, and Zurich. Reprinted in *Gesammelte Schriften*, Band 6, 1925.

5. Ibid., 24.

6. Freud, "'Civilized' Sexual Morality and Modern Nervousness," in *The Standard Edition of the Complete Works of Sigmund Freud*. First published in *Sexualprobleme*, new issue of the periodical *Mutterschutz*, Band 4, 1908. Reprinted in *Sammlung*, Zweite Folge.

7. Heidegger, *Being and Time*, 318.

8. "Conscience summons Dasein's self from its lostness in the 'they.' The Self to which the appeal is made remains indefinite and empty in its 'what.' . . . *In conscience Dasein calls itself.* . . . In its 'who,' the caller is definable in a 'worldly' way by nothing at all. . . . [In the call] Dasein addresses itself as 'Guilty!' . . . The idea of 'Guilty!' must be sufficiently formalized so that those ordinary phenomena of 'guilt' [that] are related to our concernful Being with Others will *drop out*. . . . We define the formally existential idea of the 'Guilty!' as 'Being-the-basis for a Being which has been defined by a 'not'—that is to say, as 'Being-the-basis of a nullity.' . . . This '*not*' belongs to the existential meaning of 'thrownness.' It itself, being a basis, is a nullity of itself. This means that Dasein as such is guilty. . . . Only because Dasein is guilty in the basis of its Being, and closes itself off from itself as something thrown and falling, is conscience possible. . . .

"The appeal [of conscience] calls back by calling forth: it calls Dasein *forth* to the possibility of taking over, in existing, even that thrown entity which it is; it calls Dasein *back* to its thrownness so as to understand this thrownness as the null basis which it has to take up into existence. This calling-back . . . gives Dasein to understand that Dasein itself . . . is to bring itself back to itself from its lostness in the 'they'; and this means that it *is guilty*. . . . In understanding the call, Dasein is *in thrall to its ownmost possibility of existence*. It has chosen itself. . . . What is chosen is *having*-a-conscience as Being-free for one's ownmost Being-guilty. '*Understanding the appeal*' means '*wanting to have a conscience*'" (Heidegger, *Being and Time*, 319–34).

9. Heidegger, *Being and Time*, 342.

10. Ibid., 343.

11. Ibid., 344.

12. Ibid., §74.

13. I am indebted to Tamara Johnson for bringing this point to my attention.

14. What poetic saga could establish communion among such free spirits? What, beyond the poet's saying, could enable that saying to bring people together?

For the saga to establish a harmony among us, we have to be able to see what the poet says, we have to be captivated by the spectacle that captured her and announced itself through her words, we have to see that her truth is not hers alone, but one that appropriates us all.

The difference between the poet and the rest of us is one of attunement: she sees what I overlooked because she wonders. She hears what I did not because she was listening and I was not. The world demands to be sung, but most of us most of the time are too busy rearranging it according to our own needs to pay attention when it makes its claim on us. There are moments of vision, however, that can transform us, call us out of our typical pragmatism, and project us into an ecstasy that changes how we see things. We need our poets and philosophers to give us names for the strange things that come upon us, break the patterns of our mundane lives, and open us to the realization of a truth that commands our assent.

15. *Why* does the flesh of the world require symbolic expression? What drives art into existence as a remote consequence of the big bang? The question is germane. As a matter of historical fact, flesh—and, in my view, not just human flesh—has produced art. It is my belief that flesh does indeed require (ask for, seek) beauty, as it does truth, to fulfill its existence, but this is not the place to articulate and defend this view. See "Truth in Art: Homage à Merleau-Ponty and John McCarty," in Dillon, *Merleau-Ponty's Ontology*.

16. "There is here no problem of the *alter ego* because it is not *I* who sees, not *he* who sees, because an anonymous visibility inhabits both of us, a vision in general, in virtue of that primordial property that belongs to the flesh, being here and now, of radiating everywhere and forever, being an individual, of being also a dimension and a universal" (*VI*, 142).

17. "The flesh (of the world or my own) is not contingency, chaos, but a texture that returns to itself and conforms to itself. . . . I believe that I have a man's senses, a human body—because the spectacle of the world that is my own, and which, to judge by our confrontations, does not notably differ from that of the others, with me as with them refers with evidence to typical dimensions of visibility, and finally to a virtual focus of vision, to a detector also typical, so that at the joints of the opaque body and the opaque world there is a ray of generality and light" (*VI*, 146).

18. Heidegger, *Being and Time*, 319.

19. Ibid., 321.

20. "Dass es je sein Sein als seineges zu sein hat" (Heidegger, *Being and Time*, 33).

21. See the epigram at the beginning of section 3 above.

22. It is Nietzsche's truth that the measure must be sought in the world, not before or after it, a truth both manifested and obscured by appeals to divinity.

23. What I am about to offer has little textual support just because, although Merleau-Ponty touches on the topics of anxiety, conscience, and authenticity from time to time, he offers no sustained treatment of which I am aware. Yet it is my belief and the sustaining motive of my interest in Merleau-Ponty that the whole of his philosophical endeavor was driven by the question of meaning and value in human existence, especially as that question addresses itself to transcendence and self-transcendence. The thoughts to follow are, at best, neither mine nor his, but attempts to articulate conceptual shapes emerging from the flesh of the world and demanding expression from both of us. If they are true thoughts, they belong to all of us and are anonymous in that way.

24. I should say here that, although this strategy appears elsewhere in his thought, it jars with the harmony of Heidegger's thinking. Heidegger is, above all, the thinker of horizons, the one who shows the inconspicuous context. This decontextualizing move is an aberration motivated, I think, by a genuine insight.

25. "The call [of conscience] is precisely something which *we ourselves* have neither planned nor prepared for nor voluntarily performed, nor have we ever done so. 'It' calls, against our expectations and even against our will. On the other hand, the call undoubtedly does not come from someone else who is with me in the world. The call comes *from* me and *from beyond me*.

"These phenomenal findings are not to be explained away. After all, they have been taken as a starting-point for explaining the voice of conscience as an alien power by which Dasein is dominated. If the interpretation continues in this direction, one supplies a possessor for the power thus posited, or one takes the power itself as a person who makes himself known—namely God. On the other hand one may try to reject this explanation in which the called is taken an alien manifestation of such a power, and to explain away the conscience 'biologically' at the same time. Both these explanations pass over the phenomenal findings too hastily. Such procedures are facilitated by the unexpressed but ontologically dogmatic guiding thesis that what *is* (in other words, anything so factual as the call) must be *present-at-hand*, and that what does not let itself be Objectively demonstrated as *present-at-hand*, just *is not* at all" (Heidegger, *Being and Time*, 320).

26. "One can speak neither of a destruction nor of a conservation of silence. . . . When the silent vision falls into speech, and when the speech in turn, opening up a field of the nameable and the sayable, inscribes itself in that field, in its place according to its truth—in short, when it metamorphoses the structures of the visible world and makes itself a gaze of the mind . . . , this is always in virtue of the same fundamental phenomenon of reversibility which sustains both the mute perception and the speech and which manifests itself by an almost carnal existence of the idea, as well as by a sublimation of the flesh" (Merleau-Ponty, *VI*, 154–55).

CHAPTER 4: REVERSIBILITY AND ETHICS: THE QUESTION OF VIOLENCE

Editor's note: Dillon's original essay includes the following note, which was inserted at the end of the title: "An early version of this chapter was presented at The Twenty-Second Annual International Conference of the Merleau-Ponty Circle, 18–20 September 1997, at Seattle University. I would like to acknowledge here the kind assistance rendered to me by Leonard Lawlor in the process of developing my research for this paper." A version of the chapter was published as "Reversibility and Ethics: The Question of Violence," *Bulletin de la Societe Americaine de Philosophie de Langue Francaise*, ed. Patrick Bourgeois, vol. 10, no. 2 (1998): 82–101.

1. Editor's note. Dillon uses the word "essay."

2. Merleau-Ponty, *Humanism and Terror*, 109. The original reads: "Nous n'avons pas le choix entre la pureté et la violence, mais entre différantes sortes de violence. Le violence est notre lot en tante que nous sommes incarnés. . . . Le vie, la discussion et le choix politique n'ont pas lieu que sur ce fond. Ce qui compte et dont il faut discuter,

ce n'est pas la violence, c'est son sens ou son avenir" (Merleau-Ponty, *Humanisme et Terreur*, 117–18).

3. The circularity here may be hermeneutic in the sense that it invites us to query our presuppositions thereby allowing us to thematize latent attitudes sedimented in our heritage. But hermeneutics will not give us a defensible answer to the question; at best it can only reveal our commitments. Hermeneutics is prolegomenon.

4. *American Heritage Electronic Dictionary* (Boston: Houghton Mifflin, 1992).

5. Partridge, *Origins*.

6. *American Heritage Electronic Dictionary*.

7. Partridge, *Origins*.

8. *Editor's note*: Lord Acton's famous dictum is: "Power tends to corrupt and absolute power tends to corrupt absolutely." Acton, an English historian (1834–1902), made this statement in a letter he wrote to Bishop Mandell Creighton, dated 1887 (http://en.wikipedia.org/wiki/John_Dalberg-Acton,_1st_Baron_Acton).

9. Sartre and Merleau-Ponty "disagreed over the role and efficacy of the Communist Party: Sartre moving more toward political activism, Merleau-Ponty developing a skeptical position concerning marxism as a guideline for political practice. In 1955, Merleau-Ponty published *The Adventures of the Dialectic*. This text marks the break that had already occurred. Disagreements about the role of dialectic carried into their common editorial work for *Les Temps Modernes*, and finally, in 1953, Merleau-Ponty resigned definitively from the editorial board" (Silverman and Barry, introduction to *Texts and Dialogues*, xvi).

10. Although I cannot argue the point here, I am sure that this was not Merleau-Ponty's own standpoint. In "Indirect Language and the Voices of Silence" (written in 1951–1952), he argues in favor of a theory of expression based on painting and language that points toward the universal, toward the goal of reducing or eliminating violence. For example:

> The fact that each expression is closely connected within one single order to every other expression brings about the junction of the individual and the universal. . . . A philosophy of history does not take away any of my rights or initiatives. It simply adds to my obligations as a solitary person the obligation to understand situations other than my own and to create a path between my life and that of others, that is, to express myself. Through the action of culture, I take up my dwelling in lives [that] are not mine. I confront them, I make one known to the other, I make them equally possible in an order of truth, I make myself responsible for all of them, and I create a universal life. (Merleau-Ponty, "Indirect Language and the Voices of Silence," in *Signs*, 73–75)

> L'intimité de toute expression à toute expression, leur appartenance à un seul ordre, obtiennent par le fait la jonction de l'individuel et de l'universel. . . . Une philosophie de l'histoire ne m'ôte aucun de mes droits, aucune de mes initiatives. Il est vrai seulement qu'elle ajoute à mes obligations de solitaire celle de comprendre d'autres situations que la mienne, de créer un chemin entre ma vie et celle des autres, c'est-à-dire de m'exprimer. Par l'action de culture, je m'installe dans des vies qui ne sont pas la mienne, je les confronte, je manifeste l'une à l'autre, je les rends compossibles dans un ordre de vérité, je me fais responsable de toutes, je suscite

une vie universelle. (Merleau-Ponty, "Le langage indirect et les voix du silence," in *Signes*, 91–94)

11. The standpoint taken here is that it is a mistake to separate ends from means, that in the sphere of human action one must consider both intent *and* instrument. The intent to force one's will upon another by means of compelling argument should be assessed differently from a like intent executed with firearms. And, conversely, lethal damage done to another is properly evaluated in light of motive: we distinguish between (degrees of) murder, manslaughter, and accidental death. In general, judgments are better when they seek to maximize rather than minimize consideration of relevant evidence.

12. The French is: "Si l'on condamne toute violence, on se place hors du domaine où il y a justice et injustice, on maudit le monde et l'humanité—malediction hypocrite, puisque celui qui la prononce, du moment qu'il a déjà vécu, a déjà accepté la regle du jeu. Entre les hommes considérés comme consciences pures, il n'y aurait en effet pas de raison de choisir. Mais entre les hommes considérés comme titulaires de situations qui composent ensemble une seule *situation commune*, il est inévitable que l'on choisisse" (Merleau-Ponty, *Humanisme et Terreur*, 118–19).

13. Or, at least, to choose the least violent of the available options. This modification, however, renders the standpoint nonradical.

14. The thesis that I designate with the term "semiological reductionism" is articulated in *Semiological Reductionism: A Critique of the Deconstructionist Movement in Postmodern Thought*. Here I can provide only a synopsis.

15. The French verb *violer* means "to transgress, to desecrate, to enter unlawfully, to rape." The verb is used to translate the English "rape."

16. In a pamphlet dated December 1997, issued by the Office of Affirmative Action, the University Ombudsman of Binghamton University, and bearing the title *Sexual Harassment: Definition, Policy, Response and Prevention*, the following passage appears under the heading "Safeguarding Against Sexual Harassment Charges": "Be aware of how your behavior may be interpreted by and may impact other people, and remember that *it is the impact of behavior, not the intention behind it, that is of concern*." I interpret this to mean that the precept articulated above that intent is relevant to moral assessment has been abandoned. I would extend this interpretation to speculate that at least one factor in abandoning the precept is the belief, fostered by semiological reductionism, that the presence or absence of a given motive cannot be determined.

One consequence of this standpoint is to privilege the testimony of the plaintiff: the plaintiff's interpretation of the defendant's intention is decisive; the defendant's intention, itself, is not of concern—even though it is that intention that makes the look or touch, that is, the behavior, offensive, as can be seen in another passage of the pamphlet: "Physical conduct such as unwelcome hugging or touching, *intentionally* brushing up against someone's body . . ." (from the section titled "What Is Sexual Harassment: General Description").

17. Specifically, the fallacy Irving Copi calls "converse accident" in which "one considers only unusual or atypical cases and generalizes to a rule that fits them alone" (Copi, *Introduction to Logic*, 7th ed. [New York: Macmillan, 1986], 100).

18. I am referring here to charges brought against a member of the New York City

Police Department for committing the action described against a Haitian immigrant who had been taken into custody for a minor offense.

19. The reference here is to litigation [at the time of writing] in which the plaintiff [was] Paula Jones and the defendant [was then President] William Jefferson Clinton.

20. *Editor's note*: The 1998 impeachment trial of then President Bill Clinton centered on whether or not he had had sexual relations with White House employee Monica Lewinsky and lied about it under oath. The potential DNA evidence on one of Lewinsky's dresses was a much-discussed part of the trial.

21. Once again, only a capsule version of the standpoint at hand can be given here. See M. C. Dillon, "Merleau-Ponty and the Reversibility Thesis," *Man and World*, vol. 16 (1983): 365–88; and "La carnalidad del amor: percepción e historia," *Areté*, vol. 9, no. 2 (1997): 219–34. A revised, English version of this essay is included as chapter 9 of *Beyond Romance*.

22. In the case of the sexually harassing look, words spoken, other actions performed, social and physical setting, historical narratives about the perceived behavior of the parties involved, and so on are all relevant, as is evidence attesting to the nature of the action in question.

23. See Dillon, *Merleau-Ponty's Ontology*, 113–29.

24. *Editor's note*: Dillon's hypothesis here is elaborated and defended in chapters 7 and 9 of *Beyond Romance*.

25. Editor's note. In fact, Dillon has developed this thought in considerable detail on chapters 1 and 2 of *The Ethics of Particularity* in this book.

26. This includes preemptive acts of violence. All acts of violence, even acts of self-defense, retaliation, and retribution, are essentially preemptive of further harm.

27. "Indirect Language and the Voices of Silence," in *Signs*, 74. "Toute action, tout amour est hanté par l'attente d'un recite qui les changerait en leur verité, du moment où enfin on saurait ce qu'il en a été" (*S-F*, 93).

28. The case I have in mind is Christopher Columbus. Others might be cited.

29. Or what I have latterly called an amscan.

30. See note [10] above. *Editor's note*: Because of the insertion of my own notes, I had to change the number of the note to which Dillon refers here.

31. Given the principles of universality and rational co-option underlying the thesis articulated here, it should be apparent that this figure could not take the totalitarian form of a supreme ruler, be it philosopher-king or earthly divinity.

32. Here I would cite Nazism, the Spanish Inquisition, and the holy wars and crusades of many sects.

33. The Greeks, following Socrates, corrupted the ideal of *to kalon* by elevating the mind above the flesh and pointing it toward the purity of an afterworld. Christianity exacerbated this corruption by demonizing the flesh.

It would be a mistake to interpret the values set forth here as a form of secularized Christian humanism. The values defended are secular in the extreme, and humanistic in the minimal sense that they are confined by the inability of the author to transcend the humanity he is attempting to stretch; they are Christian to the extent that Christianity draws upon a worldly source of values—as all value systems must—despite its efforts to the contrary.

CHAPTER 5: DOES MERLEAU-PONTY'S ONTOLOGY PREDELINEATE A POLITICS?

Editor's note: A version of this chapter was presented at the Twenty-sixth Annual Conference of the International Merleau-Ponty Circle, University of North Carolina at Asheville, North Carolina, in 2001. Special thanks goes to Duane Davis, director of the conference, for permission to publish this chapter, given that Dillon had pledged the paper to Duane for an anthology on Merleau-Ponty's political philosophy.

   1. *Editor's note*: This insertion reflects a connection I am reasonably certain Dillon would have made in finalizing this manuscript.

   2. "East-West Encounter," in Silverman and Barry, *Texts and Dialogues*, 26–58. Originally published as "Recontre Est-Ouest à Venice," *Comprendre*, 16 (1956). I am indebted to Thomas Busch for drawing my attention to this text.

   3. *Editor's note*: This sentence refers to a United Nations Conference Against Racism held in Durban, South Africa, in September 2001 that was deeply acrimonious and led Israel and the United States to withdraw because of perceived anti-Semitic talks and proposals.

   4. *Editor's note*: Again, this is a natural connection Dillon would almost certainly have made in his finished manuscript.

CHAPTER 6: MERLEAU-PONTY AND THE ONTOLOGY OF ECOLOGY, OR APOCALYPSE LATER

Editor's note: This chapter was presented at the Twenty-seventh International Conference of the Merleau-Ponty Circle in St. Louis in 2002. The conference paper underwent revisions by Dillon, and then posthumous minor revisions (approved by Joanne Dillon) by editors Suzanne L. Cataldi and William S. Hamrick for its publication in *Merleau-Ponty and Environmental Philosophy*, 259–71. To preserve consistency of tone with the other chapters of this book, I have reinstated Dillon's original language in a couple of places.

   1. *Editor's note*: David Abram is the author of *The Spell of the Sensuous* (New York: Vintage, 1996), and a longtime member of the International Merleau-Ponty Circle; David was present at the conference where Dillon first presented the essay.

   2. "Flesh of the world." This is Merleau-Ponty's term for the "element" of Being that is a "general thing," like earth, air, fire, and water, or "a sort of incarnate principle" that is "midway between the spatio-temporal individual and the idea" (*VI*, 139). Although I employ this term regularly to designate an ontological category patterned on the human body that undercuts the traditional bifurcation of mind and matter, body and world, by stressing that "there is reciprocal insertion and intertwining of one in the other," that, as incarnate, humans are part of the world, I am increasingly troubled by it. "Flesh of the world" suggests that the world is organic. Part of the world is organic, of course, but other parts are not, and it is a fundamental mistake to take the whole as an organism. Organisms are intentional, operate according to their own teleologies, and in that sense are purposive. Whether the world, writ large, is chaotic or governed by law, it is not driven by purpose. Water flows downhill, but it

does not want to reach the sea. Eventually, of course, it does reach the sea. And stays there for a while.

3. Whether it is possible for one voice to change language I leave moot. I prefer to think in terms of "phronesis" and its derivatives rather than "ecology" and its derivatives, but will continue here to employ the term now in currency. It is hard enough to be understood.

4. Time, as Merleau-Ponty conceives it, cannot be a circle simply because its closure stops time. Much of time, as we live it, is indeed cyclical, but the successive times are different, as the second A in the principle of identity, A=A, is different from the first, hence nonidentical. Every summer is different.

This is perilously close to the domain of metaphysical gobbledygook, but here is the argument. Either the circle is closed or it is not. If it is closed, then time stops (actually never started). If it is open, it is not a circle. This is the *arhetos* of Hegelian thought.

5. Kirk and Raven, *The Presocratic Philosophers*, 107.

6. We do not die after we spawn, as do salmon, although as Freud points out, we may both be driven by a compulsion to repeat rooted in a death-seeking teleology.

7. *Editor's note*: Dillon makes these arguments about the pragmatic limits of nature in greater detail in chapter 3 of *Beyond Romance*.

8. *Editor's note*: As previously noted, Lord Acton's dictum is that "power tends to corrupt and absolute power corrupts absolutely."

CHAPTER 7: LIFE-DEATH

Editor's note: This chapter was presented at the Twenty-eighth Annual Conference of the International Merleau-Ponty Circle, University of Western Ontario, London, Ontario, Canada, in 2003. The chapter was published as edited here as "Life-Death," in *Chiasmi International*, vol. 9 (2008): 449–58.

1. "Man, the Hero," in Merleau-Ponty, *Sense and Non-Sense*, 186. Originally published as "Le Héros, l'Homme," *Sens et Non-Sens* (Paris: Les Éditions Nagel, 1966).

2. The identification of reality and change is both (1) a preeminently metaphysical thought, and (2) a preeminently non-onto-theological thought.

3. Heidegger, *Being and Time, 303.*

4. In the section of *Zarathustra* titled "On Free Death," Nietzsche writes in praise of maturity: "Immature is the love of the youth, and immature his hatred of man and earth. . . . In the man there is more of the child than in the youth, and less melancholy: he knows better how to die and to live. Free to die and free in death, able to say a holy No when the time for Yes has passed: thus he knows how to die and to live" (Z, 185). Socrates chose to die under circumstances and at a time of his own choosing. I have questioned his motivations, or at least those attributed to him by Plato, but believe that he was more fortunate in dying as he did than was Nietzsche, who might have followed his own advice, but was in some degree a victim of bad luck.

5. The contrary can be inconceivable in a logical way (that is, one cannot conceive an infinite being because conception requires delimitation) or a psychological way if one is constrained by an unthematized preconception or unthought thought (that is,

the commitment of Plato and some logicians to the belief that ideals or essences or logical operators must exist in a place as do things). This distinction, I think, ultimately breaks down, as can be seen in the case of Merleau-Ponty's notion of perceptual faith, the contrary to which is both logically and psychologically inconceivable (and is one just because it is the other). Psychologically, the paradigm for existence is perceived things; hence, logically, it is absurd to say that I doubt the existence of the pencil I am using to write this.

6. *Editor's note*: In an endnote here Dillon refers the reader to "Conscience and Authenticity," which was published in 2003 in *Chiasmi International: Trilingual Studies Concerning Merleau-Ponty's Thought*, vol. 5. The unabridged version of that essay is included as chapter 3 of *The Ethics of Particularity* in this book.

CHAPTER 8: EXPRESSION AND THE ETHICS OF PARTICULARITY

Editor's note: This chapter was presented at the Twenty-ninth Annual Conference of the International Merleau-Ponty Circle, Muhlenberg College, Allentown, Pennsylvania, in 2004.

1. *Editor's note*: This phrase replaces Dillon's word "Elsewhere."

2. Merleau-Ponty's essay "The Primacy of Perception" appears in *The Primacy of Perception and Other Essays*, ed. James M. Edie (Evanston, IL: Northwestern University Press, 1964), 12–42.

3. I believe this is a false statement.

4. Merleau-Ponty, "The Primacy of Perception," 27.

5. "La philosophie de Hegel est une ambivalence du théologique et de anthropologique" (VI-F, 127).

6. *Editor's note*: John Ashcroft was the highly controversial attorney general of the United States, appointed by George W. Bush in 2001.

7. What is lawfulness as such? Law-governed behavior, according to Kant, is behavior that binds itself to the universal. The very idea of law is based on universality: laws apply equally to all rational beings. No person is above the law, no person is exempt from the duty to obey the law. From this formal requirement that law be universal, we can derive a criterion for duty or moral behavior: moral obligation requires us always to behave in a way that could be mandated universally, that is, for all rational beings. From this Kant arrives at the categorical imperative: "I ought never to conduct myself except in such a way *that I can also will that my maxim should become a universal law*" (*Groundwork of the Metaphysic of Morals*, 70). Reason is, by definition, universal; it is binding upon *all* rational beings.

8. *Editor's note*: My insertion replaces the word "elsewhere."

BIBLIOGRAPHY

....

Aristotle. "On Interpretation." Translated by E. M. Edghill. In *The Basic Works of Aristotle*, edited by Richard McKeon. New York: Random House, 1941.

Cataldi, Suzanne L., and William S. Hamrick, eds. *Merleau-Ponty and Environmental Philosophy: Dwelling on the Landscapes of Thought*. Albany: State University of New York Press, 2007.

Davis, Duane H., ed. *Merleau-Ponty's Later Works and Their Practical Implications: The Dehiscence of Responsibility*. Amherst, NY: Humanity Books, 2001.

Derrida, Jacques. *Of Grammatology*. Translated by Gayatri C. Spivak. Baltimore, MD: Johns Hopkins University Press, 1997.

Dillon, Martin C. "Am I a Grammatical Fiction?: The Debate Over Ego Psychology." In *Merleau-Ponty's Later Works and Their Practical Implications: The Dehiscence of Responsibility*, edited by Duane H. Davis, 309–24. Amherst, NY: Humanity Books, 2001.

———. *Beyond Romance*. Albany: State University of New York Press, 2001.

———. Introduction to *Écart & Différance: Merleau-Ponty and Derrida on Seeing and Writing*, edited by Martin C. Dillon. Atlantic Highlands, NJ: Humanities Press, 1997.

———. "La Carnalidad del Amor: Percepción e Historia." *Areté* 9, no. 2 (1997): 219–34.

———. "Merleau-Ponty and the Reversibility Thesis." *Man and World* 16 (1983): 365–88.

———. *Merleau-Ponty's Ontology*. 2nd ed. Evanston, IL: Northwestern University Press, 1997.

———. *Semiological Reductionism: A Critique of the Deconstructionist Movement in Postmodern Thought*. Albany: State University of New York Press, 1995.

Freud, Sigmund. "'Civilized' Sexual Morality and Modern Nervousness." In *The Standard Edition of the Complete Psychological Works of Sigmund* Freud, vol. 9, 1906–1908, edited by James Strachey. New York: W. W. Norton, 2000.

———. *The Ego and the Id*. Edited by James Strachey. Translated by Joan Riviere. New York: W. W. Norton, 1962.

Hass, Lawrence. *Merleau-Ponty's Philosophy*. Bloomington: Indiana University Press, 2008.

Heidegger, Martin E. *Being and Time*. Translated by John Macquarrie and Edward Robinson. New York: Harper & Row, 1962.

Liddell, Henry George, and Robert Scott. *Liddell and Scott's Greek-English Lexicon*. London: Oxford University Press, 1964.

Kant, Immanuel. *Critique of Practical Reason*. Translated by Lewis White Beck. Indianapolis: Bobbs-Merrill, 1956.

―――. *Critique of Pure Reason*. Translated by Norman Kemp Smith. New York: St. Martin's Press, 1965.

―――. *Groundwork of the Metaphysic of Morals*. Translated by H. J. Paton. New York: Harper & Row, 1964.

Kierkegaard, Søren. *Fear and Trembling*. Translated by Edward V. Hong and Edna H. Hong. Princeton: Princeton University Press, 1983.

Kirk, G. S., and J. E. Raven. *The Presocratic Philosophers*. Cambridge: Cambridge University Press, 1957.

Merleau-Ponty, Maurice. *Adventures of the Dialectic*. Translated by Joseph Bien. Evanston, IL: Northwestern University Press, 1973.

―――. *Humanism and Terror: An Essay on the Communist Problem*. Translated by John O'Neill. Boston: Beacon Press, 1969.

―――. *Humanisme et Terreur: Essai sur le Problème Communiste*. Paris: Gallimard, 1947.

―――. *Le Visible et l'invisible*. Edited by Claude Lefort. Paris: Gallimard, 1964.

―――. *Phenomenology of Perception*. Translated by Colin Smith, with revisions by Forrest Williams and David Guerrière. London: Routledge, 1981.

―――. *Sense and Non-Sense*. Translated by Hubert L. Dreyfus and Patricia Allen Dreyfus. Evanston, IL: Northwestern University Press, 1964.

―――. *Signes*. Paris: Gallimard, 1960.

―――. *Signs*. Translated by Richard C. McCleary. Evanston, IL: Northwestern University Press, 1964.

―――. *Texts and Dialogues*. Edited by Hugh J. Silverman and James Barry Jr. Atlantic Highlands, NJ: Humanities Press, 1992.

―――. *The Visible and the Invisible*. Edited by Claude Lefort. Translated by Alphonso Lingis. Evanston, IL: Northwestern University Press, 1968.

Nietzsche, Friedrich Wilhelm. *Beyond Good and Evil: Prelude to a Philosophy of the Future*. Translated by Walter Kaufmann. New York: Random House, 1966.

―――. *The Birth of Tragedy and the Case of Wagner*. Translated by Walter Kaufmann. New York: Random House, 1967.

―――. *Ecce Homo*. Translated by R. J. Hollingdale. Harmondsworth: Penguin, 1979.

―――. "Ecce Homo." In *Basic Writings of Nietzsche*, translated and edited by Walter Kaufmann, 655–800. New York: Modern Library, 2000.

―――. *The Gay Science*. Translated by Walter Kaufmann. New York: Random House, 1974.

―――. *Human, All Too Human: A Book for Free Spirits*. Translated by R. J. Hollingdale. Cambridge: Cambridge University Press, 1986.

―――. "On the Genealogy of Morals." In *Basic Writings of Nietzsche*, translated and edited by Walter Kaufmann, 437–599. New York: Modern Library, 2000.

―――. "On Truth and Lies in a Nonmoral Sense." In *Philosophy and Truth: Selections from Nietzsche's Notebooks of the Early 1870s*, translated and edited by Daniel Breazeale, 79–97. Atlantic Highlands, NJ: Humanites Press, 1990.

―――. *Philosophy and Truth: Selections from Nietzsche's Notebooks of the Early 1870s*. Translated and edited by Daniel Breazeale. Atlantic Highlands, NJ: Humanities Press, 1990.

————. *The Portable Nietzsche*. Translated and edited by Walter Kaufmann. New York: Penguin, 1982.

————. "Thus Spoke Zarathustra." In *The Portable Nietzsche*, translated and edited by Walter Kaufmann, 103–439. New York: Viking Press, 1954.

————. "Twilight of the Idols." In *The Portable Nietzsche*, translated and edited by Walter Kaufmann. New York: Viking Press, 1954.

————. *Werke, Band 1 and 2*. Herausgegeben von Karl Schlecta. Munich: Carl Hanser Verlag, 1956.

Partridge, Eric. *Origins: A Short Etymological Dictionary of Modern English*. New York: Greenwich House, 1983.

Silverman, Hugh J., and James Barry Jr. "Introduction." In *Texts and Dialogues: Merleau-Ponty*, edited by Hugh J. Silverman and James Barry Jr. Atlantic Highlands, NJ: Humanities Press, 1992.

Thomas Aquinas. *Basic Writings of Saint Thomas Aquinas*. Vol. 1, edited by Anton C. Pegis. New York: Random House, 1945.

INDEX

·····························